Vanilla Table

The essence of exquisite cooking from the world's best chefs

NATASHA MacALLER

Photography
Manja Wachsmuth

For Michael

with love and laughter

Contents

———⚬⚬⚬———

Foreword

PETER GORDON

I'VE KNOWN TASH SINCE 1996, but unfortunately I never had the pleasure of seeing her dance. However, I have had the absolute pleasure of eating her vanilla and bacon trifle in Tonga. That may sound like a rather strange combination, but trust me, in Tash's hands this finale course was completely delicious and also totally 'out there'.

We first met when Tash was involved in the wonderful foodie extravaganza 'Cuisines of the Sun' in Hawaii. There she was, this powerhouse of a woman, running around and organising the numerous star chefs and their helpers, making sure everything was where it was needed and on time. Of course, the joy of any island in the Pacific is that the day will inevitably take on a life of its own, so one does need patience and determination – traits that are required in many of the arts. I watched her corralling the teams, chefs and ingredients and she never once looked fazed as chefs with missing *mise en place* demanded another ingredient from the mainland. I knew then that we'd be good friends for a long time.

Tash then moved to live in New Zealand for part of the year and so we managed to meet up quite frequently, as she was also living in Los Angeles and popping in and out of London. I asked her to work with the pastry chefs at my New Zealand restaurants and she introduced many of her trademark American baking techniques to the kitchen, revamped our biscuit and chocolate plate and created new desserts. My chefs loved her.

Tash and I then headed off on a fabulous culinary adventure to the Heilala vanilla plantation in Tonga in 2010 and it was here that I realised Tash was also an ace at savoury foods. That wasn't really a surprise, as I had imagined she would do well at whatever she chose to put her mind to, whether it be dancing or icing cakes. However, the aforementioned bacon trifle was a revelation. We were cooking in the kitchen of a small lodge looking out onto a lagoon and Tash was extolling the virtues of vanilla in combination with crispy baked bacon bits – needless to say there were a few raised eyebrows. Yet when you put a spoonful of this dish in your mouth everything just simply comes together beautifully (see the recipe on page 103).

And so here it is, her first book, full of her own and other chefs' recipes, chefs that she has met on her travels and in their kitchens, as well as some she's admired from a distance. The pages are bursting with aromatic dishes from both the sweet and savoury sections of the kitchen and all of them have been tested, and then tested again, by Tash. It's a wonderful book, written and compiled by a wonderful woman. While she no longer dances for a living, the flavours and combinations within these pages will soon be dancing on your palate.

Peter Gordon
London, 2013

í

The Vanilla Story

NATASHA MACALLER

VANILLA IS A PASSION. It is the power behind the throne of fragrance and flavour, an integral component of most chocolate creations and the world's favourite ice cream. Its captivating scent is everywhere, hidden in more things than you can imagine (cola, perfume, dryer sheets, not to mention my Aunt Helen's Victory Garden Bundt Cakes). I believe the majority of homes around the world have some type of vanilla in their pantry. It is a universal flavour, although most people imagine it can only be added to cupcakes, custards and confections. I hope *Vanilla Table* will inspire home cooks, students and chefs to try this exotic but familiar ingredient, not only in delectable sweets but in other dishes such as Kumara Gratin layered with Vanilla Caramelised Onions, Island Crabcakes with Vanilla-Grapefruit Remoulade or Slow-Roasted Oxtail Pot Pies with Vanilla-Shiraz Gravy.

Vanilla is often used to describe something that is just ordinary, nothing special, no extras – however, vanilla is anything but plain.

———

MY DELIGHT FOR VANILLA began not in a kitchen but in a car on the way to ballet class. With my hair bobby-pinned back in a bun, dressed in a sky-blue leotard and pink tights with pink leather slippers held in place by double bands of pink elastic, Mom would pull up outside Rosalie and Alva's School of Ballet. She would dig into her gigantic purse, remove a tiny bottle and spritz me with vanilla-scented cologne. Inhaling the delicious aroma, I'd grab my ballet bag and rush gleefully into the wood-floored studio for my lesson. The vanilla seed was planted.

On weekends, I would practice on the linoleum kitchen floor, using the sink edge for balance, and perfect my *tendus* and *rond de jambs* while Mom cooked up some creation inspired by her treasured Julia Child cookbook. Some days the smell was so enticing we all fought for a taste, other times we crossed our arms and soundly rejected it as 'funny food'. Then Mom would have to resort to 'wagon wheels' macaroni and cheese.

Dessert, naturally, was always a hit, especially when it was Mom's apple pie dusted with crunchy sugar just waiting for a big scoop of plain white ice cream. Vanilla ice cream – no vanilla bean flecks or swirls back then – just plain white. And it was perfect. Dad often helped us, probably out of pure frustration as he watched our spoons bending backwards in an attempt to scrape enough of the frozen-solid vanilla goodness to top the warm pie.

Vanilla often reminds me of summer weekend visits with Great Aunt Agnes, where I learned to play the autoharp (I still have it somewhere) and paint watercolour landscapes. At cocktail hour, Aunt A always had a scotch on the rocks – for me it was a Shirley Temple – and we would sit on her very long, elegant sofa. She would take my hand and knowingly check the length of my fingernails –

they were always too short. With a tight smile she would pat my hand away, and then we would chat about my future. From the age of six, just two weeks into ballet lessons, I knew exactly what I wanted to be – a ballerina.

For breakfast, Aunt Agnes always set out the full silver service and offered fresh-squeezed orange juice and frozen waffles or eggs with toast. However, for me, the star of those treasured mornings was the fresh strawberry-topped cornflakes served with my own petite porcelain pitcher of cream. I was allowed to spoon my own vanilla-scented sugar from the Limoges sugar bowl with a silver teaspoon. I felt so grown up! The combination of crunchy cereal, strawberries and cream dusted with vanilla sugar is a comfort taste I crave to this day. This memory inspired me to create my vanilla sugar-topped shortcakes overflowing with lemon curd and fresh-picked strawberries.

Many years and hundreds of pointe shoes later as a professional ballerina, I kept a little bottle of vanilla perfume on my theatre dressing table to remind me of the decades of dedication, the joy of dancing and the enticing aroma of vanilla.

With lots of practice and a bit of luck, I was able to dance professionally into my thirties, performing in New York City's Joffrey Ballet and Boston Ballet. After five years in Boston, I transformed in four days from a Swan Lake cygnet to a second soprano dancing butterfly on Broadway in *The Phantom of the Opera*. A few months later I was transferred to the Los Angeles company of *Phantom*, and finished my stage career when we closed four years after.

Now what? The only performing art with a sell-by date is that of a dancer. A musician, a singer or an actor ages gracefully into their career; the mature dancer is a rarity. However, the craft of cooking doesn't require perfect turnout, banana-arched feet and great leg extensions, all it requires is hard work and a desire to learn. That was for me. During the ballet's seasonal layoffs I would cater parties, from sailboats to skyscrapers, to supplement my unemployment checks. After my final ballet bow, I was curious to go back to school, not only to fill in the gaps I'd missed from only gleaning recipes from cookbooks but to see if my brain still had the capacity to learn.

My next career choice was discussed at length with my partner Michael over a fine bottle of bubbles at sunrise on a Fijian beach. Was it to be a sports psychologist, a physical therapist (I was always ready to run for the ice pack when someone might be hurt in the show)... or a chef?

I chose steel-toed boots and the kitchen. With great relief, I discovered that my brain was still in good working order and I graduated first in my class. I was then, and am ever, inspired by ingredients to create food to share with others.

MY NEW CAREER BEGAN WITH JANICE. In 1996, fresh out of culinary school, I often worked as her personal assistant in her then-tiny LA garage cum office. A food and travel journalist, Janice Wald Henderson needed me to fact-check, answer phones and occasionally brainstorm about chefs and their dishes for the extraordinary event she co-created, and was mistress of ceremonies for, 'Cuisines of the Sun', one of the premier culinary events in the world. It was hard to argue that point as the venue was merely steps away from the alluring beaches of Big Island, Hawaii, where guests would mingle with chefs and winemaker luminaries invited from all over the globe.

I was flown to Hawaii – quel drag! – to assist the then hotel chef Trey Foshee with 'Cuisines'. The following year, with a new group of star chefs, I was given more responsibility and the annual event was now known in the food biz as THE place to network for chefs and cooks. Qualified volunteers would pay to fly in from everywhere, many accomplished chefs in their own right, simply to participate and work with some of the hottest chefs in the world. Quickly I became 'Ask Natasha', helping to coordinate 100 assisting chefs into teams, creating time and space for the twelve star chefs, all the while patiently explaining that there is no such thing as FedEx overnight in Hawaii but we would do our best to make it work. And we did. It was at 'Cuisines' that I met and worked closely with the majority of the chefs who have generously contributed a vanilla creation for this book.

A few years ago I experienced vanilla up-close at the First International Vanilla Food & Wine Event at the Heilala plantation in the Kingdom of Tonga. New Zealand chef Peter Gordon and I created, cooked and served an array of vanilla dishes over three days. Heilala's vanilla plantation began as an aid project and within a few years has grown into an award-winning, organic, fair trade family-run business that gives back to the village in jobs and resources. I was captivated, not only by all things vanilla, but by the generous and kind community on the pristine Pacific island of Vava'u. It was here that *Vanilla Table* began to take shape. I was so inspired by my Tongan adventure that a portion of the proceeds from this book will be donated to The Heilala Vanilla Foundation.

———— ✸ ————

EVERYBODY – NO MATTER WHAT corner of the world they live in – has a vanilla story. My dream is that the 'stories' in this book resonate with you and inspire you to remember, create and imagine your best vanilla stories too.

Vanilla 101

Vanilla Table is a culinary celebration of all things vanilla. From dishes offering earthy in-your-face vanilla flavour to others with just a sensual whisper of vanilla, the techniques and tastes of these sweet and savoury dishes will reveal many surprising unions and may prompt you to go vanilla wild! There are several expert sources for more information about vanilla (page 227), and I encourage you to explore, but as you begin (or renew) your vanilla adventures, here are a few basics.

VANILLA IS THE FRUIT of the *Vanilla planifolia* (*fragrans*) or *Vanilla x tahitensis* orchid, the only two vanilla orchid species that are cultivated, cured and commercially sold. Vanilla, discovered in Mexico and known to the ancient Totonac (or Mayan) indians, has the tiny *Melipona* bee to thank for its success. This bee is the only insect that naturally pollinates the vanilla orchid flower. Without it, the vanilla flower must be pollinated by hand in the early hours of the single day in which it blooms. It is therefore not surprising that vanilla is second only to saffron as the most expensive spice on the planet. But it is worth it – a single vanilla pod (once worth its weight in gold) will unlock a secret world of harmonious flavours.

The four distinctive styles of commercially available vanilla are Bourbon (or Madagascar), Mexican, Tahitian and Indonesian. By far the best known is *Bourbon vanilla* (no relation to American bourbon whisky). Primarily grown in Madagascar (which produces 55% of the world's vanilla), bourbon vanilla has a rich, classic flavour, some say with hints of rum, raisin and brown sugar. *Mexican vanilla* pods have a darker, earthier and spicier flavour than the others, pairing perfectly with strong flavours such as coffee and chocolate. *Tahitian vanilla*, considered the most fragrant and flowery, goes gracefully with delicate cakes, creams and fruit. Grown only in small geographical areas, it is also the most expensive vanilla. *Indonesian vanilla* production has increased dramatically in the past few years. The curing method is quite different, yielding a woody, smoky aroma making Indonesian vanilla a good partner for roasted meats, marinades and other preparations requiring high heat and long cooking.

VANILLA PODS When selecting vanilla pods (although often called vanilla beans, the fruit of the vanilla orchid is a pod), check that they are lustrous and supple. If the pod seems brittle, find a fresher one. If you are lucky enough to find them dusted with white powdery crystals – naturally occurring vanillin – choose those. Vanillin is the strongest of the 250 organic chemical components found in a cured vanilla pod, yet it's strangely absent in the fresh-picked fruit. Only through the drying and curing process does the captivating fragrance of vanilla unleash its magical dance on our senses.

SINGLE FOLD EXTRACT Pure vanilla extract and paste are readily available as 'single fold'. A fold is the concentration of vanilla per litre of liquid. Food service and gourmet food manufacturers use double fold, triple fold, and all the way to thirty fold! Double extract or paste, found in gourmet grocers, is well worth using as it goes twice as far and has not lost the layers and nuances that the higher folds lack.

VANILLA PASTE Recipes often call for whole pods to be 'split in half and seeds scraped out' (often known as 'vanilla caviar'). Vanilla paste is simply vanilla seeds suspended in vanilla extract, natural gum thickeners and a bit of sugar (some brands add more sugar than others so be sure to read the label).

VANILLA POWDER A recent addition, powder comes in many guises. The finest I've used is from Heilala, who slow-dry whole pods, then mill and sieve them into a fine powder. It possesses the goodness of a fresh pod without added moisture and is terrific for making vanilla salt flakes.

QUICK GUIDE to the relative strength of vanilla products: 1 tsp of paste = 1 tsp of extract = seeds of 1 pod = 1 tsp powder.

STORE YOUR VANILLA in a dark glass bottle to protect it from light. Pods, extract, paste, powder and sugar are best kept in a cool dark pantry (not refrigerated) and tightly sealed. Properly stored, extract will last 4–5 years and pods for at least two. Syrup can be refrigerated for up to a month.

A FINAL NOTE about imitation vanilla. If it is in your pantry, throw it out. Fake vanillin is distilled from a blend of wood pulp and coal tar processed with various chemicals to extract the 'vanilla' flavour. Use 100% pure vanilla. Although more expensive than imitation, a little bit goes a long way and produces the finest results.

Starter Plates

'Ota Ika' Ceviche   10

Hearts of Palm & Papaya Salad   12

Butternut Squash Soup Shooters   14

Shaved Fennel & Kerikeri Orange Salad   16

Smoked Trout Johnnycake Stacks   18

Caramelised Garlic & Ricotta Custard Cups   20

Seared Scallops & Roast Tomatoes   22

Ho Farm Tomatoes & Big Island Goat Cheese Salad   24

Vanilla & Cocoa Nib Crusted Foie Gras   26

Pâté au Poulet with Tipsy Cherries   28

Fennel Flan with Orange Gelée   31

Heirloom Tomato Bisque   34

Meia Esfera De Salmão Marinado   36

'Ota Ika' Ceviche
with coconut black sesame wafers

Sounds like the lyrics of an island song, but this is the name of the Tongan version of ceviche. Known in Fiji as kokoda, Hawaii as poke and ceviche in South America, ota ika is a light, quick and easy dish. Use the freshest local fish you can. Our Tongan host, John Ross, spear-caught a parrotfish – beautiful and delicious! Fresh fish paired with the aroma of fresh coconut and vanilla makes this an ideal summer dish. Serve with a local amber beer (Ikale is the local Tongan beer) or chilled crisp white wine. I enjoy ota ika with a glass of Prosecco – a bit of fizz pairs beautifully with the fragrance of vanilla.

GF OPTION   **SERVES 4**

fresh opakapaka, snapper, sea bass or other firm white fish	2 fillets	110 g	4 oz
red bell pepper/red capsicum, chopped	⅓ cup	55 g	2 oz
red onion, chopped	¼ cup	20 g	¾ oz
green mango or green papaya, cut into 3-cm/1¼-in pieces	⅓ cup	55 g	2 oz
fresh or canned coconut cream	⅓ fl cup	80 ml	2½ fl oz
vanilla paste	½ tsp		
lime juice, plus zest of 1 lime	¼ fl cup	60 ml	2 fl oz
sweet chilli sauce	1 Tbsp	15 ml	½ fl oz
hot sauce, to taste	4 dashes		
kiwi fruit, peeled, cut into 3-cm/1¼-in pieces	½	30 g	1 oz
Asian/nashi pear or jicama, cut into small cubes	½ cup	60 g	2 oz
parsley, finely chopped/minced	1 Tbsp		
COCONUT BLACK SESAME WAFERS			
shredded coconut, unsweetened	¾ cup	65 g	2¼ oz
black sesame seeds	2 tsp		
vanilla sugar (page 222)	2 Tbsp	30 g	1 oz
plain or gluten-free flour	⅓ cup	50 g	1¾ oz
egg, large	1		
egg whites	2	60 ml	2 fl oz
1 lime and ½ orange zested	4 tsp		
butter or coconut oil, melted and cooled	2 Tbsp	30 ml	1 fl oz
TO SERVE			
spring/green onions or chives for garnish, chopped	1 Tbsp	20 g	¾ oz

Cut the boned raw fish fillets into 6-cm/2½-in pieces and place in a non-reactive metal or glass bowl. Add the pepper/capsicum, onion, mango, half the coconut cream, vanilla paste, lime juice and zest, sweet chilli sauce and hot sauce. Gently fold together, cover and chill for 1 hour.

Just before serving, fold in the kiwi fruit, Asian pear, parsley and remaining coconut cream. Season with sea salt and pepper to taste and gently combine. Chill for up to 30 minutes if wished.

Coconut black sesame wafers

In a small mixing bowl, whisk together the coconut, sesame seeds, sugar, flour and large pinch of sea salt. Add egg, egg whites, zests and butter or coconut oil. Cover and chill for 30 minutes.

Preheat oven to 180°C/350°F/gas mark 3 (160°C/325°F fan).

Spread batter in a thin, even layer as teardrops or circles on lightly oiled baking paper or mat on a baking tray/cookie sheet.

Bake until golden brown, turning tray halfway through and checking often to keep from burning; about 10 minutes. Lower oven temperature if needed. Carefully lift wafers from sheet to cooling racks. If you want sharper edges to the wafers, transfer from the tray to a cutting board and use a cookie cutter to cut out desired shapes, then use a palette knife or small spatula to transfer to cooling racks. If needed, return to oven for a few minutes to soften and reshape.

When cooled, store in an airtight container.

To serve

Spoon the ceviche into 4 coconut shells or martini glasses, sprinkle with spring/green onions or chives, and garnish with a coconut black sesame wafer. Serve immediately. *NM*

Hearts of Palm & Papaya Salad
with baby greens

This spontaneous salad was invented at the Nuku'alofa farmers market within minutes of arriving in the capital city of Tonga. Planning to serve our guests an orange and fennel salad (see page 16), I soon discovered there was not a single fennel bulb to be found in this tropical island kingdom, so off I went on a hearts of palm quest. On our visit, chef Peter Gordon and I not only learned the technique of picking mature vanilla pods, but discovered first hand from host Caroline Hudson of Ika Lahi Lodge how one finds the core of a palm tree by peeling away the fibrous outer layers to reveal the soft flavourful heart. Thankfully, there are now varieties of palm grown for commercial use that develop heart 'branches', which means the tree doesn't have to be destroyed to extract the delicious and tender core.

GF SERVES 4

COCONUT–LIME VANILLAGRETTE

lime juice	2 Tbsp	30 ml	1 fl oz
rice wine vinegar	1 Tbsp	15 ml	½ fl oz
light palm sugar, grated (or 2 tsp honey)	1 Tbsp	30 g	1 oz
ginger, fresh grated	1 tsp		
wasabi powder	¼ tsp or to taste		
vanilla pod seeds (or ½ tsp paste)	½ tsp		
poppy seeds	½ tsp		
coconut oil	1 Tbsp	15 ml	½ fl oz
grapeseed oil	1 Tbsp	15 ml	½ fl oz
fine sea salt	¼ tsp		
SALAD			
prosciutto, thin slices	8–10 pc	100 g	3–4 oz
mixed baby greens (e.g. spinach, mesclun, etc.)	4 cups	175 g	6 oz
hearts of palm, fresh, or 1 can hearts of palm,* drained	2 cups	250 g	9 oz
papaya, firm	half	250 g	9 oz
chives, finely chopped/minced	¼ cup	25 g	1 oz

* If not available, use fresh bamboo shoots, which can be found at Asian grocers.

Coconut–lime vanillagrette
Whisk together the lime juice, vinegar, palm sugar, ginger, wasabi powder, vanilla seeds and poppy seeds until well blended. Whisk in oils until combined and season to taste with salt. Set aside until ready to serve.

Salad
Heat a small sauté pan over medium heat. Pan fry the prosciutto until crispy, drain on paper towels and set aside.

Wash and drain baby greens.

Cut hearts of palm in half lengthways, then into randomly sized batons.

Peel, remove the seeds and slice papaya into thin strips.

Toss hearts of palm, greens and chives together. Add papaya. Drizzle the salad with the vanillagrette to lightly coat salad leaves. Decorate with crispy prosciutto slices and extra chives. Serve immediately. *NM*

Butternut Squash Soup Shooters

A delicious, year-round, make-ahead-of-time starter that can be served as an amuse bouche or a first course. You can combine hearty squash with pumpkin, adjusting sugar and lemon juice depending on the natural sweetness of the varieties used.

GF **SERVES 6–8**
[OR 60 ML/24 X 2 FL OZ GLASSES]

BUTTERNUT SQUASH			
butternut squash, halved and seeds scooped out	1 large	1 kg	2 lb
brown sugar, packed	3 Tbsp	50 g	1¾ oz
unsalted butter in small pieces	2 Tbsp	25 g	1 oz
sea salt and pepper	to taste		
SOUP			
grapeseed oil or vegetable oil	¼ fl cup	60 ml	2 fl oz
unsalted butter	2 Tbsp	25 g	1 oz
white/brown onions, 4 medium, peeled, halved and thinly sliced	3 cups	500 g	1 lb
vanilla pod, split and scraped	1		
chicken or vegetable stock	4 fl cups	1 L	1 qt
lemon juice	2 Tbsp	30 ml	1 fl oz
crème fraîche for garnish (optional)			
baby sage leaves for garnish			

Butternut squash

Heat oven to 180°C/350°F/gas mark 4.

Place prepared squash in foil-lined baking pan cut-side up. Sprinkle with brown sugar, dot with butter and add a few grinds of salt and pepper. Bake until fork-tender – about 45 minutes. Remove from oven and set aside. (This can be done up to a day ahead of time.)

Soup

Place oil and butter in large soup saucepan/pot (2 L/2 qt) and warm over medium–low heat until sizzling. Add sliced onions and sweat until translucent, stirring occasionally. Add vanilla seeds and pod. Continue to cook over low heat until onions are caramel coloured, about 20 minutes, stirring occasionally. Add stock and bring to a simmer.

Remove vanilla pod (rinse and dry for another use).

Scoop out squash, add to soup pan/pot and discard skin. Add 1–2 Tbsp lemon juice or to taste. Use a hand-/stick-blender to blitz soup until smooth. The soup should be thick but easy to sip. If it is too watery, gently simmer, stirring, until reduced. Adjust lemon juice and add salt and pepper as preferred. Serve hot with a dollop of crème fraîche, a sprinkling of fresh sage leaves, and for some crunch serve with Parmesan cheese straws. *NM*

Shaved Fennel & Kerikeri Orange Salad

Kerikeri, in the Bay of Islands, New Zealand, grows acres of oranges, kiwi fruit, lemons and, most recently, olives. This welcoming orchard town has been growing Kerikeri oranges - a full-flavoured Valencia variety - since the 1920s.

GF SERVES 4			
ROASTED SHALLOTS			
shallots	3	135 g	4½ oz
extra virgin olive oil	1 Tbsp	15 ml	½ fl oz
ROASTED SHALLOT VINAIGRETTE			
garlic cloves, caramelised*	2 or 1 tsp	10 g	
white wine vinegar	¼ fl cup	60 ml	2 fl oz
orange vincotto or aged balsamic vinegar	2 Tbsp	30 ml	1 fl oz
orange zest	2 tsp		
Dijon mustard	1 tsp		
vanilla paste	½ tsp		
sea salt and cracked pepper	to taste		
SALAD			
pancetta or bresaola, thinly sliced	6-8 slices	100 g	3-4 oz
mixed baby lettuces	4 cups	175 g	6 oz
fresh basil leaves, torn	½ cup	50 g	1¾ oz
fennel bulbs, with bruised or brown outside leaves discarded	2 med	500 g	1 lb
chives or spring/green onions, finely chopped/minced	¼ cup	30 g	1 oz
oranges, preferably unsprayed, peeled, seeded and cut into segments	2		

* See method for caramelising garlic on page 20.

Roasted shallots

Preheat oven to 180ºC/350ºF/gas mark 4. Trim shallot root ends, leaving papery skin attached. Place in a small foil-lined baking pan and drizzle with olive oil. Roast in oven about 30–35 minutes or until soft when pierced with the tip of a knife and golden brown.

Roasted shallot vinaigrette

In a small bowl, peel then mash the roasted shallots and caramelised garlic to make a smooth paste.

Whisk in remaining ingredients and season to taste with salt and pepper.

Cover and chill until ready to use.

Salad

Layer meat slices together then cut into small squares. Over medium heat add the pancetta to a dry pan and fry until crispy. Drain on paper towels and set aside.

Rinse and drain salad leaves and basil.

Cut fennel bulbs in half lengthways. Remove and discard core and shave fennel into wafer-thin slices.

Toss fennel, greens, basil and chives or spring/green onions together. Add orange segments and drizzle dressing over all. Add pancetta just before serving and toss salad to lightly coat with the dressing.

Serve immediately. *NM*

Smoked Trout Johnnycake Stacks

with vanilla citrus sauce

Johnnycakes, originally known as journeycakes, are a cornmeal flatbread credited to the American tribes of 1800s New England. Additional native ingredients - black beans and wild rice - layered with plentiful trout transform these crusty-outside, moist-inside cakes into a substantial course. If trout is unavailable, use another delicate smoked fish, such as gurnard or tarakihi. By substituting oil and water for the butter and milk, these Johnnycakes taste just as delicious and are gluten- and dairy-free.

GF SERVES 4

VANILLA CITRUS SAUCE [MAKES 120 ML/4 FL OZ/½ FL CUP]

egg yolk, large	1	30 ml	1 fl oz
garlic clove, crushed/minced	1		
lime juice	1 Tbsp	15 ml	½ fl oz
lime zest	½ tsp		
orange zest	1 tsp		
vanilla paste	½ tsp		
agave syrup or honey	2 tsp	10 ml	
grapeseed oil	½ fl cup	120 ml	4 fl oz

JOHNNYCAKE BATTER [MAKES ABOUT 12]

fine cornmeal	¾ cup	115 g	4 oz
fine sea salt	½ tsp		
brown sugar	1 Tbsp	15 g	½ oz
milk or water	1¼ fl cups	300 ml	10 fl oz
butter or vegetable oil	2 Tbsp	30 g	1 oz
black beans, cooked, drained	¾ cup	100 g	3½ oz
wild rice, cooked, drained	¾ cup	90 g	3 oz
red onion, finely chopped (reserve a little for the garnish)	½	90 g	3 oz
hot sauce	1 tsp		
lime zest	1 tsp		
butter or vegetable oil, melted (for frying pan/skillet)	¼ fl cup	60 ml	2 oz

TO SERVE

smoked trout, gurnard or other delicate fish, in pieces	1–2 filets	200 g	7 oz
microgreens such as micro coriander/cilantro or watercress	small handful		
red onion, diced, reserved			

Vanilla citrus sauce

In a small bowl, whisk yolk with a pinch of sea salt, garlic, lime juice, citrus zests, vanilla paste and agave until well blended.

Using a whisk or hand-/stick-blender, whisk egg mixture continuously, then drizzle oil in a slow, steady stream until sauce begins to come together and thicken. If too thick, whisk in an additional teaspoon of water until well combined. Cover and chill until ready to use.

Johnnycake batter

In a medium bowl, whisk cornmeal, salt and sugar.

In a small saucepan/pot, heat milk and butter (or water and vegetable oil) to a simmer. Slowly pour milk mixture into the cornmeal, whisking to prevent lumps.

Combine beans, wild rice, onion, hot sauce and zest and gently fold into the batter. Cover and chill the batter for at least 1 hour (or up to a day), until just before serving.

Heat a heavy or cast-iron frying pan/skillet over medium heat. Add a pat of butter and wait for the sizzle.

Using a tablespoon, spoon batter into the sizzling butter and cook until crisp and golden brown on one side. Gently turn over and repeat. Place Johnnycakes on baking tray/cookie sheet in oven to keep warm while cooking the rest. Add additional butter or oil to pan as needed, making sure the pan doesn't get too hot or the fat will burn.

To serve

Place a Johnnycake on the plate, top with sauce then smoked fish and a sprinkling of microgreens. Stack layers 1 or 2 more times. Top the stack with more sauce and garnish with micro coriander/cilantro and diced red onion. *NM*

Caramelised Garlic & Ricotta Custard Cups

Some of the most memorable moments of the LA production of 'Phantom of the Opera' happened backstage. Long before 'Food TV', the cast, crew and orchestra often held cooking competitions, one of which produced a cookbook, Fun With Garlic! I created a garlic, ricotta and vanilla custard, that is surprisingly easy to make. Delicate and savoury, this custard can be made ahead of time and is sublime paired with a glass of creamy Champagne.

GF **SERVES 6**

CARAMELISED GARLIC			
garlic head, recipe needs 6 caramelised cloves	1		
oil	2 tsp	10 ml	
CUSTARD CUPS			
butter to grease cups	1 tsp		
vanilla pod	1		
apple sauce/applesauce or ¼ apple, peeled and grated	1 Tbsp	15 ml	½ fl oz
whipping cream	½ fl cup	120 ml	4 fl oz
milk	1 fl cup	240 ml	8 fl oz
caster/superfine sugar	½ tsp		
fine sea salt	½ tsp		
white pepper	¼ tsp		
eggs, large	3		
ricotta	½ cup	90 g	3 oz
Parmesan, finely grated	¼ cup	20 g	¾ oz
ground nutmeg	pinch		

Caramelised garlic
Preheat oven to 180ºC/350ºF/gas mark 4.

Cut top off garlic head to expose cloves. Peel away just the outer layer of the garlic bulb skin, leaving the skins of the individual cloves. Wrap loosely in foil and drizzle over the oil. Pinch the foil closed at the top, place in a baking pan and cook in oven 30–35 minutes until squishy, caramelised and golden brown.

Custard cups
Butter 6 small (120 ml/4 fl oz) custard cups. Set inside a baking dish large enough to hold the cups.

Cut the vanilla pod in half but don't split and scrape it, to keep the custard ivory coloured. Squeeze 6 caramelised garlic cloves into a saucepan and add apple sauce/applesauce, vanilla pod, cream, milk, sugar, salt and pepper. Bring just to a simmer, turn off heat and cool about 20 minutes.

Turn the oven to 160ºC/325ºF/gas mark 3.

In a large jug/pitcher, whisk the eggs well, then add ricotta. Place a sieve/strainer over the jug/pitcher and strain the milk mixture into the eggs, pressing the garlic through with the back of a spoon. Discard the vanilla pod or rinse, dry and save for another use. Add Parmesan, salt, pepper, a pinch of nutmeg and whisk together.

Pour custard into cups. Lift pan into the oven, then fill with very hot water to come halfway up the outside of the cups. Bake for 20 minutes until custard has browned and set but is still jiggly in the centre. Serve warm as is or top with a spoonful of green pea pesto (page 34). *NM*

Seared Scallops & Roast Tomatoes

with vanilla, ginger & lemongrass dressing

'Depending on the size of the scallops, you'll need 3 to 4 per portion. Buy them with the coral roe still attached as it has a wonderful flavour, but make sure they're cleaned well and the rubbery muscle is removed.'

PETER GORDON

GF **FOR 6 STARTERS**

scallops with roe attached, out of their shells and cleaned	about 24	500 g	18 oz
olive oil	3 Tbsp	45 ml	1½ fl oz
cherry tomatoes	24	220 g	8 oz
dried chilli flakes (more or less to taste)	¼ tsp		
sea salt flakes	to taste		
fresh lemongrass stem	4 in long	10 cm	
pandan leaf, roughly chopped (or ⅛ tsp pandan extract)*	6 in	15 cm	
vanilla pod, piece, split in half	¾ in	2 cm	
ginger, finely chopped	½ tsp		
lime juice	2 Tbsp	30 ml	1 fl oz
mirin	4 Tbsp	60 ml	2 fl oz
sake	4 Tbsp	60 ml	2 fl oz
soy sauce	1½ Tbsp	20 ml	¾ fl oz
toasted sesame oil	½ tsp		
sunflower oil	1½ Tbsp	20 ml	¾ fl oz
watercress or rocket leaves	2 cups	170 g	6 oz

* Pandan leaves and extract can be found in most Asian grocery stores.

Preheat oven to 180°C/350°F/gas mark 4.

Brush the scallops gently with 1 Tbsp of the olive oil and leave on a tray, covered tightly, to come to room temperature.

Cut the cherry tomatoes in half and sit on a baking tray/cookie sheet lined with baking paper, cut sides facing up. Sprinkle with the chilli flakes and a little flaky sea salt. Drizzle with the remaining olive oil and bake until they just begin to colour and shrivel – about 20 minutes.

To make the dressing, cut 2 cm/1 in off the base of the lemongrass stem. Remove the 2 outer leaves, chop finely and place in a small pan with the pandan leaf, vanilla pod, ginger, lime juice, mirin, sake and soy sauce.

Bring to the boil, then simmer for 6 minutes.

Strain through a sieve/strainer into a jam jar with a screw-top lid.

Slice the inner stem of the lemongrass as thin as you can and put in the jar with the lemongrass liquor and the sesame and sunflower oils.

Give it a good shake, adding salt or extra lime juice if needed.

Heat up a heavy-based pan or frying pan/skillet (or the barbecue if it's summertime) and grill the scallops for 90 seconds on each side – more or less depending on size. They're best cooked medium rare.

To serve, divide the greens amongst your plates and sit the scallops on top. Place 8 cherry tomato halves around the scallops then drizzle generously with the dressing.

The first time I saw vanilla orchids growing was in Tonga in 2010, when I was cooking there with Tash, the author of this book. We were visiting the Heilala plantation and it was incredible to think that these fat green aromaless pods could ever become the richly sweet and luscious beans we know of as vanilla. How the Aztecs ever figured out how to create such beauty from something so plain is one of the world's great wonders. **PG**

Ho Farm Tomatoes &
Big Island Goat Cheese Salad
with vanilla li hing mui dressing

'Li hing mui is a very popular snack in Hawaii. When growing up, I ate them like potato chips. There are leis made up of strung-together packages of li hing mui that people give as gifts. Li hing mui, called "crack seed" here on the islands, are dried preserved plums and are Chinese in origin. Found in Asian grocer shops, they can be sweet, salty, sour, wet or dried. Other fruit, including lemons, mangoes and other stone fruit, are also given the li hing mui treatment. The nuances are all about the balance of sweet/salty/sour, with so many variations they are never consistently the same taste. This salad uses a dessert port, a dessert vermouth, and seductive vanilla.'

ALAN WONG

GF SERVES 4

LI HING MUI JUICE			
rock salt plum	1½ Tbsp	25 g	¾ oz
White Li Hing Mui	1 Tbsp	15 g	½ oz
Sweet Li Hing Mui	1 Tbsp	15 g	½ oz
Lemon Peel Li Hing Mui	1 Tbsp	15 g	½ oz
King Plum Li Hing Mui	3 Tbsp	40 g	1½ oz
LI HING MUI DRESSING			
port, A Ramos Pinto 2005 Late Bottled Vintage*	⅔ fl cup	150 ml	5 fl oz
vermouth, A Cocchi Vermouth Di Torino*	¾ cup	180 ml	6 fl oz
li hing mui juice	¼ fl cup	60 ml	2 fl oz
pure vanilla extract	1 Tbsp	15 ml	½ fl oz
dried prunes, cut in half	about 10	70 g	2½ oz
SALAD			
cherry tomatoes	24	220 g	8 oz
goat cheese, rolled into balls	12 pieces	120 g	4 oz
macadamia nuts, lightly toasted	½ cup	70 g	2½ oz
mixed baby lettuce	2 cups	170 g	6 oz
vanilla pods, split lengthways, halved	2		

* The two alcohols have a lot of vanilla nuances in them so that's why they are specific. If you can't get these, ask your local off licence/bottle shop for recommendations.

Li hing mui juice
Add 300 ml/10 fl oz/1¼ fl cups water to all the ingredients, bring to the boil and simmer for 5 minutes. Cool, strain and then add to the dressing.

Li hing mui dressing
Heat the port and vermouth in a small saucepan. Leave to boil 5 minutes to burn off the alcohol, then remove from heat and decant to a bowl. Add the li hing mui juice, vanilla and prunes, whisking well. Set aside.

Salad
Strain the dressing, discarding prunes. Place dressing on the bottom of a bowl. Arrange the mixed baby lettuce, tomatoes, goat cheese balls and lightly toasted macadamia nuts on top, garnish with the vanilla pods.

Vanilla & Cocoa Nib Crusted Foie Gras

with huckleberry gastrique

NEAL FRASER

SERVES 4			
VANILLA AND COCOA NIB CRUST			
vanilla powder	2 tsp	10 g	
apple cider gelée, or pear or apple jam	2 Tbsp	50 g	1¾ oz
cocoa nibs	2 Tbsp	20 g	¾ oz
toasted pistachios	⅓ cup	50 g	1¾ oz
kosher salt or sea salt flakes	1 tsp		
black pepper, cracked	1 tsp		
QUINCE			
water	4 fl cups	1 L	1 qt
honey	⅓ fl cup	80 ml	2½ fl oz
quince	2	600 g	1¼ lb
vanilla pod, split and scraped	1		
HUCKLEBERRY GASTRIQUE			
honey	⅓ fl cup	80 ml	2½ fl oz
sherry vinegar	3½ Tbsp	50 ml	1¾ fl oz
veal or duck stock	3½ Tbsp	50 ml	1¾ fl oz
fresh huckleberries (or blueberries)	½ cup	50 g	1¾ oz
TO SERVE			
foie gras, Grade A	4 pieces	4 x 60 g	4 x 2 oz
sea salt & black pepper	to taste		
thick slices of brioche, toasted	8		

Vanilla and cocoa nib crust
In a food processor, mix all ingredients for the crust. Blend/pulse the mixer until slightly chunky. Reserve.

Quince
Put the water into a large saucepan/pot and add the honey. Peel, core, seed and cut quince into large pieces. Add vanilla pod and bring to a simmer, cooking until fork-tender. Remove quince and set aside. Continue cooking the liquid until reduced to a syrup. When cool, cut the quince into large dice. When ready to serve, reheat gently in the reduced syrup.

Huckleberry gastrique
In a saucepan, caramelise honey until golden brown. Add sherry vinegar and simmer to reduce by half. Add veal stock and reduce by half. Add huckleberries and cook to asauce consistency. Set aside.

To serve
Season foie gras with salt and black pepper. Heat a black steel or cast-iron pan until very hot. DO NOT ADD OIL. Add foie gras and cook till golden brown, about 1 minute. Gently turn over and cook over medium heat until just cooked through, approximately 1 minute more. Remove from pan and drain on paper towels for 20 seconds.

Take a generous handful of the vanilla and cocoa nib crusting mixture and press into one edge of the foie gras. Repeat with the remaining pieces. Divide warm quince on serving plates. Top with a piece of foie gras, then drizzle each plate with huckleberry gastrique. Serve immediately with toasted brioche on the side.

Pâté au Poulet

with tipsy cherries & vanilla brioche soldiers

In 1980, during my first venture to New York City, the dream of dancing with American Ballet Theatre was my full-time mission. On the way to daily ballet lessons at Columbus Circle, I'd walk by this tiny shop, from where the most marvellous smells would escape. It was the Silver Palate, where boldly flavoured food was created. The cookbook soon followed and their Lemon Chicken, Salmon Mousse and Pâté Maison became a favourite at my parents' dinner parties. Inspired by this memory, the combination of earthy chicken livers enhanced with vanilla and spices, layered with vanilla-brandied cherries is a decadent make-ahead starter.

SERVES 8			
TIPSY CHERRIES			
vanilla liqueur, such as Navan or Calvados* brandy	⅔ fl cup	150 ml	5 fl oz
dried sour cherries, halved	1 cup	110 g	4 oz
PÂTÉ AU POULET			
unsalted butter	2 Tbsp	30 g	1 oz
chicken livers	1½ cups	450 g	16 oz
bay leaf	1		
shallots, peeled and chopped	3	170 g	6 oz
carrots, peeled and chopped	2	120 g	4 oz
vanilla liqueur or Calvados	2 Tbsp	30 ml	1 fl oz
unsalted butter, softened	½ cup	115 g	4 oz
quatre épices or mixed spice	½ tsp		
vanilla paste	2 tsp		
TO ASSEMBLE AND SERVE			
quince or gooseberry paste	½ cup	120 g	4½ oz
brioche soldiers (page 30)			

* If wished, substitute the liqueur with 4 Tbsp apple juice and 1 Tbsp pure vanilla extract.

Tipsy cherries
In a small saucepan, warm liqueur over low heat and add the cherries, swirling to coat. Turn off heat and set aside.

Pâté au poulet
Ready 4 glass bowls or small preserving jars (sized 180 ml/ 6 fl oz/¾ cup).

Melt 1 Tbsp butter over medium heat in a sauté pan. Season livers with a pinch of sea salt and freshly ground cracked pepper, then sauté 3–5 minutes until tender but firm and browned on all sides. Remove from pan.

Add additional 1 Tbsp butter to pan, then add bay leaf with shallots and carrots, sautéing until tender and caramelised. Add livers back to pan with liqueur and sauté 1 minute longer. Remove bay leaf.

Spoon livers and vegetables into the bowl of a food processor fitted with a steel S blade. Add 115 g/4 oz/½ cup butter, pinch of sea salt, spices and vanilla paste. Process until smooth and creamy.

To assemble and serve pâté
Divide the cherries into the 4 jars and press into the bottom, discarding liqueur. Scrape the pâté into a large piping/pastry bag or a zipper-type plastic bag (seal and cut a corner off before piping). Insert the tip of the piping/ pastry bag into the container, touching the cherry layer. Squeeze the bag from the top, keeping the tip touching the pâté (this prevents air pockets), until the jar is ¾ full. Repeat with remaining jars and level the top with a small spoon. Alternatively, spoon the pâté into jars and smooth the top with a tiny spoon.

Warm the quince or gooseberry paste in a saucepan or microwave and pour over the top of each jar, gently swirling the jar to distribute evenly.

Cover and refrigerate for at least 3 hours. Allow to stand at room temperature for 1 hour before serving. Serve with toasted vanilla brioche soldiers and a Pinot Gris, Riesling or Zinfandel. *NM*

VANILLA BRIOCHE SOLDIERS			
active dry yeast	1 Tbsp	10 g	
white sugar	3 Tbsp	45 g	1½ oz
milk, warm (about 40°C/110°F)	⅓ cup	80 ml	2½ fl oz
eggs, large	2		
vanilla paste	2 Tbsp	30 g	1 oz
unbleached bread/high-grade flour	2½ cups	300 g	10½ oz
fine sea salt	¼ tsp		
unsalted butter, softened	⅓ cup	80 g	3 oz
egg white, lightly beaten, to glaze	1	30 ml	1 fl oz

Vanilla brioche soldiers

In a stand-mixer or regular mixing bowl, sprinkle the yeast then 1 Tbsp of the sugar into the warm milk. Gently stir then set aside until the yeast floats to the top forming a puffy raft, about 10–15 minutes.

In a small bowl, beat the eggs with the vanilla paste until well blended, and set aside.

Place bowl with the puffy yeast raft on the mixer with paddle attachment, or use a wooden spoon. Add the flour, remaining sugar and salt. Mix on low speed for 30 seconds, then add the egg mixture.

The dough will look rough at first, but continue mixing until the dough is smooth and slightly elastic. Add the softened butter and continue mixing until the dough pulls away from the sides and is elastic – about 7 minutes – stopping and scraping the bowl and spoon or paddle as needed. Remove bowl from the mixer and cover with a damp towel in a warm spot away from direct sun and free of draughts. Leave to rise until doubled in size, about 1 hour.

Transfer the dough onto a floured work surface and gently deflate. Knead a few times and form into a loaf. Carefully lift into pan, cover with a towel and leave to rise in a warm place for a further hour.

Preheat oven to 190°C/375°F/gas mark 5 (180°C/350°F fan). Grease a loaf tin/pan with butter.

Bake for 10 minutes then turn down heat to 180°C/350°F/ gas mark 4 (160°C/325°F fan) and bake for an additional 20 minutes. Remove from oven and cool for 10 minutes. Remove from pan, place on rack and cool.

When completely cool, cut into thick slices, toast and cut into soldiers to serve with pâté. *NM*

One of the finest ways to test a stand-mixer is to make a batch of brioche. Most recipes call for a dough hook and the brioche dough gets kneaded for up to 30 minutes as the mixer strains and whines. If it is a lower grade mixer it will overheat and just stop. This easy recipe adapted from Jim Dodge uses a bowl and biceps or a regular paddle attachment. The scent of vanilla and butter escaping from the oven while this bakes is absolutely heavenly! **NM**

Fennel Flan

with orange gelée, cashew foam & vanilla oil

JOSIAH CITRIN

GF SERVES 6			
VANILLA OIL			
vanilla pod	1		
extra virgin olive oil	½ fl cup	120 ml	4 fl oz
ORANGE GELÉE			
fresh cardamom seeds	½ tsp		
fennel seeds	¼ tsp		
coriander seeds	¼ tsp		
star anise, whole	1		
clove, whole	1		
fresh-squeezed orange juice	3 fl cups	700 ml	24 fl oz
agar agar	1 tsp		
CHLOROPHYLL			
water	2 Tbsp	30 ml	1 fl oz
spinach leaves	2 x 5-oz bags	285 g	10 oz
sea salt	to taste		
FENNEL FLAN MIX			
unsalted butter	1 Tbsp	15 g	½ oz
sweet onion, medium, sliced	½	100 g	3½ oz
fennel, trimmed to the bulb, cored and sliced	1	200 g	7 oz
water	¼ fl cup	60 ml	2 fl oz
whipping cream	1½ fl cups	350 ml	12 fl oz
chlorophyll (see above)	1 Tbsp	15 ml	½ fl oz
eggs, large, lightly beaten	2		

Vanilla oil

Split the vanilla pod in half lengthways and scrape the seeds out using a small knife. Add the scraped seeds and the pod to the olive oil in a bowl and mix well with a whisk. Let the oil marinate at room temperature for 24 hours.

Strain the oil through a chinois (fine-meshed conical sieve/strainer) and transfer into a squeeze bottle.

Orange gelée

Toast all the spices in a sauté pan. Place them in muslin/cheesecloth. Tie the muslin/cheesecloth closed with a string.

Put the orange juice and spice sachet into a saucepan/pot and bring to the boil. Bring the heat to a low simmer and reduce the orange juice until 120 ml/4 fl oz/½ fl cup remains, constantly skimming the scum from the surface. Strain the reduced juice through a chinois into another pan/pot and bring it back to the boil.

Whisk in the agar agar and cook for 3 minutes on low heat, whisking constantly to dissolve. Strain the juice again through the chinois.

Put 1 Tbsp of orange juice reduction into each of six shot glasses and chill.

Chlorophyll

Heat water, add spinach and salt and bring to the boil. Cook until spinach is soft to the touch but still green. Transfer to a blender and purée until smooth. Strain the mixture through a chinois into a stainless steel bowl then set that bowl over a bowl of ice. Stir the mixture to chill. This will maintain the vibrant green colour.

Fennel flan mix

Melt the butter in a saucepan/pot over low heat. Add the sliced onions and cook until soft and translucent (about 5 to 7 minutes), stirring often to keep them from colouring. Add the fennel and continue cooking until the fennel is tender (about 8 minutes). Add the water, bring the pan/pot to the boil over medium heat and let the liquid reduce by half.

Transfer the fennel-onion mixture to a blender and purée until smooth. Strain the purée through a chinois and into a stainless steel bowl then set that bowl over a bowl of ice.

CASHEW FOAM			
whole milk	1 fl cup	240 ml	8 fl oz
double/heavy cream	1 fl cup	240 ml	8 fl oz
star anise	1		
gelatin sheets, softened in cold water	3		
toasted cashews	1 cup	110 g	3¾ oz
fleur de sel	to taste		
EQUIPMENT			
chinois sieve/strainer ● whipped cream dispenser and CO₂ charger			

I can distinctly remember the scent of vanilla in my grandma's house when she was making crème brûlée. To this day, a fragrant vanilla bean or a great crème brûlée brings back wonderful memories of the woman we loved, whom we all called 'Mimi'. **JC**

Stir the purée to chill. Once the purée is chilled, fold in the cream, chlorophyll and the eggs and pass through a chinois. Let the flan mix rest in the refrigerator for at least 3 hours.

Cashew foam
Combine the milk, cream and anise in a large saucepan/ pot and bring to the boil. Add drained, softened gelatin leaves to the milk mix and let it dissolve. Strain the milk mixture through a chinois and transfer into a blender with the toasted cashews. Blend until the mixture is smooth. Strain the mixture through a chinois and into a stainless steel bowl then set that bowl over a bowl of ice. Stir the mixture to chill.

Fill a whipped cream dispenser halfway with the cashew cream and charge with one CO₂ charger. Chill for at least 1 hour.

To finish
Preheat the oven to 90°C/200°F (lowest setting).

Spoon 3 Tbsp of the flan mix into each of the shot glasses on top of the set orange gelée. Cover each shot glass with a piece of aluminum foil. Place the glasses in a deep baking pan and add 2 cm/1 in of water. Place in the oven and cook until the flans tremble like jelly/Jell-O but are not runny with liquid (about 25 minutes). Once the flans are cooked, keep them in a warm place.

To serve
Wipe the shot glasses clean, remove the foil and top with the cashew foam. Drizzle with the vanilla oil and a sprinkle of fleur de sel. Serve immediately.

Heirloom Tomato Bisque

with green pea pesto

What to do with all those gorgeous homegrown tomatoes? A traditional bisque adds shellfish and a roux. This version is vegetarian and gluten-free as it is thickened with vanilla-caramelised onions rather than a flour-based roux.

GF SERVES 4 [MAKES 1 L/1 Q]

BISQUE

heirloom tomatoes, fresh*	12 med	1 kg	2 lb
brown sugar	2 tsp	10 g	
fine sea salt	2 tsp		
unsalted butter	3 Tbsp	45 g	1½ oz
vanilla pod, split and scraped	1		
brown onion, peeled and chopped	1	140 g	5 oz
garlic cloves, peeled & chopped	2	10 g	
bay leaf, bruised	1		
chicken or vegetable stock	1½ fl cups	350 ml	12 fl oz
cracked pepper, fresh	1 Tbsp		
juice of 1 lemon	3 Tbsp or to taste	45 ml	1½ fl oz
sea salt flakes	to taste		
cream/crème fraîche/Greek yogurt	½ cup	120 g	4½ oz

GREEN PEA PESTO

peas, fresh or frozen	1 cup	130 g	4½ oz
garlic clove, chopped	1	15 g	½ oz
extra virgin olive oil	5 Tbsp	75 ml	2½ fl oz
basil leaves, chopped	2 tsp	15 g	½ oz
lemon juice	2 tsp or to taste	10 ml	
Parmesan cheese	2 Tbsp		
sea salt and cracked pepper	to taste		
crème fraîche to serve, if wished	¼ cup	60 g	2 oz

*If fresh tomatoes are not available substitute whole tinned/canned tomatoes – 2 tins/cans/800 g/28 oz/4 cups.

Bisque

Preheat oven to 190ºC/375ºF/gas mark 5.

Line a baking tray/cookie sheet with lightly greased foil, then place halved tomatoes cut-side up on sheet. Sprinkle with sugar and salt and roast for 40 minutes, until bubbly and lightly browned on top.

Melt the butter in a 1½–2 L/1½–2 qt soup saucepan/pot with vanilla seeds and pod. Add onion and cook until translucent. Add garlic, bay leaf and stock. Add roasted tomatoes (or tinned/canned) and simmer, stirring occasionally, for 20 minutes (30 for tinned/canned).

Add pepper and season to taste with lemon juice and salt. Simmer an additional 5 minutes then remove vanilla pod and discard.

Purée liquid with a hand-/stick-blender or food mill until smooth. Gently whisk in cream, yogurt or crème fraîche.

Green pea pesto

Simmer peas in salted water for 2 minutes. Drain well then pour into a food processor bowl with the S blade. Add garlic, oil, basil and lemon juice. Whizz to a fine purée then add Parmesan with salt and pepper to taste.

Set aside or chill until ready to serve.

To serve

Top the bisque with green pea pesto and crème fraîche (if wished) and serve immediately with warm buttered toast. May be refrigerated and reheated next day, or you can serve the bisque cold. *NM*

Meia Esfera de Salmão Marinado

Marinated Salmon Sphere

FRANCESCO CARLI

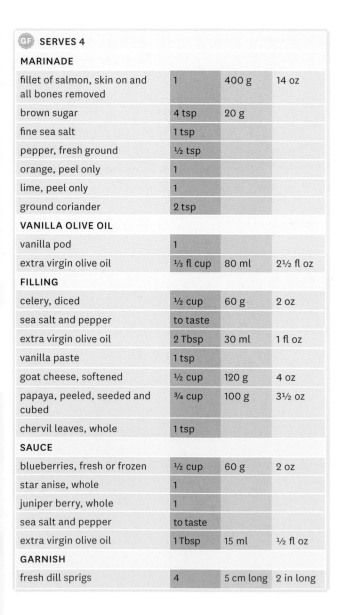

GF SERVES 4			
MARINADE			
fillet of salmon, skin on and all bones removed	1	400 g	14 oz
brown sugar	4 tsp	20 g	
fine sea salt	1 tsp		
pepper, fresh ground	½ tsp		
orange, peel only	1		
lime, peel only	1		
ground coriander	2 tsp		
VANILLA OLIVE OIL			
vanilla pod	1		
extra virgin olive oil	⅓ fl cup	80 ml	2½ fl oz
FILLING			
celery, diced	½ cup	60 g	2 oz
sea salt and pepper	to taste		
extra virgin olive oil	2 Tbsp	30 ml	1 fl oz
vanilla paste	1 tsp		
goat cheese, softened	½ cup	120 g	4 oz
papaya, peeled, seeded and cubed	¾ cup	100 g	3½ oz
chervil leaves, whole	1 tsp		
SAUCE			
blueberries, fresh or frozen	½ cup	60 g	2 oz
star anise, whole	1		
juniper berry, whole	1		
sea salt and pepper	to taste		
extra virgin olive oil	1 Tbsp	15 ml	½ fl oz
GARNISH			
fresh dill sprigs	4	5 cm long	2 in long

Marinade
Place salmon in a flat dish and evenly cover with the brown sugar, salt, pepper, orange peel, lime peel and coriander. Cover, chill and leave to marinate for 24 hours.

Discard the marinating liquid and pat the salmon dry. Cut salmon in thin slices and with the slices line the insides of 4 silicone hemisphere moulds, reserving some slices to cover the filling.

Vanilla olive oil
Cut the vanilla pod lengthways and scrape out seeds. Place the pod and seeds in a small saucepan/pot and cover with olive oil. Leave it to rest for a few hours in a warm place. This will make more than needed, so save extra for another use. Set aside.

Filling
Season celery with salt, pepper and olive oil. Add vanilla to goat cheese, then combine with celery mixture.

In a separate bowl, season the papaya with salt, pepper and chervil leaves. Set aside.

Line the salmon with half of the filling, leaving a hole in the middle. Place the papaya cubes in centre of each dome, then cover with the rest of the filling. Close with the reserved salmon slices.

Cover and refrigerate until set, about 3 hours.

Sauce
In a blender, purée all the ingredients, strain and reserve until ready to serve.

To serve
De-mould the salmon spheres onto a cutting board with the flat side down. Using a small sharp knife, cut a small slice to expose the layers, or cut a cake-wedge shape out of each. Carefully transfer onto individual plates. Using a teaspoon or squeeze bottle, paint the plate with blueberry sauce and dot with vanilla oil pearls. Finish each hemisphere with a dill sprig and serve immediately.

Main Plates

Roasted Lobster   40

Slow-Roasted Oxtail Pot Pies   42

Vanilla Lacquer Duck Leg   45

Goat Cheese & Vanilla Ravioli   48

Pineapple Marinated Fish   50

The Pork Chop   52

Seared Scallops with Vanilla Parsnip Purée   54

Scotch Fillet Steak   56

New Zealand Cassoulet   58

Crispy Salmon Fillet   60

Steamed Barramundi & Fregola Salad   62

Chicken Stroganoff with Chanterelles & Vanilla   64

Roasted Lobster

with citrus, vanilla & white pepper vinaigrette

'A beautiful and easy recipe to bring out all the flavours and sweetness of the lobster.'

NEIL BRAZIER

GF SERVES 4

CITRUS, VANILLA & WHITE PEPPER VINAIGRETTE

orange juice	2 Tbsp	30 ml	1 fl oz
lemon juice	2 Tbsp	30 ml	1 fl oz
Chardonnay vinegar or white wine vinegar	⅓ fl cup	80 ml	2½ fl oz
rapeseed/canola oil	1½ fl cups	350 ml	12 fl oz
vanilla pods, split and scraped	2		
cracked white pepper	1 Tbsp		
LOBSTER			
lobster,* average size	2	2 x 750 g	2 x 1½ lb

* This recipe was made with classic New England lobster, however, you can just as easily substitute the sublime New Zealand crayfish, also known as rock lobster.

I've had so many good vanilla memories – a big one, though, is back at school when all my friends had just passed their driving tests and the craze was to have a vanilla-scented 'tree' air freshener hanging from the rearview mirror. The sweet smell of vanilla wafted around everyone's cars and, even after getting out, the vanilla was strong enough to stick its aroma to your clothes for the rest of the day. Positively mouth-watering, and made you want to eat vanilla until it came out of the ears! **NB**

Citrus, vanilla and white pepper vinaigrette
In a medium bowl, mix everything together, including vanilla seeds and pods, and season with salt to taste. Leave to infuse in the refrigerator for at least 24 hours. Allow the vinaigrette to come to room temperature before using.

To prepare the lobster
Fill a large 6-L/6-qt saucepan/pot with a tight-fitting lid ¾ full of water. Bring water to the boil, then turn off heat. Place lobsters into the water, cover immediately with the lid and leave to stand for 1 minute.

Remove lobsters and, using a tea towel and/or gloves, remove the claws and place them back in the steaming water for a further 5 minutes.

Twist and remove the tail from the head of the lobster. Using a pair of scissors, and with the hard part of the lobster tail in the palm of your hand, cut down the sides of the soft part of the tail so you can remove the lobster tail meat whole. Pull the vein out of the top of the lobster meat.

For the claws, remove each knuckle and push the meat out with the end of a fork. Then pull down on the bottom pincer, snapping it off and, with that, the cartilage from inside the lobster should come out with the pincer. With the back of a large knife, gently break the shell and remove the claw meat in one piece if possible.

To finish and serve
Around 7 to 8 minutes before you are ready to serve, put the tail piece back in the tail shell and dress liberally with the vanilla and white pepper vinaigrette.

Cook with the claw meat, dressed on a tray, in the oven at 180°C/350°F/gas mark 4, or under the grill/broiler, until just cooked through, approximately 5 minutes.

Remove from the shell if you wish and serve with anything you fancy, such as a simple leaf salad or roasted vegetables drizzled with vanilla oil (see page 222).

Slow-Roasted Oxtail Pot Pies

with vanilla Shiraz gravy

When I was 10, one of my most favourite dinnertime treats that I could prepare solo was Banquet pot pies. Often on special offer at 49 cents, this frozen meal in a tin was so simple. But it was an agonising 45-minute wait for it to bake and bubble, then another 10 minutes before it cooled enough to eat a spoonful of crumbly pastry, meat and sauce - or the roof of my mouth would catch on fire! Here is my grown-up version, that can be started up to a day ahead.

SERVES 4

OXTAIL FILLING

vegetable oil	3 Tbsp	45 ml	1½ fl oz
oxtail, evenly sized, cut 5-cm/2-in thick	12 pieces	1 kg	2 lb
plain/all-purpose flour, seasoned with salt and pepper	⅓ cup	45 g	1½ oz
Shiraz or spicy red wine	½ bottle	375 ml	12½ fl oz
garlic heads, halved crosswise	2	120 g	4½ oz
onion, peeled and quartered	1	200 g	7 oz
shallots, peeled and halved	4	170 g	6 oz
carrot, peeled and cut in 5-cm/2-in pieces	2	120 g	4 oz
parsnip, peeled and cut in 5-cm/2-in pieces	1	60 g	2 oz
vanilla pods, split	2		
peppercorns	10		
beef stock or demi-glace	4 fl cups 2 fl cups	1 L 475 ml	1 qt 16 fl oz
thyme sprigs	10		

POT PIE PASTRY CRUST

plain/all-purpose flour	1 cup	120 g	4¼ oz
wholemeal/wholewheat flour	⅓ cup	40 g	1⅓ oz
white sugar	2 tsp	10 g	
fine sea salt	¼ tsp		
paprika	¼ tsp		
unsalted butter, cut in 1-cm/½-in pieces, chilled	⅓ cup + 1 Tbsp	100 g	3½ oz
egg yolk	1	30 ml	1 fl oz
ice water	¼ cup	60 ml	2 fl oz
cider vinegar	½ tsp		
yolk for eggwash	1	30 ml	1 fl oz

Oxtail filling

Heat oil in a large, heavy-bottomed saucepan/pot with a lid over medium heat.* Dredge the oxtail pieces in seasoned flour and place the pieces in the pan/pot in one layer. Brown meat on all sides, then remove from pan/pot. Add wine, reduce by half then add meat back in pan/pot. Reserve leftover flour to thicken filling.

Tuck the garlic heads, onion, shallots, carrot and parsnip in spaces between the oxtail. Add vanilla pods, peppercorns, beef stock and top with thyme sprigs.

Bring to a simmer, cover the pan/pot and leave to gently simmer for about 4 hours, until the meat falls off the bone. Check liquid after 2 hours and meat after 3 hours. Cool for 30 minutes then refrigerate overnight if wished.

Pot pie pastry crust

Sift into a bowl the flours, sugar, salt and paprika.

Cut in chilled butter with a pastry cutter or blend/pulse in a food processor until butter is pea-sized. Whisk yolk, water and vinegar together and drizzle into the dry mixture, using a fork to toss and incorporate or blend/pulse the food processor just until it begins to come together. Flatten into a pad, wrap in plastic and chill for 1 hour.

On a lightly floured surface, roll out the dough into a 1-cm/½-in thick round. Fold over twice and roll out again to same thickness, being careful not to overwork the dough. Cut with a cookie cutter into 6 circles, 1 cm/½ in larger than the baking ramekins. Place on baking paper-lined tray. Wrap and chill again until ready to bake.

---

* Slow-cooker directions: dredge oxtails in flour mix then brown on all sides with oil in a large frying pan/skillet. Reduce wine as above. Add meat to slow-cooker and following same method as above, add 1 additional cup of stock (240 ml/8 fl oz) to pan/pot. Cook on low for 4–6 hours, adding additional liquid as needed. Finish with same procedure, described on next page.

TO FINISH			
port wine	2 Tbsp	30 ml	1 fl oz
shallots, peeled and quartered	7	340 g	12 oz
anya/peewee potatoes, whole	about 18	500 g	9 oz
carrots, peeled, cut into large dice	2	120 g	4 oz
Worcestershire sauce	1 Tbsp	15 ml	½ fl oz
Shiraz wine	2 Tbsp	30 ml	1 fl oz
reserved flour	1 Tbsp	15 g	½ oz
parsley, chopped	1 Tbsp		
peas, fresh or frozen	1 cup	150 g	5 oz
egg yolk plus 1 tsp water	1	30 ml	1 fl oz

To finish

Skim and discard the fat from the top of the cooked meat. Remove the oxtail from the pan/pot and pull the meat from the bones. Set meat and garlic halves aside, discarding bones, vanilla pods and thyme. If pan/pot is chilled, heat and purée sauce, decanting into a smaller pan/pot.

To the pan/pot add the port, shallots, baby potatoes and carrots. Bring to a simmer and cook until the potatoes and carrots are fork-tender, adding water if needed.

Add the Worcestershire sauce. Stir together the second measure of wine with the reserved 1 Tbsp flour until smooth, then add to the sauce. Gently heat and stir to thicken, sprinkle in the parsley and fold in the oxtail meat and peas until heated through.

Preheat oven to 220°C/425°F/gas mark 7 (200°C/400°F fan).

Divide filling into six 240-ml/8-fl oz/1-fl cup baking ramekins. Brush sides with eggwash and top each with pot pie lid. With leftover dough, roll and cut into strips, then wrap rims with dough strips. Press with tines of small fork to create decorative ridges if wished. Seal edges, brush eggwash over pastry then slit tops to vent.

Place pies on tray and bake for 15 minutes, until golden brown and bubbly. Serve with a glass of Shiraz or beer. *NM*

Vanilla Lacquer Duck Leg

with Shanghai dim sum & lychee lime relish

PAUL JOBIN

SERVES 6			
VANILLA LACQUER DUCK LEGS			
hoisin sauce	½ fl cup	120 ml	4 fl oz
sea salt	1 Tbsp	15 g	½ oz
Chinese five spice	1 Tbsp	10 g	
Shaoxing rice vinegar	½ fl cup	120 ml	4 fl oz
Sichuan pepper, freshly ground	1 Tbsp	10 g	
ginger, fresh, peeled & grated	⅓ cup	75 g	2½ oz
vanilla pods, chopped	2		
honey	⅔ cup	150 ml	5 fl oz
star anise, whole	2		
light soy sauce	¾ fl cup	180 ml	6 fl oz
chicken stock	6 fl cups	1½ L	1½ qt
shallot, peeled, finely sliced and fried	1	60 g	2 oz
duck legs	6	225–300 g each	8–10 oz each
SHANGHAI DIM SUM FILLING			
spring onion, sliced on bias	about 6	200 g	7 oz
sesame oil	2 tsp	10 ml	
peanut oil	4 tsp	20 ml	
white sugar	2 tsp	10 g	
coriander/cilantro, roughly chopped	¾ cup	60 g	2 oz
SHANGHAI DIM SUM DOUGH			
plain/all-purpose flour, sifted	2 cups less 2 Tbsp	200 g	7 oz
duck fat or shortening	¼ cup	60 g	2 oz
water	5 Tbsp	75 ml	2½ fl oz
oil, for frying			
sea salt, to season			

Vanilla lacquer duck legs

In a blender, blitz the hoisin sauce, salt, five spice and rice vinegar.

Add the Sichuan pepper, ginger, vanilla, honey, star anise and soy sauce and blitz again until smooth.

Pour into a bowl, whisking in chicken stock and fried shallot.

Preheat the oven to 160°C/325°F/gas mark 3. Place the duck legs into a deep roasting pan, pour in the lacquer, place on stovetop and bring to the boil. Remove from heat and place in preheated oven.

Braise, turning the duck every 30 minutes for about 1½ hours. Remove the duck legs to a tray to cool.

Strain the lacquer, discard the solids and skim off the fat.

Shanghai dim sum filling

In a mixing bowl, stir the ingredients together.

Shanghai dim sum dough

In a mixing bowl, rub duck fat into flour.

Add water and mix to a smooth silky dough for 5 minutes, until a sheen develops.

Wrap in clingfilm/plastic wrap and rest for 20 minutes.

Cut the dough into 18 equal pieces and roll each piece of dough through a pasta machine.

Trim each sheet into a rectangle, place a strip of filling on the long edge and roll up, sealing it with water.

Squeeze one end shut and poke it into the open end to resemble a donut. Squeeze to secure.

Store at room temperature on non-stick baking paper until ready to cook.

Heat frying oil to 180°C/350°F, deep-fry until the dim sum float. Drain on absorbent paper and season with sea salt.

LYCHEE LIME RELISH			
slightly green banana	1	200 g	7 oz
lychees, whole, peeled	⅔ cup	130 g	4½ oz
black sesame seeds, toasted	1 Tbsp	10 g	
coriander/cilantro, chopped	1 Tbsp	10 g	
mint leaves, chopped	2 tsp		
garlic cloves, peeled, sliced and fried	3–4	15 g	½ oz
ginger, peeled, julienned and fried	1 Tbsp	15 g	½ oz
red onion, peeled, sliced and fried	half	75 g	2½ oz
sesame oil	1 tsp		
peanut oil	1 Tbsp	15 ml	½ fl oz
dark palm sugar (Gula Malacca)	2 Tbsp	30 g	1 oz
lime juice	2 Tbsp	30 ml	1 fl oz
fish sauce	4 tsp	20 ml	¾ fl oz
TO SERVE			
freeze-dried lychees (optional)			

Lychee lime relish (best made fresh on the day)
Cut banana into small dice and slice lychees in half. Place in a mixing bowl and add sesame seeds, aromatic herbs, garlic, ginger, red onion and oils. Fold just to mix.

Toss in the sugar, lime juice and fish sauce, and gently fold together.

To finish and serve
Place the duck legs into the simmering lacquer, allow to warm through, approximately 15 minutes, drain and place onto 3 crispy dim sum, top with the lychee lime relish and crushed freeze-dried lychees, if wished.

My vanilla memory is my grandmother telling me that a whiff of vanilla would calm us grandchildren. I admit I didn't know back then that vanilla was actually a bean – I thought it came in a miniature bottle until I started cooking. During my bachelor days as a restaurateur, a few years back, I had an abundance of used beans (and not enough jars of sugar to put them in) which I semi-dried in the New Zealand sunshine. I then placed this bounty into a stocking (you can just wonder where the stocking may have come from!), knotted it and hung it in the wardrobe to combat mildew, moisture and smelly boys' shoes. I remember a visitor commenting that they knew I was a chef because my cottage smelt of dessert... not sure whether this wooed the girls though. PJ

Goat Cheese & Vanilla Ravioli

with grilled asparagus tips & beurre noisette dressing

JASON DELL

SERVES 4			
PASTA DOUGH			
fine semolina	¾ cup	125 g	4½ oz
'00' pasta flour*	1 cup	125 g	4½ oz
egg, large	1		
egg yolks, large	3	90 ml	3 fl oz
water	1½ tsp		
sea salt	pinch		
GOAT CHEESE FILLING			
soft goat cheese	½ cup + 1 Tbsp	150 g	5¼ oz
vanilla paste (I use Heilala)	1½ tsp		
fresh chives, chopped fine	1½ Tbsp		
chopped preserved lemon	½ tsp		
toasted macadamia nuts, chopped	¼ cup	50 g	1½ oz
additional semolina for dusting baking tray/cookie sheet	2 Tbsp		
BEURRE NOISETTE			
unsalted butter	¼ cup	60 g	2 oz
TO SERVE			
asparagus tips, blanched or chargrilled	12 pieces		
good quality Reggiano Parmesan cheese, finely grated	¼ cup	20 g	¾ oz
chives, snipped fine	¼ cup	20 g	¾ oz
macadamia nuts, toasted and roughly chopped	¼ cup	30 g	1 oz

* '00' indicates the flour has been very finely ground. You can also use a plain/all-purpose flour to make pasta.

Pasta dough
In a food processor, blend/pulse all ingredients together until well combined. Remove to a bench and knead dough by hand until smooth. Wrap in clingfilm/plastic wrap and rest in the refrigerator for 30 minutes before rolling.

Goat cheese filling
Combine the goat cheese, vanilla, chives, preserved lemon and macadamia nuts in a food processor. Blend/pulse until just combined. Adjust seasoning. Cover and chill.

To make ravioli
Roll pasta out through pasta machine to second-last setting.

Place large teaspoons of filling onto pasta at intervals approx 3 cm/1 in apart. Brush lightly around filling with water, then carefully place a second sheet of pasta on top.

First use an inverted cookie cutter (i.e. not the sharp edge) on the top layer of pasta to help keep the filling enclosed and to pinch the pasta sheets together, but DO NOT cut through. Then, using a second cookie cutter with a wider diameter, cut the ravioli out by pressing down firmly on the cookie cutter.

Place ravioli on a tray/sheet dusted with fine semolina and chill until required.

Beurre noisette
Place butter in a small saucepan over medium heat, stirring occasionally, and cook until nutty brown. Set aside until serving.

To serve
When ready to serve, blanch the ravioli in plenty of salted boiling water and cook till al dente. Remove with a slotted spoon into a bowl. Season with salt and pepper, add the asparagus tips, and drizzle over the beurre noisette. Arrange in pasta bowls, sprinkle over the grated Parmesan, chives, macadamia nuts and lastly drizzle over a little more beurre noisette.

Pineapple Marinated Fish

with grilled fruit & spicy pineapple vanilla vinaigrette

'This requires an extraction juicer to make, but it is a great machine to own for many reasons. The recipe is also very fine for finishing grilled pork ribs, as well as marinating a fatty fish for the grill or a hot wok, or as a dressing for luxuriously rich fruits!'

NORMAN VAN AKEN

GF SERVES 4

PINEAPPLE VANILLA VINAIGRETTE

pineapple juice (must be freshly extracted from 1 large pineapple)	3 fl cups	700 ml	24 fl oz
juice of jalapeño, stems and seeds discarded	1½ Tbsp	20 ml	¾ fl oz
vanilla pods, split in half lengthways and scraped	2		
cider wine vinegar	2 Tbsp	30 ml	1 fl oz
lime, squeeze or more of one	2 Tbsp	30 ml	1 fl oz
extra virgin olive oil	1 cup	240 ml	8 fl oz
tamari or light soy sauce	2 Tbsp	30 ml	1 fl oz
Kosher or sea salt and freshly cracked black pepper	to taste		

GRILLED FISH AND FRUIT

bamboo skewers soaked in water for at least 30 minutes	8–12		
grey triggerfish, hapuku, bass or similar firm white fish	4 equal pieces	150 g each	4–6 oz each
selection of fresh fruit such as mango, pineapple, nectarines, figs with skin on, thickly sliced			

Pineapple vanilla vinaigrette

Gently simmer the freshly extracted pineapple juice, jalapeño juice and scraped vanilla pods, with seeds, into a saucepan/pot and simmer until reduced down to 250 ml/8 fl oz/1 fl cup, stirring occasionally.

Place the reduction in a clean mixing bowl. Whisk in the remaining ingredients, season with salt and pepper, then cover and chill until needed.

Grilled fish and fruit

Soak skewers in water.

Pat fish dry and place in a baking dish. Brush each piece with a generous portion of the vinaigrette and allow fish to marinate for 20–30 minutes as the grill heats up.

Carefully skewer fruit, brush with marinade and set aside.

When ready to cook, wipe the grill lightly with oil and place fruit skewers and fish on the grill. Carefully turn when sides of fish turn opaque and fruit has seared.

Serve immediately with additional vinaigrette on the side.

Every child has a memory of vanilla. I challenge anyone to not be able to conjure a once-lost memory when a vanilla pod is split and set before them. To test this theory, I went to my pastry chef's shop. She was curious as to why I was investigating her prized pods but I left her to wonder and continue her tasks. I returned to my desk and found myself with the smiling countenance of my long departed 'Nana'. She was delighted to see me after many years in Heaven. When I was 10, my grandmother, Nana, came to live with us. She had lived in New York City her entire life, and was now in the hinterlands of northern Illinois watching over my two sisters, Bette and Jane, and me. They were golden times. I came to adore Nana, as she bathed me in a kind of unconditional approval steeled with great expectations. She also allowed me to bring her one bourbon every night before our dinner. That bourbon joined my memories as I sat with the vanilla pod. And without taking a drop, I was drunk as an Irishman. **NVA**

The Pork Chop
with caramelised pear & onion compote

Ahh. . . the cardboard pork chop incident. It was to be a small London dinner party with my partner's childhood friends. Friends I had never met. Friends I had hoped to impress with a memorable meal. It was memorable - and not so good. Even a large steak knife was no match for those chops. Nine years later, whispered tales of the Tower Bridge Pork Chop can still be heard. If I had only known the secret of succulent pork chops that day! It's brine: I can't wait for Tony and Margaret to try these.

GF SERVES 4

bone-in pork loin chops* rind on (2½–4 cm/1–1½ in thick)	4	220 g each	7 oz each
vanilla oil (page 222) for brushing chops	1 Tbsp	15 ml	½ fl oz
GINGER BEER BRINE			
water	4 fl cups	1 L	1 qt
fine sea salt	4 Tbsp	60 g	2¼ oz
brown sugar	2 Tbsp	30 g	1 oz
ginger ale/ginger beer	bottle	500 ml	17 fl oz
yellow mustard seed	1 Tbsp	10 g	
fresh ginger, chopped	2-in piece	20 g	¾ oz
vanilla pods**	1–2		
peppercorns	10		
fresh bay leaves, bruised	3		
PEAR-ONION COMPOTE			
grapeseed or vegetable oil	5 tsp	25 ml	1¼ fl oz
medium onions, peeled and chopped in 1-cm/½-in pieces	2	325 g	11 oz
grainy mustard	2 Tbsp	30 g	1 oz
runny honey	2 tsp	10 ml	
apple cider or white wine vinegar	2 tsp	10 ml	
vanilla paste	2 tsp	10 ml	
white wine such as Riesling or Gewürztraminer	½ fl cup	120 ml	4 fl oz
chicken stock	¾ fl cup	180 ml	6 fl oz
pear, large, firm, peeled, cored and cut into 1-cm/½-in pieces	1	200 g	7 oz
fresh thyme sprigs	4		

* If you are fortunate enough to get a pork chop with crackling skin on, here's Brendan the Butcher's tip: pour boiling water over scored pork skin until it curls back. Brine as indicated and, just before grilling, pack pork skin with butter and a layer of salt.

** Smoky oven-cured Indonesian vanilla pods are ideal for this dish.

Ginger beer brine
Put pork chops in a large sealable plastic bag.

In a large jug/pitcher, stir the brine ingredients together, pour into the pork chop bag and seal.

Place sealed bag in a dish and refrigerate for 2–6 hours or overnight, turning the bag over occasionally.

Pear-onion compote
In a sauté pan, over medium–low heat, heat oil and onions. Stir occasionally, until they are caramelised – about 20 minutes. While onion mixture is cooking, mix mustard, honey, vinegar and vanilla paste in a small bowl. Set aside.

Deglaze the pan with the wine and scrape up the bits of browned onion with a wooden or silicone spoon until nearly dry. Add stock occasionally and reduce by half, then add the pear and thyme. Simmer the compote until pears are fork-tender, caramelised and the liquid is reduced. Fold in the mustard mixture and add sea salt and fresh cracked pepper to taste.

Turn off heat, cover and keep warm while chops are cooking. Can be made a day ahead and reheated just before serving.

To grill the chops
Remove chops and discard brine. Rinse under running cold water and pat dry.

Brush both sides with vanilla oil and allow 20 minutes to let meat come to room temperature.

Heat barbecue grill to medium–high. Place chops on hot grill and cook without moving them for 3 minutes. Lift chops, make a quarter turn and return to grill for an additional 3 minutes. Turn chops over and repeat steps for an additional 5–6 minutes. Place chops crackling side on grill, holding with tongs or leaning on a rack and cooking until crispy, 3–5 minutes. Remove from grill, loosely cover and allow to rest for 10 minutes.

Serve chops immediately with warmed pear-onion compote and a chilled glass of Gewürztraminer, Riesling or Rosé. *NM*

Seared Scallops with Vanilla Parsnip Purée

ELIZABETH FALKNER

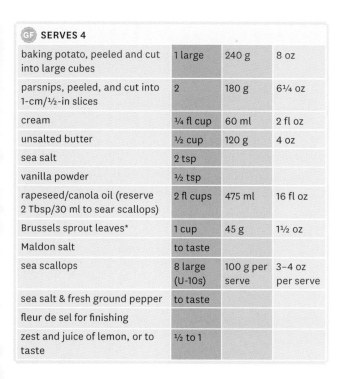

GF SERVES 4			
baking potato, peeled and cut into large cubes	1 large	240 g	8 oz
parsnips, peeled, and cut into 1-cm/½-in slices	2	180 g	6¼ oz
cream	¼ fl cup	60 ml	2 fl oz
unsalted butter	½ cup	120 g	4 oz
sea salt	2 tsp		
vanilla powder	½ tsp		
rapeseed/canola oil (reserve 2 Tbsp/30 ml to sear scallops)	2 fl cups	475 ml	16 fl oz
Brussels sprout leaves*	1 cup	45 g	1½ oz
Maldon salt	to taste		
sea scallops	8 large (U-10s)	100 g per serve	3–4 oz per serve
sea salt & fresh ground pepper	to taste		
fleur de sel for finishing			
zest and juice of lemon, or to taste	½ to 1		

AUTHOR'S NOTE: The photo opposite shows this dish served with flash-fried basil leaves as there was not a single Brussels sprout leaf to be found in all of London when Elizabeth's dish was photographed. If sprouts are hard to come by, you can, as I did here, substitute 30 g/1 oz/1 cup of fresh basil leaves, and lessen frying time to 15 seconds.

Place potato in a small saucepan, cover with water and bring to the boil. Cook potato until tender. Do the same with parsnips in a separate saucepan. (They cook at different times.) Drain and either use ricer or food processor to purée the two together.

Add the cream and 4 Tbsp (55 g/2 oz) of butter along with salt and vanilla powder. Reserve in a warm spot.

Heat the rapeseed/canola oil in a medium saucepan to 180°C/350°F and drop the Brussels sprout leaves in for a minute or until crispy. Drain on paper towels then season with Maldon salt. Set aside until ready to plate.

Heat a large non-stick sauté pan on high heat. Add 2 Tbsp of the rapeseed/canola oil. Dry the scallops off very well and season with salt and pepper. Add to the sauté pan and sear until very brown on one side and then flip over and turn off the heat. Remove the scallops and set in a warm spot. Wipe out the pan with a paper towel.

Put a large spoonful of the parsnip and vanilla purée in the centre of each plate. Place 2 or 3 scallops on each plate. Divide the Brussels sprout leaves over each.

Add the remaining butter to the sauté pan and brown. Quickly add the lemon juice and zest. Drizzle on each plate, sprinkle with the fleur de sel and serve immediately.

Scotch Fillet Steak

with chilli-vanilli sauce

A garlicky, spicy chilli sauce simmered with a single vanilla pod adds a seductive aroma to the umami flavour of beef as it is spooned over a freshly grilled scotch fillet. Outside of New Zealand and Australia this cut is known as a rib-eye, entrecôte or Delmonico. Richly flavoured and well-marbled, this boneless steak is ideal for grilling on the barbecue or pan cooking.

GF SERVES 4

CHILLI-VANILLI SAUCE			
garlic cloves, peeled & crushed	3 large	15 g	½ oz
red jalapeño or chilli peppers, seeds optional, finely chopped	2–3	45 g	1½ oz
palm sugar or brown sugar	½ cup	100 g	3½ oz
vanilla pod, split and scraped	1		
water	½ fl cup	120 ml	4 fl oz
lime juice and zest of ½	1 Tbsp	15 ml	½ fl oz
kaffir lime leaves	2		
fish sauce	1 tsp		
fine sea salt	2 tsp		
rice wine vinegar	1 Tbsp	15 ml	½ fl oz
SCOTCH FILLET STEAK			
scotch fillet or rib eye steaks	4	225 g ea	8 oz ea
oil for coating steaks	2 Tbsp	30 ml	1 fl oz
salt to season for the grill	to taste		
TO SERVE			
coriander/cilantro for garnish	1 cup	85 g	3 oz

Chilli-vanilli sauce

Combine the garlic, jalapeño (seeds optional), sugar, vanilla pod and seeds, water, lime juice and zest, lime leaves, fish sauce and salt in a small saucepan.

Bring to the boil over medium–high heat. Lower the heat and simmer until the mixture begins to thicken and the garlic–pepper bits begin to soften. After about 3 minutes, whisk in vinegar and allow to cool completely.

Remove lime leaves and transfer the vanilla pod to a tall bottle. Using a funnel, fill the bottle with the sauce and refrigerate. Will keep refrigerated for 2 weeks.

Scotch fillet steak

Heat a barbecue flat-top grill or a frying pan/skillet to high. Pat steaks dry, then brush both sides with oil. Season with salt and sear on the first side, without moving the steak, over high heat about 3 minutes. Flip over and cook an additional 5–7 minutes. Remove steaks from heat and rest 5 minutes.

To finish and serve

Thinly slice steaks against the grain and fan onto plate. Drizzle with warmed chilli–vanilli sauce* and a scattering of coriander/cilantro if wished. Serve with a luscious red wine. *NM*

* To make a great chilli-vanilli vinaigrette, whisk into the chilli-vanilla sauce a dash of toasted sesame oil, 120 ml/4 fl oz/½ cup of grapeseed oil and 1 Tbsp/30 ml/1 fl oz rice wine vinegar. Drizzle over a handful of salad leaves and steak slices.

New Zealand Cassoulet

This hearty meal-in-a-bowl was created for Marsden Estate Winery in Bay of Islands, New Zealand. It uses a variety of beans, local lamb and 'Brendan's sausages' from the local butcher, Churchill's. Served with baby root vegetables and a bottle of Marsden's Syrah, this turns a cold-night friends-and-family gathering into a celebration!

GF   **SERVES 6**

THREE BEAN MEDLEY			
dried beans, 3 colourful, e.g. cranberry, cannellini & turtle	⅔ cup each	150 g each	5 oz each
ONE-POT CASSOULET			
vegetable oil	3 Tbsp	45 ml	1½ fl oz
lamb shoulder, boned, cut in 4 pieces,	1	750 g	1½ lb
with lamb bones if possible	3–4 bones	450 g	1 lb
lardons*/thick cut bacon	1 cup	250 g	9 oz
white onions, medium, peeled and diced	2	250 g	9 oz
carrots, medium, peeled and cut into large dice	1½ cups	250 g	9 oz
fresh thyme sprigs	10		
rich red wine, e.g. Syrah	1⅔ fl cup	400 ml	14 fl oz
garlic cloves, peeled and sliced	12	140 g	5 oz
allspice berries**	3		
vanilla pod, sliced lengthways	2		
cracked black pepper	2 tsp		
lamb or beef stock	4 fl cups	1 L	1 qt
fennel bulb, medium, diced	1	250 g	9 oz
BRENDAN'S FENNEL–VANILLA SAUSAGE			
pork or sausage meat, chilled	4½ cups	1 kg	2¼ lb
vanilla paste	1 tsp		
sea salt	1 Tbsp	15 g	½ oz
fennel seed, toasted	2½ Tbsp	20 g	¾ oz
iced water	⅓ fl cup	80 ml	2½ fl oz
TO FINISH AND SERVE			
vegetable oil	1 Tbsp	15 ml	½ fl oz
fresh parsley, chopped	¼ cup	20 g	¾ oz
fresh thyme leaves, chopped	½ tsp		
lemon juice	3 Tbsp	45 ml	1½ fl oz

* A French term for lightly smoked thick-cut bacon pieces.

** If fresh lamb is strongly scented, use 4 allspice berries.

Three bean medley
Rinse then cover beans in 2½ L/2½ qt cold water with 1 Tbsp salt and bring to the boil. Cover and leave to stand 1 hour.

One-pot cassoulet
Heat oil in large heavy saucepan/pot over medium heat. Pat meat dry. Brown meat and bones on all sides then remove from pan/pot and set aside. In pan/pot, add lardons, onions, carrots and thyme then cook until lightly caramelised. Deglaze pan/pot with half the wine and return meat, bones and vegetables to pan/pot. Rinse and drain beans well then add to pan/pot with garlic, allspice, vanilla, pepper, additional wine and the stock to just cover. Top up with additional water if needed. Cover and cook 1 hour, barely simmering, then add fennel. Cook an additional 2–2½ hours until meat and beans are fork-tender.

Brendan's fennel–vanilla sausage
Leave fat on pork and grind through a mincer or use a blender. Grind through twice or blend till smooth. Add to mixing bowl with vanilla paste, salt, fennel seed and ice water, mixing thoroughly. Divide into 12 pieces.

Roll out a piece of clingfilm/plastic wrap 25-cm/10-in long and place sausage portion into the middle. Fold the clingfilm/plastic wrap over the meat leaving a few inches either side.

Holding the ends of the plastic with your thumb and finger, wind around in circles so plastic is wrapping around the meat creating a sausage shape. When it has wrapped around roughly 6 times, cut the plastic away from the box. Repeat process with remaining pork, then knot each end of plastic to seal, like a plastic-wrapped sausage.

Bring a pan of water to a simmer, drop in the sausages and gently simmer for 12 minutes. Cool and then refrigerate until ready to serve. (Alternatively if you don't have time to wrap and poach sausages you can make 12 quick patties 1½ cm/½ in thick.) Chill until ready to serve cassoulet.

To finish and serve
Peel off plastic and sauté the sausages or the sausage patties in a lightly oiled frying pan/skillet over medium–high heat, turning them over twice until golden brown.

To serve, remove bones, allspice berries and vanilla pods and discard. Break up meat into bite-size pieces. Slice sausages lengthways. Divide cassoulet into warmed bowls, top with 1 or 2 sausages and serve with baby root vegetables and a crusty baguette if wished. *NM*

Crispy Salmon Fillet

with fennel broth & creamy polenta

One of the challenges for a chef hosting a dinner party is finding moments to socialise with guests while calmly cooking an impressive meal. Of course, that's the challenge for home cooks as well. So I created this, my first savoury vanilla dish, for just these occasions. I call it elegant comfort food. Everything except for the actual cooking of the salmon is done ahead of time, allowing you to enjoy your guests' company.

GF **SERVES 4**

FENNEL BROTH			
fennel bulb, trimmed, cored and fronds reserved	½ (or 3 small)	150 g	5 oz
carrot, medium, peeled	1	125 g	4 oz
onion, finely chopped	½ cup	80 g	3 oz
water or vegetable stock	3 fl cups	700 ml	24 fl oz
lemon juice	2 Tbsp	60 ml	2 fl oz
parsley, finely chopped/minced	2 Tbsp		
sea salt and pepper	to taste		
POLENTA			
water (or add 8 fl oz/1 fl cup chicken or vegetable stock to ¾ L/¾ qt/3 fl cups water)	4 fl cups	1 L	1 qt
fine sea salt	1 Tbsp	15 g	½ oz
brown sugar, packed	1 Tbsp	15 g	½ oz
polenta (not quick-cooking)	1 cup	140 g	5 oz
mascarpone or thick plain Greek yogurt	⅓ cup	85 g	3 oz
vanilla paste	1 Tbsp	15 ml	½ fl oz
SALMON			
wild or locally caught salmon, skin on, boned	4 equal pieces	450 g	1 lb
grapeseed or vegetable oil for brushing	1 Tbsp	15 ml	½ fl oz

* Polenta can be made 20 minutes ahead of serving and kept covered on the stove (do not leave to stand longer or it will solidify). Just before serving, stir in the mascarpone and vanilla paste. This will make more than you need for this dish, but you can serve leftover polenta with fried eggs for breakfast.

Fennel broth

Using a mandoline or sharp knife, cut fennel into very thin slices. Place in bowl, cover with water and set aside.

Cut carrot in half and cut one half into 5-cm/2-in chunks and the other into matchstick-sized pieces. Reserve fennel fronds, matchstick carrots and 2 Tbsp of onion.

In 1-L/1-qt saucepan/pot add water or stock, fennel, carrot chunks and rest of onion. Bring to a gentle simmer. Reduce by half, add lemon juice, parsley, and season with salt and pepper. Remove from heat and set aside.

Polenta

Bring water, salt and sugar to the boil in a 2 L/2 qt pan/ pot. Stream in polenta, stirring constantly with a wooden spoon. Reduce heat to medium, stirring an additional 3 minutes. Reduce heat to low, cover and simmer polenta*, stirring briefly every 10 minutes for about 40 minutes total. Remove from heat, stir in mascarpone and vanilla paste until blended. Serve warm.

Salmon

Strain broth and heat liquid to a simmer with reserved vegetable pieces.

Heat a heavy-bottomed sauté pan on high heat and turn on your extractor fan! Pat salmon pieces dry, brush with oil and sprinkle with sea salt. Sear salmon in pan skin-side down, cooking 4–5 minutes, depending on thickness, until edges become a white-pink. Carefully turn salmon over and cook another 2 minutes. Turn off heat and leave to rest in the pan. The fish will continue to cook as the pan cools. If you prefer your fish a little more done, leave a few minutes longer.

To serve

Place a large spoonful of polenta in each bowl and place salmon on top. Pour the steamy broth around the polenta and top salmon with a spoonful of vanilla aioli (page 222). Serve immediately. *NM*

Steamed Barramundi & Fregola Salad

with vanilla & black pepper vinaigrette

'Fregola, a Sardinian dried pasta similar to Israeli couscous, pairs perfectly with barramundi and this fresh citrus-and-vanilla-infused vinaigrette.'

CHRISTINE MANFIELD

SERVES 4

BLACK PEPPER VINAIGRETTE			
lemon juice	5 tsp	25 ml	1 fl oz
orange juice	2½ Tbsp	40 ml	1½ fl oz
rice vinegar	2 Tbsp	30 ml	1 fl oz
aged balsamic vinegar	4 tsp	20 ml	⅔ fl oz
vanilla pod seeds	½ a pod		
freshly ground black pepper	1 tsp		
sea salt	½ tsp		
muscovado sugar	1½ tsp	10 g	
Colonna orange-infused extra virgin olive oil	5 tsp	25 ml	1 fl oz
extra virgin olive oil	1 fl cup + 2 Tbsp	275 ml	9⅓ fl oz
FREGOLA			
medium fregola	1¼ cups	225 g	8 oz
STEAMED BARRAMUNDI			
barramundi* fillets, boneless, skinless	4	700 g	1½ lb
lettuce or Chinese cabbage/ Napa leaves to wrap fish	4		
salt and pepper	to taste		

* Other firm white fish are suitable, such as sea bass, grouper and tarakihi.

Black pepper vinaigrette
Whisk all ingredients together with hand-/stick-blender till emulsified. Makes 350 ml/12 fl oz/1½ cups.

Fregola
Cook fregola in a medium saucepan of boiling salted water until al dente, about 8 minutes. Drain in a colander and allow to cool, shaking colander occasionally to drain all excess water from pasta.

Return to pan to keep warm.

Steamed barramundi
Fill a steamer pan/pot with about 5 cm/2 in of water. Heat to a simmer. Use a bamboo steamer basket or pan/pot steamer insert, making sure the steamer does not touch the simmering water.

Wrap each fillet in a leaf, tucking in the leaf ends to make a little package. Place the wrapped fish in a single layer in the steamer basket and place lid on top. Allow the fish to gently steam for about 8 minutes, then turn off the heat.

To serve
Immediately plate each dish with a helping of fregola then unwrap each fillet, discarding the leaves, and place on top of the pasta. Drizzle all over with the black pepper vinaigrette. Serve warm.

Chicken Stroganoff with Chanterelles & Vanilla

JONATHAN WAXMAN

SERVES 4

SPAETZLE (GERMAN NOODLE)

egg yolk	1	30 ml	1 fl oz
egg, large	1		
cream	1 fl cup	240 ml	8 fl oz
plain/all-purpose flour	1½ cups	180 g	6½ oz
kosher or sea salt	1 tsp		
freshly ground pepper	¼ tsp		
unsalted butter, melted	¼ fl cup	60 ml	2 fl oz
olive oil	2 Tbsp	30 ml	1 fl oz

CHICKEN

chicken breast (organic, skin on and boneless)	2 whole	approx 170 g	approx 6 oz
unsalted butter	½ cup	120 g	4 oz
shallots	2	90 g	3 oz
fresh chanterelle mushrooms,* washed and dried	4 cups	240 g	8½ oz
Tio Pepe**	1 Tbsp	15 ml	½ fl oz
vanilla seeds, 1 pod	1 tsp		
crème fraîche	½ cup	120 g	4 oz

* Or, if unavailable, a selection of field mushrooms.

** This classic bone-dry sherry from Andalucia, Spain enhances the flavour of pure vanilla.

Spaetzle

In a small bowl, beat the egg yolk, egg and cream together.

In a medium bowl, combine flour, salt and pepper. Add butter and the egg mixture to the flour mixture and mix by hand until well blended. Do not overmix at this stage. Cover the bowl and refrigerate. Allow the batter to rest for at least 1 hour.

In a large saucepan/pot, bring 1 L/1 qt of salted water to a simmer. Prepare a bowl of ice water.

Using a colander, force the batter in batches through the holes into the simmering water. The spaetzle will cook in 3 minutes. When they float to the top, use a slotted spoon to scoop the noodles into the bowl of ice water to prevent overcooking. When cold, drain and dry. Add olive oil to prevent spaetzle sticking together. Set aside until needed.

Chicken

Slice the chicken breast into 8 slices per breast. Season with sea salt and pepper.

Using a heavy casserole pan, add half the butter and brown the chicken slices. Remove the chicken and add remaining butter to the pan. Add the shallots and chanterelles and cook until browned slightly. Add the Tio Pepe and the vanilla, cook for 2 minutes, then stir in the crème fraîche.

Reintroduce the chicken slices. Heat to a simmer and add the spaetzle. Toss well, season and serve hot.

When I was young, my parents would go out for the evening leaving me in charge of we three boys (aged 10, 9 and 6), and dinner was up to our own design. The first meal I remember making was a batch of shortbread cookies from The Joy of Cooking. The recipe I reproduced on my Mom's handy Sunbeam Mixmaster and the ingredients could not have been simpler: sugar, flour, butter, salt and pure vanilla extract. When I unscrewed the top of the vanilla, I was filled with instant euphoria. Little did I know it was 40 proof! The cookies were eaten still piping hot from the oven. The recipe asked that you let them 'cure' for a week or so, but we were famished, and the smell of those vanilla-laced cookies was intoxicating! **JW**

Blue Plates* & Brunch Plates

❧

* The 'blue plate' is a US invention. Literally a plate, it was made up of three compartments – one each for main, side and dessert.
Most popular during the Depression Era of the 1920s and '30s, the cheap and cheerful daily 'Blue Plate Special' was affordable to most.
Meatloaf, fried chicken and sandwiches were some of the rotating daily choices on the chalkboard menu – all for '2 bits' (25 cents).

Monty's Surprise: The Baked Apple

The baked apple – how simple, how comforting. Stuffed with chestnut & vanilla streusel, drizzled with speckled vanilla syrup and served warm from the oven with feijoa ice cream, this recipe makes a dimpled and freckled backyard apple delicious, nutritious and divine!

SERVES 4

CHESTNUT & VANILLA STREUSEL			
brown sugar, packed	1 cup	225 g	8 oz
white sugar	1 cup	200 g	7 oz
plain/all-purpose flour	1¼ cups	120 g	4½ oz
chestnut flour*	½ cup	170 g	6 oz
vanilla powder	2 tsp		
cinnamon	1 tsp		
ground cardamom	½ tsp		
nutmeg, fresh grated	½ tsp		
fine sea salt	1 tsp		
lemon zest	1 tsp		
unsalted butter, cut into small dice, chilled	¾ cup	170 g	6 oz

TO BAKE			
large apples suitable for baking such as Monty's Surprise,** Bramley or MacIntosh (whatever is local)	4	200 g ea	7 oz ea
brown sugar for baking pan	¼ cup	55 g	2 oz
vanilla syrup (page 222) for drizzling	½ fl cup	120 ml	4 fl oz

* You can find this at speciality grocers, Italian grocers or online, or substitute almond or hazelnut flour.

** 'Monty's Surprise' is a New Zealand heirloom apple and is excellent for eating and baking. Many heritage apples have high levels of beneficial plant compounds and most are found in the skin, so eat the whole apple!

Chestnut & vanilla streusel
In a stand-mixer with paddle attachment, mix all but the lemon zest and butter on low speed until well combined. Add lemon zest. Turn mixer off and add chilled butter all at once.

Turn mixer to slow and process until streusel is combined but still chunky, like your favourite granola. Do not walk away from mixer because the streusel will clump into a large ball. If this happens, sift the streusel through a wire sieve/strainer or tamis, then chill well.

Store chilled in a container with a tightly-fitting lid until ready to use. (This will keep 3 weeks chilled or you can freeze for up to 3 months. Use extra streusel as a topping for muffins, scones or enjoying more baked apples!)

To bake
Preheat oven to 180°C/350°F/gas mark 4.

Wash and core the apples. With a paring knife, cut a shallow ring just through the peel two-thirds of the way up the apple, this helps prevent the cooking apple pulp from exploding out the top. Set apples in a 20 x 20-cm/8 x 8-in baking dish. Pack the centres with the streusel and mound a bit on the top. Pour in a small amount of water, just to cover the bottom of the pan, then sprinkle apples with brown sugar. Place in oven and bake just until fork-tender, about 30–35 minutes.

To serve
Put warmed apple on plate, drizzle with vanilla syrup and serve with a scoop of feijoa–vanilla ice cream (page 225). *NM*

Coronation Chicken

on squashy poppy buns

Hands-down my favourite sandwich: a little sweet, a little spicy and scented with vanilla. These petite sliders – the filling created, they say, for the Queen's coronation – are perfect for picnics, brunches and parties.

MAKES 12			
CHICKEN SALAD			
chicken, boneless skinless breast and/or thighs, cooked	3 cups	450 g	1 lb
mayonnaise	½ cup	115 g	4 oz
Greek yogurt	¼ cup	60 g	2 oz
curry powder, mild	1½ tsp		
mango chutney	2 Tbsp	30 g	1 oz
chives, finely chopped/minced	1 Tbsp		
red onion, diced small	¼ cup	35 g	1¼ oz
slivered almonds, toasted	2 Tbsp	20 g	¾ oz
dried mango, chopped	2 Tbsp	35 g	1¼ oz
red bell pepper/capsicum, diced small	¼ cup	45 g	1½ oz
lime juice	2 Tbsp	30 ml	1 fl oz
orange zest	1 tsp		
vanilla paste	1 tsp		
BUNS			
plain/all-purpose flour	2 cups	250 g	9 oz
baking powder	1 Tbsp		
poppy seeds	2 tsp		
sea salt	½ tsp		
unsalted butter, chilled	⅓ cup	75 g	2½ oz
runny honey	2 tsp	10 ml	
vanilla paste	1 tsp		
butternut or pumpkin squash, cooked and puréed	1 cup	250 g	9 oz
milk, as needed	2 Tbsp	30 ml	1 fl oz
TO SERVE			
tomatoes, cherry, thinly sliced	12	110 g	4 oz
Iceberg lettuce leaves	4	170 g	6 oz
chives to garnish	1 Tbsp		

Chicken salad
Cut or tear the cooked chicken into bite-size pieces and set aside. Mix the mayonnaise, yogurt and curry powder until smooth. Add remaining ingredients to mayonnaise mixture until well combined. Fold in the chicken pieces. Cover and chill until ready to serve.

Buns
Preheat oven to 200°C/400°F/gas mark 6 (190°C/375°F fan).

Combine flour, baking powder, poppy seeds and salt. Cut butter in small pieces and work into flour with a pastry cutter or forks until butter is the size of small peas.

Stir honey and vanilla paste into puréed squash and fold into flour mixture, adding just enough milk, if needed, to make a soft dough.

Turn dough onto a lightly floured surface. With floured hands, flatten to about 1½-cm/½-in thickness. Knead slightly then gently fold over, rotate 90°, pat out and fold again twice more, dusting with flour if necessary. Work quickly to prevent butter from melting.

Roll dough to 1½ cm/½ in thick. Using a floured cookie cutter, cut into 4-cm/1½-in rounds. Place buns closely together in a 20-cm/9-in square baking pan. Bake until puffed and very lightly browned, 18–20 minutes. Cool for 15 minutes.

To serve
Split open and fill buns with chicken filling. Top with tomatoes, finely shredded lettuce and a sprinkling of chopped chives, and arrange on serving platters. *NM*

Monte Cristo Tropicana

Duke's Tropicana Grill, the 'dive' coffee shop attached to the infamous Tropicana Motel where rockers lived and wrote hit music, was a Hollywood hangout. I was drawn there not to catch a glimpse of Rickie Lee Jones, Tom Waits or the ghost of Janis Joplin, but to enjoy the BEST Monte Cristo this side of Disneyland! Mom and I would wind down Laurel Canyon Boulevard for these Duke's sandwiches as a Sunday brunch treat. Alas, Duke's and the Tropicana are long gone, but the stories and tributes remain.

SERVES 4

MONTE CRISTO BATTER			
plain/all-purpose flour	2 Tbsp	30 g	1 oz
baking powder	¾ tsp		
eggs, large	2		
milk	½ fl cup	120 ml	4 fl oz
whipping cream	½ fl cup	120 ml	4 fl oz
vanilla paste	1 tsp		
APPLE–ONION BUTTER			
apple sauce/applesauce	⅓ cup	150 g	5½ oz
caramelised onions (page 223)	2 Tbsp	50 g	1¾ oz
vanilla paste	¼ tsp		
TO ASSEMBLE			
vanilla brioche (page 74) or Challah egg bread*	8 slices		
gouda	8 slices	230 g	8 oz
turkey or chicken	4 slices	115 g	4 oz
ham	4 slices	115 g	4 oz
butter and oil for frying, each	2 Tbsp	30 ml	1 oz

* Challah is a rich bread traditionally made with eggs, similar to brioche.

Monte Cristo batter
Sift flour, baking powder, a pinch of sea salt and a pinch of sugar in a flat-bottomed bowl large enough to accommodate a sandwich. Whisk eggs, milk, cream and vanilla paste in a small bowl, then stir into dry ingredients. Chill for 30 minutes.

Apple–onion butter
Simmer apple sauce/applesauce in a small saucepan/pot until reduced to a thickened 'butter'. Finely mince caramelised onions, then stir into pan/pot with the vanilla paste.

To assemble
Spread 1 Tbsp apple–onion butter on one side of each brioche slice. Top four pieces with a slice of cheese, then turkey and ham, then a second slice of cheese. Place brioche on top, apple–onion butter side down, and press sandwich down with your hand so it compresses and sticks together.

Over low–medium heat, warm a large frying pan/skillet, add butter and oil then wait until butter foams and sizzles. Quickly dip each sandwich in batter, then let excess batter drip back into bowl. Place sandwich in pan and cook about 3 minutes each side until golden brown and crispy outside with custardy cheesy insides. Drain on paper towels and keep warm in oven if wished. Repeat with remaining sandwiches.

Cut each sandwich in half (or quarters if wished) and serve with your favourite fruit compote – mine is plum – or with heirloom tomato bisque (page 34). *NM*

Jefferson's Coffeecake

Thomas Jefferson was quite the gourmand and even wrote his own cookbook. Well before Julia Child and Cordon Bleu, Jefferson's years in France had an astonishing influence on American food. As the third US President, he introduced French cuisine, French wines and installed a French chef in the White House (which remained unchanged until President Obama brought in an American chef). Jefferson introduced new fruits, vegetables and spices, including figs and, most importantly, vanilla. He enjoyed cooking, baking and entertaining, penning hundreds of recipes, including vanilla ice cream and one for 'coffeecake'. As a British teacake doesn't contain tea, the American coffeecake has no coffee, but both are designed to be enjoyed with a hot beverage. Inspired by Jefferson's recipe, this coffeecake is stuffed with figs, almonds and vanilla. He always served coffeecake warm, so be sure to present it à la Jefferson.

SERVES 6–8

VANILLA BRIOCHE			
active dry yeast	1 Tbsp	10 g	
white sugar	3 Tbsp	45 g	1½ oz
milk, warm (about 40ºC/110ºF)	⅓ cup	80 ml	2½ fl oz
unbleached bread/high grade flour	2¾ cups	330 g	11¾ oz
fine sea salt	¼ tsp		
eggs, large, beaten	2		
vanilla paste, or seeds of 4 vanilla pods	2 Tbsp	30 ml	1 fl oz
unsalted butter, softened	⅓ cup	100 g	3 oz
egg, lightly beaten with 1 tsp water to glaze brioche	1		

BROWNED BUTTER FIG FILLING			
dried figs, or fresh figs	2 cups / 24	340 g / 1 kg	12 oz / 2 lb
unsalted butter	½ cup	110 g	4 oz
vanilla pod, split, scraped & cut in 4 pieces	1		
cinnamon stick	1		
orange juice	½ fl cup	120 ml	4 fl oz
water	½ fl cup	120 ml	4 fl oz
cider vinegar or lemon juice	1 tsp		

ASSEMBLE			
almond paste or marzipan	½ cup	120 g	4 oz

Vanilla brioche

In a stand-mixer or large bowl, sprinkle yeast and 1 Tbsp sugar into milk, give a quick stir and set aside until yeast floats to top and forms a puffy raft, 10–15 minutes. With the dough hook, or using a wooden spoon, add flour, remaining sugar and salt. Mix on low speed, adding eggs and vanilla. Turn speed to medium–low and continue mixing until the dough is slightly elastic, 5–8 minutes. Add softened butter and continue mixing until dough pulls away from the sides and is elastic, which may take up to 15 minutes. Cover with a damp towel and leave to rise in a warm spot until doubled in size, about 1 hour.

Browned butter fig filling

Top and quarter figs. Melt butter over medium heat in a pan, add vanilla, cinnamon and a pinch of sea salt. Gently cook and stir until it froths and begins to turn golden brown. Add orange juice, water and figs (dried figs will take a bit longer to absorb the liquid). Cook down, gently stirring until sauce thickens. Add vinegar or lemon juice to blend. Remove from heat and cool before filling brioche.

Assemble, second rise and bake

Line sturdy baking tray/cookie sheet with baking paper or mat. Transfer dough onto a lightly floured work surface. Roll to form a rectangle about 1-cm/½-in thick. Crumble and sprinkle almond paste over surface, leaving a 1-cm/½-in edge clear around the sides. Cover almond paste with fig filling.

Starting at long edge closest to you, gently lift dough and roll away to form a spiral. Seal edge, carefully turn over, placing seam-side down on baking tray/cookie sheet. Shape into a 'C', cover with a towel and leave to rise for about 45 minutes.

Preheat oven to 190ºC/375ºF/gas mark 5 (180ºC/350ºF fan). Bake 10 minutes, then turn down to 180ºC/350ºF/gas mark 4 (170ºC/325ºF fan), and bake an additional 25 minutes. Cool on tray 15 minutes. Carefully transfer to a cooling rack for another 15 minutes. Serve warm with crème fraîche if wished. *NM*

Crunchy Cornflake Fried Chicken

This is crispy, crunchy, delicious comfort food. Ruth, our babysitter, made the best fried chicken. She also ironed our clothes beautifully. We later learned her secret – a bottle of scotch hidden in the laundry basket! Ruth shook those chicken drumsticks in a big flour-and-spice-filled paper bag then plopped a huge spoonful of Crisco shortening to melt in the electric frying pan/skillet. I've added a crispy cornflake coating to satisfy my love of cornflakes, and finished with a sprinkling of vanilla salt flakes. Here I've used boneless, skinless chicken thighs. If you're making fried chicken like Ruth, simply increase the cooking time by a few minutes for bone-in chicken pieces. Serve as is, or with buttermilk dressing spiked with hot sauce.

SERVES 4–6

VANILLA YOGURT MARINADE			
plain pouring yogurt or buttermilk	2 fl cups	475 ml	16 fl oz
pure vanilla extract	4 tsp	20 ml	¾ fl oz
sea salt	1 tsp		
brown sugar	2 tsp	10 g	
chicken thighs, boneless, skinless	8–12 pieces	750 g	1½ lb
CORNFLAKE COATING			
cornflakes	4 cups	160 g	5½ oz
COOK AND SERVE			
plain/all-purpose flour	1½ cups	185 g	6½ oz
ground white pepper	¼ tsp		
onion powder	½ tsp		
paprika	¼ tsp		
eggs	2		
oil for frying			
vanilla salt flakes (page 222)	to taste		

Vanilla yogurt marinade

Whisk yogurt, vanilla, salt and sugar together. Rinse and pat chicken pieces dry. Arrange chicken in a casserole dish, then pour over yogurt marinade. Move chicken pieces around to evenly distribute marinade. Cover tightly and refrigerate for 2 hours or up to overnight.

Cornflake coating

Spread cornflakes on a baking tray/cookie sheet in one layer and toast in a 120ºC/250ºF/gas mark ½ oven for 30–45 minutes until lightly golden brown. Remove from oven and set aside in a large bowl. Lightly crunch the cornflakes in your hands – very fun – so some flakes are broken and some remain whole.

Cook and serve

Place a cooling rack inside a baking tray/cookie sheet and set aside. Heat the oven to 150ºC/300ºF/gas mark 2. Take chicken out of fridge. In a flat bowl or cake tin, mix flour and spices together. Then, in another bowl or tin, whisk eggs with a few tablespoons of water.

Arrange the four dishes in a line: marinated chicken, flour, egg, cornflakes. Using one hand as the wet hand and one as the dry, remove a piece of chicken from marinade, lightly coat in flour, then dip in egg, and finally crust with cornflakes. Arrange on a large baking tray/ cookie sheet or plate. Repeat with the remaining chicken pieces.

Warm a large frying pan/skillet over medium heat. Add 3 cm/1 in oil and attach a sugar/candy thermometer to the frying/skillet pan. When oil reaches 180ºC/350ºF, place a few chicken pieces in pan, making sure oil does not go below 160ºC/325ºF. Cook for 4–5 minutes, turning halfway through. Drain on paper towels then transfer to cooling rack in a pan. Bake pieces in oven an additional 5–10 minutes, adjusting for size and if bone-in to ensure chicken is cooked through. Sprinkle with vanilla salt flakes and keep warm in oven or serve immediately. *NM*

Labneh

with vanilla-roasted rhubarb and pistachios

'Draining the yogurt for the labneh (a yogurt cheese of Middle Eastern origin) is best started the night before. This will give it a rich and creamy texture. Four to six hours will also do, although the labneh might not be as thick. In any case, squeezing the yogurt bundle a couple of times throughout the process will help release the water. If you want to avoid draining altogether, use a thick Greek or Arab yogurt as it is. This won't be as rich and dessert-like but still wonderfully fresh: perfect for a late brunch.'

YOTAM OTTOLENGHI

GF SERVES 4

natural full-fat yogurt	3⅓ cups	800 g	28 oz
icing/powdered sugar	⅔ cup	80 g	3 oz
fine sea salt	¼ tsp		
rhubarb	3½ cups	400 g	14 oz
Muscat de Beaumes de Venise	⅓ fl cup +1 Tbsp	100 ml	3½ fl oz
caster/superfine sugar	⅓ cup	70 g	2½ oz
vanilla pod	½		
lemon skin, half peeled into strips and half grated	1		
pistachios, coarsely chopped	2 Tbsp	20 g	¾ oz

Put the yogurt in a medium bowl with icing/powdered sugar and salt. Mix well and transfer to the middle of a clean muslin/cheesecloth or linen cloth. Tie into a bundle using an elastic band or string and hang it over a bowl in the fridge for up to 18 hours.

Preheat oven to 180°C/350°F/gas mark 4.

Wash, pat dry and cut the rhubarb into 6-cm/2-in batons and mix with the Muscat, caster/superfine sugar, vanilla pod (cut open and scraped), vanilla seeds and lemon strips. Put in an ovenproof dish just large enough to accommodate the rhubarb snugly. Roast, uncovered, for 20 minutes or until the rhubarb is tender but not mushy. Set aside to cool.

Just before serving, take the yogurt from the fridge and give it a good squeeze to release any extra liquid. Remove from the cloth and place in a bowl. Stir in the grated lemon zest and spoon into serving dishes. Spoon the rhubarb on top with some of the cooking juices and sprinkle with pistachios.

Vanilla seeds make anything look luxurious. I scrape them into a cake glaze (icing/powdered sugar, vanilla seeds and lemon juice or vodka whisked together until smooth) and drizzle over simple sponges. Or I fold into an easy white icing (whipped up cream cheese, mascarpone, butter, icing/powdered sugar and vanilla seeds) and spoon over cupcakes or fruit cakes. **YO**

Apricot, Almond & Vanilla Clafoutis

MAGGIE BEER

SERVES 4			
unsalted butter, for greasing	1 tsp		
flaked/slivered almonds	½ cup	50 g	1¾ oz
dried apricots	¾ cup	150 g	5¼ oz
verjuice	½ fl cup	120 ml	4 fl oz
water	½ fl cup	120 ml	4 fl oz
vanilla pod, scraped	1		
plain/all-purpose flour, sifted	3½ Tbsp	35 g	1¼ oz
caster/superfine sugar	⅓ cup	75 g	2½ oz
milk	⅓ fl cup	90 ml	3 fl oz
whipping cream	½ fl cup	120 ml	4 fl oz
free-range eggs, large	3		
crème fraîche to serve	1 cup	250 g	9 oz

Preheat the oven to 190°C/375°F/gas mark 5 (180°C/350°F fan).

Grease a 1-L/1-qt flan dish with unsalted butter and dust with a little caster/superfine sugar. Set aside.

Place the flaked/slivered almonds onto a lined baking tray/cookie sheet, place into the preheated oven and toast for 10 minutes or until golden brown. Remove from the oven and set aside to cool.

Meanwhile, place the dried apricots into a medium saucepan and pour over the verjuice and water. Add the scraped vanilla seeds and pod, place over a medium to high heat, bring to simmering point and allow to cook for 5 minutes until the apricots are plump and soft. Remove the apricots and vanilla pod from the liquid, discard the pod and roughly chop the apricots and place in a bowl. Continue to simmer the verjuice liquid until it has reduced to 2 Tbsp, then remove and add to the cut apricots.

In another mixing bowl, place the flour and sugar, whisk in the milk and cream, add the eggs and whisk until smooth.

Place the chopped apricots into the base of the flan dish, then pour over the mixture, sprinkle the toasted almonds over the top and place into the preheated oven. Bake for about 30–35 minutes.

Remove from the oven and allow to stand for 5–10 minutes. Then serve warm with crème fraîche.

I have a vanilla memory so firmly imprinted in my mind that just writing this I can return to that day. It was our first trip ever to Bali, in the early '80s, when, exhausted, Colin and I ran away for a week and had friends take over the restaurant while we were away. We heard about a vanilla plantation and hired a car to take us there, an adventure in itself. I'll never forget this huge shed, high as the tallest trees around, with carpets on the floor and ladies sitting cross-legged with stacks of vanilla beans in front of them, which they were sorting. That overpowering scent, wonderful as it was, almost knocked me out and I realised how attuned those women must be to the headiness of the vanilla or they could never have coped. The beans were plump and shiny and we bought a kilo from them and duly declared them as we came back into the country. A memory I'll never, ever forget! **MB**

Roasted Stone Fruit

with vanilla, cinnamon & red wine

GALE GAND

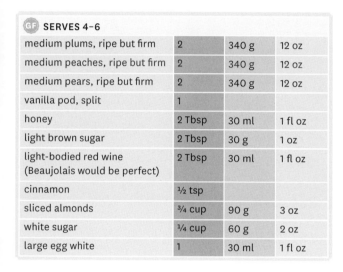

GF SERVES 4-6			
medium plums, ripe but firm	2	340 g	12 oz
medium peaches, ripe but firm	2	340 g	12 oz
medium pears, ripe but firm	2	340 g	12 oz
vanilla pod, split	1		
honey	2 Tbsp	30 ml	1 fl oz
light brown sugar	2 Tbsp	30 g	1 oz
light-bodied red wine (Beaujolais would be perfect)	2 Tbsp	30 ml	1 fl oz
cinnamon	½ tsp		
sliced almonds	¾ cup	90 g	3 oz
white sugar	¼ cup	60 g	2 oz
large egg white	1	30 ml	1 fl oz

Preheat the oven to 200°C/400°F/gas mark 6.

Quarter the fruit and remove all seeds and pits. Do not peel. Combine the vanilla pod, honey, sugar, wine and cinnamon in a 22-cm/9-in baking dish. Add the fruit and toss to coat.

Bake until tender, 20–30 minutes. When the fruit is done, remove it and reduce the oven temperature to 180°C/350°F/gas mark 4.

Meanwhile, toss the almonds and sugar together, then add the egg white and mix well to coat. Lightly grease a baking sheet and spread the almond mixture on it.

Bake the almonds, turning them with a spatula every 5 minutes, until golden brown and caramelised, about 10–12 minutes.

Serve the fruit warm or at room temperature, with the almonds sprinkled on top.

Canelés

'Canelés are a sweet pastry with a very dark caramelised crust. They are a speciality from the Bordeaux region in France. Extremely textural, the canelé has a crunchy, almost chewy exterior, then a soft-set custard-like centre. Typically they are flavoured with rum, however, I developed this recipe using orange zest, Cointreau and, of course, the best vanilla in the world from Heilala.'

AL BROWN

MAKES 24-ISH
DEPENDING ON THE SIZE OF YOUR FLUTED CANELÉ MOULDS

milk	4 fl cups	1 L	1 qt
orange zest, finely grated, 1	2 Tbsp	30 g	½ oz
butter	7 Tbsp	100 g	3½ oz
Heilala vanilla pod, split and scraped	1		
white sugar	2½ cups	500 g	17½ oz
sea salt	pinch		
eggs whole, large	4		
egg yolks, large	4	120 ml	4 fl oz
plain/all-purpose flour	1⅔ cups	200 g	7 oz
Cointreau liqueur	2½ Tbsp	40 ml	1½ fl oz

In a small saucepan, add milk, orange zest, butter and vanilla. Place on medium heat and bring up to a simmer, but DO NOT BOIL. Remove from heat and whisk in sugar and salt. Allow mixture to cool.

In a large bowl, whisk whole eggs and yolks together. Pour milk mixture into eggs while continuously whisking. Now whisk in flour a little at a time until batter is smooth, then finish by stirring through the Cointreau.

Pour batter through a coarse sieve/strainer and refrigerate overnight.

Remove batter from refrigerator and bring up to room temperature 30 minutes prior to baking for best results.

Preheat oven to 200°C/400°F/gas mark 6.

Place canelé moulds on a baking tray/cookie sheet and heat in the oven for 5 minutes or so. Remove and coat insides with baking spray. Fill moulds almost to the top with batter and return to oven. Bake for 1 hour. The canelés will reach a dark caramel colour.

Cool on a wire rack before de-moulding. Serve at room temperature.

Adding a vanilla pod to your bulk sugar container is a wonderful way to impregnate the vanilla flavour through the granules. However, if you want to take it to the next level, dry out (completely) a couple of whole vanilla pods, then finely grate them into a cup of caster/superfine sugar to sprinkle on all manner of desserts, such as apple pie, banana fritters, etc. **AB**

Lilikoi Quiche Lorraine

'Lilikoi' is Hawaiian for passionfruit and this dish uses this delicate fruit to enhance a classic French quiche Lorraine. I also add a bit of New Zealand's native flora and up the presentation with a pastry fern-frond garnish. This savoury brunch dish, infused with tart passionfruit woven into a rich vanilla filling (and what a heavenly marriage!), is presented 'floating' in a 'sea' of colourful rock salt.

SERVES 8			
QUICHE FILLING			
passionfruit	8		
rock salt, food grade*	1 cup	250 g	8 oz
butter	1 Tbsp	15 g	½ oz
shallots, peeled and chopped	2	60 g	2 oz
pikopiko (fresh fern tips),† coarsely chopped	¼ cup	40 g	1½ oz
horopito pepper, ground or cayenne pepper	¼ tsp ⅛ tsp		
nutmeg, fresh grated	⅛ tsp		
eggs, large	2		
whipping cream	⅓ fl cup	80 ml	2½ fl oz
vanilla paste	½ tsp		
passionfruit juice	2 tsp	10 ml	
vanilla candied bacon bits (page 223)	¼ cup	30 g	1 oz
mild goat cheese,‡ crumbled	3 Tbsp	35 g	1¼ oz
PASTRY FRONDS			
puff pastry, frozen	½ sheet	20 x 20 cm	9 x 9 in
Parmesan cheese, finely grated	2 Tbsp		
parsley, chopped, to sprinkle	1 Tbsp		
horopito or cayenne pepper to sprinkle			
VANILLA PASSION MOUSSE			
mild goat cheese, chilled	¼ cup	60 g	2 oz
passionfruit juice, chilled	1 Tbsp	15 ml	½ fl oz
pure vanilla extract	¼ tsp		
TO ASSEMBLE AND SERVE			
rock salt	1 cup	250 g	8 oz
food colouring, 3 colours			
3 small spray bottles			

* Any kind of coarse salt can be used but make sure it is food grade and not snow-melting sidewalk salt!

† Fiddlehead fern shoots or asparagus tips can be substituted.

‡ Substitute a milder cheese such as fromage frais or quark for the goat cheese if wished.

Preheat the oven to 180ºC/350ºF/gas mark 4. Take puff pastry sheet out of freezer to thaw.

Quiche filling
Halve passionfruit, scrape out shells, strain and reserve juice. Pour rock salt into a small glass dish or roasting pan, then wedge and level passionfruit shells into salt. Set aside.

Melt butter over medium heat in a small sauté pan. Add shallots and stir occasionally until caramelised, about 15 minutes. Add fern tips and cook for 3 minutes, then turn off heat. Add pepper, nutmeg and a pinch of sea salt, stir until combined. In a small bowl, beat eggs, cream, vanilla paste and passionfruit juice until smooth. Fold in bacon bits and crumbled cheese, then shallot mixture. Pour filling into prepared shells. Bake 12–15 minutes, depending on size of shells, until sides are set but the centre is still jiggly. Remove from oven and cool to room temperature.

Pastry fronds
Roll out half a sheet of pastry to ¾ cm/⅓ in thick and sprinkle with Parmesan cheese, parsley and pepper. Roll back up and freeze until firm enough to slice.

Turn oven up to 200ºC/400ºF/gas mark 6.

Remove from freezer and cut into 1-cm/16½-in thick spirals. Unroll a bit of the end, leaving a 4-cm/1½-in 'tail.' Place spirals on sides with their tails flat on lined baking tray/cookie sheet. Bake 6–8 minutes until golden and crisp. Cool on rack.

Vanilla passion mousse
In a small bowl, whip goat cheese with passionfruit juice and vanilla until you have a fluffy mousse, adding a bit of water or milk to thin if needed. Scoop into a piping/pastry bag with a star tip or use a small spoon to top each quiche with a swirl of mousse.

To assemble and serve
Divide and spread second measure of rock salt into 3 trays. Dilute food colourings with water, then fill each bottle. Spray each salt tray with a different colour, then leave to dry in turned off oven. Spoon coloured salts into individual serving bowls, or let the kids be creative with the colours! Nest a quiche shell in the coloured salt. Top with a pastry frond and a sprinkling of parsley. *NM*

Jack's Chicken Meatloaf
with melted onion-carrot jam

My Halloween trick-or-treat buddy Jack has a very interesting palate… at 5 years old his favourite foods were raw broccoli and blue cheese. Go figure. The following year I brought my healthy meatloaf laced with apricot and vanilla to eat before the Halloween sugar fest. He had a taste, then finished his plate without a word. As I chaperoned the now Ninja Turtle Jack house-to-house collecting a plastic pumpkin full of candy, he whispered to me 'Mytasha - your meatloaf is my favourite forever'. Jack's meatloaf has been in his cookbook of favourite recipes ever since.

GF OPTION · SERVES 4-6

quinoa, dried (makes 180 g/ 6 oz/1+ cup cooked)	⅓ cup	65 g	2¼ oz
chicken stock/broth or water	1 fl cup	240 ml	8 fl oz
caramelised onions (page 223)	¾ cup	180 g	6 oz
low-sugar apricot jam	¼ cup	85 g	3 oz
maple syrup	2 Tbsp	30 ml	1 fl oz
bourbon, e.g. Jack Daniel's*	2 Tbsp	30 ml	1 fl oz
vanilla paste	1 Tbsp	15 g	½ oz
grainy mustard	3 Tbsp	45 g	1½ oz
egg, beaten	1		
ground chicken or turkey	3¼ cups	560 g	20 oz
panko or GF breadcrumbs	½ cup	20 g	¾ oz
poultry seasoning (optional)	1 tsp		
fine sea salt	½ tsp		
pimentón paprika powder**	¼–½ tsp		

MELTED ONION-CARROT JAM [MAKES 1½ CUPS]

grapeseed or vegetable oil	3 Tbsp	45 ml	1½ fl oz
butter	2 Tbsp	30 g	1 oz
onions, large, peeled and thinly sliced	2	340 g	12 oz
vanilla pod, split	1		
carrots, medium, peeled and grated	6	340 g	12 oz
bourbon, e.g. Jack Daniel's*	2 Tbsp	30 ml	1 fl oz
apple cider vinegar	2 tsp	10 ml	
brown sugar	1 Tbsp	15 g	¾ oz
sea salt and cracked pepper	to taste		

* Substitute apple juice if wished.

** Pimentón is a Spanish smoked paprika that adds a bit of smoky, spicy heat to dishes. It can be found in most large supermarkets and gourmet shops.

Preheat oven to 180°C/350°F/gas mark 4.

In a small saucepan, combine quinoa and chicken broth. Bring to the boil, turn down to a simmer, cover and cook for about 15 minutes, until seeds are translucent little spirals and liquid is absorbed. Turn off heat, stir and cool to room temperature.

Oil a 1-L/1½-qt loaf tin/pan and set aside.

In a large bowl, blend caramelised onions, apricot jam, maple syrup, bourbon, vanilla paste, mustard and egg. Gently fold in ground meat and quinoa until combined. Fold breadcrumbs with seasonings and combine into meat mixture.

Pat meatloaf into tin/pan, smoothing top. (You may freeze and hold at this point, but thaw in the fridge before baking.)

Bake covered with foil for 30 minutes. Remove foil and bake an additional 35 minutes until the sides are bubbly, juices run clear and temperature in the centre reads 70°C/160°F on a thermometer (a thermometer is important when cooking chicken and turkey to ensure that the poultry is thoroughly cooked). Cool 15 minutes before unmoulding, to make slicing easier.

Melted onion-carrot jam

Over medium heat, pour oil into a medium saucepan/pot or sauté pan. Add butter. When oil begins to sizzle, put onions in all at once with vanilla pod and stir to coat with the oil. Add carrot and cook until onions are translucent and carrots are soft. Add bourbon, vinegar and sugar. Season with salt and pepper to taste.

Turn down heat, stirring occasionally, until onions are meltingly soft and caramelised – this will take about 20 minutes. Take off heat, remove and reserve vanilla pod and purée jam in blender if wished. Spoon into a clean jar, add vanilla pod and seal. Store chilled until ready to use.

Serve warmed spooned over meatloaf, with a side of succotash. *NM*

The Lobster Roll

*The purist's Lobster Roll. No avocado. No massive veggies.
Just a splash of vanilla. Fragrant, fun and delicious.*

SERVES 6			
LOBSTER			
lemon, quartered	1		
bay leaves	2		
peppercorns	10		
lobsters, whole* or lobster tails	2 2	500 g ea 110 g ea	1 lb ea 4 oz ea
LOBSTER ROLL FILLING			
mayonnaise	¼ cup	120 g	4½ oz
lemon juice and zest	½ lemon		
paprika	¼ tsp		
chives, chopped	1 Tbsp		
vanilla paste	½ tsp		
celery, 2 ribs, finely chopped	⅓ cup	80 g	3 oz
hot sauce	to taste		
vanilla salt flakes (page 222)	½–¾ tsp		
cracked black pepper	to taste		
TO SERVE			
hot dog rolls, split top	6		
lettuce leaves, shredded	4	60 g	2 oz
small tomatoes, sliced thinly	3	125 g	4 oz

** Crayfish, also known as rock lobster, is New Zealand's
alternative to lobster. The small coastal town of Kaikoura
is renowned for its crayfish – 'kai' food + 'koura' crayfish =
heavenly.*

Lobster

Add lemon, bay leaves and peppercorns to a large
saucepan/pot. Fill with cold water and bring to the boil.
Add lobsters, cover and cook for 12–15 minutes, until bright
orange/red. Plunge into ice water until cool then pat dry,
crack open and remove the meat. Cut or shred lobster into
bite-size pieces.

Lobster roll filling

In a medium bowl mix mayonnaise, lemon juice, zest,
paprika, chives (reserving 1 tsp for sprinkling), vanilla
paste, celery, hot sauce, vanilla salt and pepper to taste.
Gently mix in lobster meat. Adjust seasoning if needed
and chill until ready to serve.

To serve

Warm a frying pan/skillet over medium heat. Split the
rolls and toast dry in the frying pan/skillet cut-side-down
until golden brown. Fill rolls with lobster, shredded lettuce
and thin slices of tomato. Sprinkle with more chives and a
dusting of paprika.

Serve with onion rings and cucumber pickles. *NM*

Sharing Plates

Smoked Salmon Tartine

This divine quick-to-make sharing plate can be assembled a few hours before the guests arrive and is easily doubled. Velvety smoked salmon with creamy vanilla sauce is an unexpected combination: the vanilla adds a surprise layer of fragrance and flavour to the stunning overall taste. Pair with a buttery Chardonnay or a classic gin martini.

SERVES 6–8			
VANILLA SAUCE [MAKES 240 ML/8 FL OZ/1 FL CUP]			
egg yolks	2	60 ml	2 fl oz
lemon juice	1 Tbsp	15 ml	½ fl oz
vanilla paste	1 tsp		
runny honey	1 Tbsp	15 ml	½ fl oz
grapeseed oil	1 fl cup	240 ml	8 fl oz
HERB CHEESE SPREAD			
mild goat cheese, softened	⅔ cup	150 g	5¼ oz
ricotta, softened	¼ cup	50 g	1¾ oz
fresh herbs such as tarragon, dill, basil and chervil, chopped	1 Tbsp		
vanilla pod seeds	1 tsp		
cracked black pepper	10 grinds		
ASSEMBLE AND SERVE			
ciabatta, or baguette	1 loaf	40–45 cm	16–18 in
olive oil, for brushing bread	1 Tbsp	15 ml	½ fl oz
vanilla caramelised onions, chopped (page 223)	½ cup	120 g	4 oz
sliced smoked salmon	1 pack	225 g	8 oz
capers, rinsed then patted dry	3–4 tsp	20 g	¾ oz
lemon zest, to taste	2 tsp		
fresh herbs or microgreens			

Vanilla sauce

In a medium bowl, whisk yolks with a pinch of sea salt, lemon juice, vanilla paste and honey until well blended.

Tuck a twisted tea towel around base of bowl to hold it steady. While whisking egg mixture continuously, drizzle oil in a slow, steady stream until sauce begins to come together and thicken. If too thick, whisk in a teaspoon of water until well combined. Alternatively, use a hand-/stick-blender to emulsify the sauce.

Cover and chill until ready to use.

Herb cheese spread

In a small bowl, combine the cheeses, fresh herbs, vanilla seeds and pepper until smooth and creamy.

Assemble and serve

Preheat oven to 180°C/350°F/gas mark 4.

Split the bread lengthways and brush both sides with olive oil. Toast in oven oiled-side-up until golden brown, about 7 minutes. Remove and cool.

Spread bread with herb cheese spread and arrange on a serving platter. Top with the chopped caramelised onions and smoked salmon. Drizzle with vanilla sauce. Sprinkle with capers, lemon zest and additional fresh herbs or microgreens. Use a sharp serrated knife to cut into slices. *NM*

Kumara Gratin
with vanilla caramelised onions

Kumara is the New Zealand name for the sweet potato: it was a staple of the Maori long before the Pakeha (white Europeans) touched the shores of Aotearoa. The flesh colour ranges from pale yellow to rich red. This recipe uses the sweeter and darker-fleshed variety, which in the US is, rather deceptively, known as a red yam. With melt-in-your-mouth, hot-out-of-the-oven layers of oozey cheese, kumara and vanilla caramelised onions, this dish is a moreish accompaniment to roasted chicken or The Pork Chop (page 52).

GF SERVES 4–6

kumara or sweet potato, orange	2	500 g	1 lb
vegetable oil for baking pan	1 tsp		
caramelised onions (page 223)	1 cup	230 g	8 oz
Parmesan cheese, grated	1¼ cup	100 g	3½ oz
mild gouda cheese, grated	1¼ cup	100 g	3½ oz
fresh cracked pepper	to taste		
cream	1 fl cup	240 ml	8 fl oz

Preheat the oven to 180°C/350°F/gas mark 4.

Peel and very thinly slice the kumara into a bowl or tray and set aside.

Lightly oil a small loaf tin/pan or individual 240 ml/8 fl oz ramekins. Begin with a double layer of kumara, followed by a layer of caramelised onions. Scatter a bit of both cheeses on top and sprinkle with pepper.

Repeat layers 2–3 more times, finishing with the cheeses and pepper. Press the layers with the palm of your hand to level the top.

Slowly pour the cream a bit at a time over all and allow it to settle into the gratin. (Can be refrigerated at this point to bake the next day if wished.)

On a foil-covered baking tray/cookie sheet (less mess!), bake for about 1 hour, until the top is golden brown and the kumara is fork-tender (test with a skewer). Leave to cool 20 minutes to set the gratin, which makes slicing easier. *NM*

Island Crabcakes

with vanilla-grapefruit remoulade

For this dish, I used delicate paddle crab (also known as swimmer crab), found in the waters around New Zealand, Australia and the Pacific Islands. For best flavour and sustainability, use locally caught crustaceans, or substitute other local fish such as ling, cod, halibut or locally caught scallops. These dairy-free small-bite crabcakes are perfect for parties and easy to make. Serve with vanilla-grapefruit remoulade and your favourite rosé or Champagne.

GF OPTION   **MAKES 24–30**

VANILLA–GRAPEFRUIT REMOULADE

red grapefruit (for remoulade, crabcakes and garnish)	1 large	225–275 g	8–10 oz
shallot, peeled & chopped	1	30 g	1 oz
garlic clove, peeled & chopped	1		
mayonnaise	½ fl cup	120 ml	4 fl oz
vanilla paste	¾ tsp		
runny honey	½ tsp		
Dijon mustard	1 Tbsp	15 g	½ oz
pimentón* smoked paprika	⅛ tsp		
parsley, finely chopped/minced	1 tsp		

CRABCAKES

crabmeat, picked and free of shell, squeezed dry	2 cups	250 g	1 lb
grapefruit juice	2 Tbsp	30 ml	1 fl oz
grapefruit zest	1 tsp		
eggs, large, beaten	3		
mayonnaise	½ fl cup	120 ml	4 fl oz
vanilla paste	1 tsp		
Dijon mustard	1 tsp		
pimentón smoked paprika	1 tsp		
Worcestershire sauce	1 Tbsp	15 ml	½ fl oz
hot sauce	1 tsp		
red onion, finely chopped	⅓ cup	80 g	2¾ oz
red bell pepper/capsicum, finely chopped	¼ cup	40 g	1½ oz
parsley, finely chopped	¼ cup	40 g	1½ oz
panko dry breadcrumbs†	1½ cups	175 g	6¼ oz
oil for frying			

* Pimentón is a Spanish smoked paprika that adds a bit of smoky, spicy heat to dishes. It can be found in most large supermarkets and gourmet shops.

† You can also use gluten-free rice crumbs.

Vanilla–grapefruit* remoulade

Zest grapefruit and set aside. Using a small knife, cut top and bottom off grapefruit and slice the peel away from sides in a downward motion until all the pith has been removed. Hold the fruit over a bowl to catch the juice and using a small knife separate the segments from the membrane, allowing the segments to fall into the bowl. Squeeze the remaining juice from the membrane into the bowl. You should have enough juice for both recipes.

In a small bowl, mix chopped shallot and garlic into mayonnaise. Mix in remaining ingredients plus 2 tsp of grapefruit juice and 1 tsp of zest from the grapefruit, combining well. Cover and chill until ready to serve. Reserve remaining zest and grapefruit segments in juice for crabcakes and garnish.

Crabcakes

In a small bowl, combine crabmeat, 2 tbsp of grapefruit juice and 1 tsp zest. Mix well. In a medium bowl blend remaining ingredients (except breadcrumbs). Gently fold crab into egg mixture, then sprinkle in breadcrumbs and a few grinds of salt and pepper, and mix to combine. Shape into small 60-g/2-oz patties and place on a clingfilm-/plastic wrap-covered plate. Chill for 1 hour.

Warm frying pan/skillet to medium heat and flick in a little water from your fingers – if it sizzles the pan is ready. Coat pan with a thin film of oil, then add the crabcakes a few at a time, being careful not to overcrowd the pan. Cook 3–5 minutes on each side until golden brown. Drain on paper towels.

To serve

Chop about 6 grapefruit segments into small pieces and gently stir into chilled remoulade sauce. Serve with the crabcakes. *NM*

* If grapefruit is not for you, substitute a large thin-skinned juice orange. Follow the same method but add a few drops of lime juice for tartness.

Normandy Caramelised Apple Tart

This flavourful tart was inspired by visits to a tiny French village near Carrouges, tucked into the Normandy countryside: a place of simple yet amazing tastes – Pont L'Évêque and Livarot cheeses, sea-salty prawns, oysters, crab, local apple cider and the famous apple brandy, Calvados. The combination of a tarte tatin and a British custard tart, handmade by my friend Gabrielle, is sublime. She generously sprinkles vanilla sugar over the parbaked crust, then layers last-of-the-season apricots, topping them with caramelised apples freshly picked from her garden, and lastly pours in a vanilla custard to bake and bubble in the oven!

SERVES 8–10

PASTRY/CRUST			
plain/all-purpose flour	2¾ cups	325 g	11½ oz
white sugar	1 Tbsp	15 g	½ oz
unsalted butter cut into small pieces, chilled	1 cup	225 g	8 oz
ice-cold water	9–12 Tbsp	90–120 ml	3–4 fl oz

VANILLA FILLING			
egg yolks	6	180 ml	6 fl oz
whipping cream	1¼ fl cup	300 ml	10 fl oz
cornflour/cornstarch	1½ Tbsp	15 g	½ oz
lemon juice	2 tsp	10 ml	
light brown sugar, packed	¾ cup	150 g	5 oz
pure vanilla extract	1 Tbsp	15 ml	½ fl oz

CARAMELISED APPLES			
white sugar	½ cup	100 g	3½ oz
lemon juice	a few drops		
firm, tart apples, e.g. Granny Smith, Cox's Orange, Honeycrisp, peeled, cored and quartered	3–4	450 g	2 lb

ASSEMBLE AND BAKE			
vanilla sugar for sprinkling on crust (page 222)	3 Tbsp	45 g	1½ oz
apricots, fresh, halved and stoned	6–8	450 g	1 lb
or apricots dried,* halved	1 cup	170 g	6 oz
Calvados	2 Tbsp	30 ml	1 fl oz

If using dried apricots, soak in additional Calvados or water to rehydrate.

Pastry/Crust
In a medium bowl, whisk together the flour, sugar and a pinch of sea salt. Blend in the butter with your fingertips or a pastry blender until the butter is pea-sized. Slowly drizzle in the ice water, tossing gently with a fork just to combine. Test a small handful – if it doesn't hold together, add a bit more water. Do not overwork the dough.

Turn out onto a lightly floured work surface and pat into a pad. Fold over twice, then twice again. Gather dough together into a ball then flatten into a 15-cm/6-in disk. Wrap tightly in plastic and put in freezer for at least 1 hour.

Vanilla filling
Whisk together egg yolks and cream.

In a small bowl, dissolve cornflour/cornstarch in lemon juice. Add remaining ingredients and a large pinch of sea salt and whisk together. Cover and chill until ready to bake.

Finish the tart dough
Grease a 30-cm/12-in tart or quiche pan and set aside. On a lightly floured work surface, roll dough into a 33-cm/13-in disk. (You may have extra dough, so wrap tightly and freeze for another use.) Lift dough over rolling pin, lay into the tart pan and smooth bottom and sides to fit snugly. Place in freezer and chill for 30 minutes.

Caramelised apples
Preheat the oven to 180°C/350°F/gas mark 4.

In a small clean saucepan/pot, make the caramel. Place sugar and enough water to just moisten in pan/pot over medium–high heat. Add a few drops of lemon juice and brush down the sides of the pan/pot with water.

Meanwhile, butter a baking pan and place the apple quarters in the pan with the outsides down.

When the caramel begins to turn golden brown (this should only take a few minutes), remove from the heat and swirl a few times to even the colour. Pour the caramel over the apples and place in oven for about 15 minutes, until just fork-tender, basting caramel over the apples occasionally.

Remove from oven and allow to cool in pan.

Assemble and bake
Remove the pastry/crust from the freezer and mark the crust all over with the tines of a fork.

Place a piece of baking paper on top of the dough and fill with baking beans/pie weights. Par-bake for 15 minutes or until the paper releases easily from the crust. Remove from oven and lift out baking paper and baking beans/pie weights. Sprinkle crust with vanilla sugar and return to the oven. Bake an additional 12–15 minutes, until crust is dry and barely light brown. Remove from oven.

Place a layer of apricots in the bottom of crust and arrange the caramelised apples and caramel syrup on top. Drizzle with Calvados if using. Pour the custard filling over all and place tart on a baking tray/cookie sheet in the oven.

Bake at 180°C/350°F/gas mark 4 (160°C/325°F fan) for 50–60 minutes until custard is just set.

Remove from oven and cool to room temperature before slicing and serving.

To serve
Serve warmed or at room temperature with roasted toasted crème fraîche sherbet (see below). *NM*

MAKES 1 L / 1 QT			
ROASTED APRICOT PURÉE			
fresh apricots, small	6–8	225 g	8 oz
brown sugar	2 Tbsp	30 g	1 oz
ground ginger	¼ tsp		
CRÈME FRAÎCHE SHERBET			
white sugar	1½ cups	280 g	10½ oz
boiling water	⅔ fl cup	150 ml	5 fl oz
crème fraîche	2½ cups	560 g	20 oz
buttermilk	¾ fl cup	180 ml	6 fl oz
lemon juice	¼ fl cup	60 ml	2 fl oz
vodka	4 tsp	20 ml	¾ fl oz
pure vanilla extract	4 tsp	20 ml	¾ fl oz
walnuts, toasted and roughly chopped	½ cup	70 g	2½ oz

Roasted Toasted Crème Fraîche Sherbet
with roasted apricots and toasted walnuts

Roasted apricot purée
Preheat oven to 200°C/400°F/gas mark 6.

Stone and halve apricots and place cut-side-up on a lined baking tray/cookie sheet. Sprinkle with sugar, ginger and a pinch of sea salt and roast for 25–30 minutes until lightly caramelised.

Cool, then slip off and discard the skins. Mash or purée apricots with a hand-/stick-blender. Chill until ready to use.

Crème fraîche sherbet
Dissolve sugar and a pinch of sea salt in boiling water. Whisk in crème fraîche in 3 stages to combine, then whisk in buttermilk, lemon juice, vodka and vanilla. Lightly cover and chill 2 hours or overnight. Freeze in ice-cream maker according to manufacturer's instructions.

Scoop into storage container then add a swirl of the puréed apricots and sprinkle with walnuts. Fold over a few times, then cover and freeze. *NM*

The Tonga Trifle

The trifle 'reveal' took place on Vava'u Island, Tonga for Heilala's First Annual Vanilla Harvest Event. As the massive bowl was paraded around the tables after a three-course luncheon I detected agonised sighs coming from the guests as they protested: 'No! No! Not the trifle!', then whispers of 'bacon bits in a dessert?' But, of course, I love the sweet-salty combination of crispy bacon, oozey vanilla caramel and hot fudge sauce. Needless to say, as the guests pushed back their chairs post-trifle I noticed all that remained in the bowl were a few cake crumbs and toasted almonds. And the bacon bits? Gone!

SERVES 12

VANILLA RUM BUTTERCAKE

plain/all-purpose flour	3½ cups	425 g	15 oz
baking powder	1 tsp		
bicarb of soda/baking soda	½ tsp		
fine sea salt	½ tsp		
unsalted butter	1 cup	225 g	8 oz
white sugar	1⅔ cups	340 g	12 oz
large eggs, room temperature	4		
Greek yogurt or sour cream	1 cup	250 g	8 oz
dark rum	1 Tbsp	15 ml	½ fl oz
vanilla paste	1 Tbsp	15 ml	½ fl oz

VANILLA AND RUM BUTTER GLAZE

brown sugar	1 cup	170 g	6 oz
golden or corn syrup	2 tsp	10 ml	
water	2 Tbsp	30 ml	1 fl oz
salted butter	5 Tbsp	75 g	2½ oz
dark rum	1 Tbsp	15 ml	½ fl oz
pure vanilla extract or liqueur	1 Tbsp	15 ml	½ fl oz

JIM'S WHITE CHOCOLATE PASTRY CREAM

plain/all-purpose flour	1 Tbsp	15 g	½ oz
cornflour/cornstarch	1 Tbsp	10 g	
white sugar	¼ cup	60 g	2 oz
large egg, room temperature	1		
whole milk	1½ fl cups	350 ml	12 fl oz
white chocolate, chopped	½ cup	60 g	2 oz
unsalted butter, softened	2 Tbsp	30 g	1 oz
pure vanilla extract	2 tsp	10 ml	
light rum	1 Tbsp	15 ml	½ fl oz

Vanilla rum buttercake

Preheat the oven to 160ºC/325ºF/gas mark 3. Have all ingredients at room temperature. With 2 tsp of butter, grease a Bundt/tube tin/pan (or 2 loaf tins/pans) and set aside.

In a medium bowl, sift together flour, baking powder, bicarb of soda/baking soda and salt.

In the bowl of a stand-mixer with a paddle attachment or a hand-held mixer, cream butter and sugar at medium speed, until light and fluffy.

Bring speed to low and add eggs, one at a time, until mixed, scraping down sides of bowl between each egg.

In stages, with mixer on low speed, alternate flour mixture and yogurt, ending with flour. Add rum and vanilla paste and combine well.

Spoon into prepared tin/pan, smooth top and bake for 50–60 minutes, until a wooden toothpick inserted in centre comes away clean.

Vanilla and rum butter glaze

In a small saucepan, heat sugar, golden syrup and water, with a big pinch of sea salt. Simmer to dissolve, then stir in butter. Continue to simmer for 1 minute, being careful not to boil. Remove from heat and stir in rum and vanilla.

While cake is still warm, prick all over with a long skewer, then slowly spoon over the glaze, allowing it to soak in. Allow cake to cool completely before unmoulding.

Jim's white chocolate pastry cream

Sift flour, cornflour/cornstarch and sugar into a bowl. Add egg and whisk until light and without any lumps. In a small stainless saucepan/pot, bring milk to a simmer. Whisk half of the milk into egg mixture until blended, then pour mixture back into pan/pot. Stirring constantly, cook over medium–high heat until pastry cream comes to a simmer and thickens.

Remove pan/pot from heat and whisk in chocolate, butter, vanilla and rum. Blend until smooth.

Cover the surface with clingfilm/plastic wrap while cooling to prevent a skin forming. Refrigerate until needed.

VANILLA CARAMEL SAUCE

unsalted butter	1 cup	225 g	8 oz
white sugar	2 cups	400 g	14 oz
lemon juice	1½ Tbsp	25 ml	¾ fl oz
whipping cream, warmed	1¾ fl cups	420 ml	14 fl oz
pure vanilla extract	1 Tbsp	15 ml	½ fl oz

HOT FUDGE SAUCE

dark chocolate, chopped	2 cups	250 g	8 oz
white sugar	¼ cup	50 g	1¾ oz
fine sea salt	¼ tsp		
golden syrup or light corn syrup	½ fl cup	120 ml	4 fl oz
filtered water	¾ fl cup	180 ml	6 fl oz
dark cocoa powder	¾ cup	70 g	2½ oz
vanilla paste	1 Tbsp	15 ml	½ fl oz
pure vanilla extract	1 Tbsp	15 ml	½ fl oz

TO ASSEMBLE (THE TONGA TRIFLE CHECKLIST!)

whipping cream with 2 tsp/10 ml pure vanilla extract	1 fl cup	240 ml	8 fl oz
vanilla rum buttercake, cooled	1		
generous amount of gold rum*	½ fl cup	120 ml	4 fl oz
white chocolate pastry cream	1 batch		
bananas, ripe with green tips (peeled weight)	4	450 g	1 lb
vanilla caramel sauce	1 batch		
hot fudge sauce	1 batch		
sliced almonds, toasted	½ cup	45 g	1½ oz
unsweetened shredded coconut, toasted	½ cup	45 g	1½ oz
streaky/lean bacon, chopped, cooked crispy and drained on paper towels, or vanilla candied bacon (page 223)	¾ cup	250 g	8 oz

I use New Zealand's Stolen Rum.

Vanilla caramel sauce

Prepare an ice bath by filling a large metal bowl halfway with ice and cold water.

Melt butter in a large saucepan. Stream in sugar and big pinch of sea salt. Stir gently with a wooden or heat-resistant spoon until combined, to prevent lumps. When the sugar begins to caramelise, add lemon juice, which slows the sugar from caramelising too quickly. Continue cooking, stirring occasionally, until sugar is a deep golden brown. Take off heat and stir in the warm cream in 4 stages, being careful to prevent splattering. Place pan/pot in an ice bath, add vanilla and stir sauce occasionally as it cools and thickens. Cover and refrigerate until needed. Will keep for 2 weeks.

Hot fudge sauce

Melt chocolate in double boiler, stirring occasionally, over barely simmering water. Turn off heat and keep warm. Whisk sugar, salt, golden syrup, water and cocoa powder to a simmer in a heavy saucepan/pot over medium heat. Reduce heat to low and simmer 1–2 minutes, slowly whisking to dissolve cocoa powder and to prevent burning on bottom of pan. Drizzle in melted chocolate and cook 2 minutes more, whisking continuously until thickened and glossy. Stir in vanilla paste and extract.

To assemble and serve

Whisk cream with vanilla until whipped.

Slice cake into pieces and make a layer in bottom of trifle dish or a large tall-sided glass bowl (4 L/4 qt). Add a generous splash of rum, and top with one-third of the pastry cream.

Slice bananas into rounds and arrange a third around sides and centre of bowl.

Add spoonfuls of vanilla caramel sauce, then dollops of whipped cream.

Drizzle over a third of the fudge sauce, then sprinkle surface with ⅓ almonds and coconut.

Repeat layers, beginning with the rum-splashed cake slices, 2 more times.

Finish the top layer with whipped cream and fudge sauce. Lightly cover with clingfilm/plastic wrap and refrigerate for 3 hours or up to a day to allow the flavours to infuse.

When ready to serve, let trifle come to room temperature. Top with a generous amount of bacon bits and pass around the table with a large serving spoon – enjoy! *NM*

⸺ ✦ ⸺

I love to perch over my stand-mixer and inhale the scent of vanilla just after it has been added into the creamed butter and sugar. **NM**

New England Cider Baked Beans

My earliest New England autumn memory is of flinging myself into a brightly coloured pile of leaves and looking up at the clear blue sky - such moments are always ones to treasure. Autumn/Fall is also the time to get out the slow-cooker and make baked beans! The secret addition of vanilla gives richness to this pot of flavourful goodness!

GF · SERVES 8

dried pinto beans	1½ cups	275 g	10 oz
white haricot or navy beans, dried	1½ cups	275 g	10 oz
bacon, thick cut, lightly smoked	10 slices	285 g	10 oz
medium onions, peeled and quartered	1½	225 g	8 oz
apple (Granny Smith, Bramley), peeled, cored and quartered	1	200 g	7 oz
vanilla pods, split	2		
bay leaves	2		
garlic cloves, small, peeled and halved	2		
Dijon mustard	2 Tbsp	30 g	1 oz
dry mustard powder	1 Tbsp	15 g	½ oz
treacle or molasses	⅓ fl cup	80 ml	2½ fl oz
maple syrup, Grade B	¼ fl cup	60 ml	2 fl oz
sea salt	2 tsp	10 g	
hard apple cider*	½ fl cup	120 ml	4 fl oz
unfiltered apple juice	2 fl cups	475 ml	16 fl oz

* Known as 'hard' cider in the US, New England craft cider is fast putting the pinch on beer. Choose your local favourite, making sure you save a pint to savour with your supper!

Soak beans in 1½ L/1½ qt water with 2 Tbsp of salt. Cover and leave for 12 hours or overnight.

Rinse and drain the beans.

Cut the bacon slices into quarters and layer half the bacon in the bottom of a 3½-L/3½-qt slow-cooker. Spoon the beans into the pot then bury the onions, apple, vanilla, bay leaves and garlic in the beans and layer remaining bacon on top.

In a small saucepan, simmer the Dijon, dry mustard, molasses, maple syrup, salt and cider, stirring to dissolve the salt.

Pour the hot mustard mixture over the beans. Add apple juice and enough additional water to just cover beans.

Cook covered on low heat for 5–7 hours, until beans are fork-tender. *NM*

Devilish Eggs
with vanilla candied bacon

Yum. These eggs bewitch everyone who tries them: the marriage of vanilla with bacon and pink peppercorns is a culinary ménage-a-trois!

GF SERVES 6			
eggs	6		
VANILLA CANDIED BACON			
vanilla sugar (page 222)	2 Tbsp	45 g	1½ oz
pink peppercorns, crushed	¼ tsp		
smoked bacon slices	4	125 g	4 oz
TO FILL AND SERVE			
mayonnaise	5 Tbsp	75 g	2½ oz
vanilla paste	½ tsp		
mild curry powder	¼ tsp		
white wine vinegar	½ tsp		
tarragon fresh, finely chopped	½ tsp		
pink peppercorns, cracked, for garnish	¼ tsp		
vanilla salt flakes (page 222)	¼ tsp		

Place eggs in a small saucepan/pot, covered by 2½ cm/1 in of cold water. Warm on medium–high heat and leave to come to a rolling boil. Immediately turn off the heat, cover with a lid and leave to stand for 12 minutes. Drain eggs and rinse in cold water until eggs are cool. Crack and carefully peel away shell. Chill until needed.

Vanilla candied bacon
Preheat oven to 180ºC/350ºF/gas mark 4.

Mix vanilla sugar and pink pepper in a pie tin or small bowl. Dredge the bacon slices in the mixture and place bacon on a tray/sheet lined with baking paper.

Cook 25–30 minutes, turning over halfway through baking. (Do not be tempted to increase oven temperature as bacon will burn.) Remove from oven and drain on a cooling rack.

Chop bacon into bits. If not crispy enough, heat in a small, dry pan until crispy. Cool completely and store chilled in an airtight container. (This will make more than you need but save for other dishes in this book.)

To fill and serve
Slice the eggs in half lengthways and remove yolks. Arrange the whites on a plate and set aside. Grate the cooked yolks into a small bowl and add the mayonnaise, vanilla paste, curry powder, vinegar, tarragon and a pinch of sea salt. Mash with a fork to a creamy consistency. You can press through a sieve/strainer to make it completely smooth if wished. Fill a piping/pastry bag with a star tip and pipe the filling into the egg whites.

Sprinkle with vanilla candied bacon bits, pepper and a few flakes of vanilla salt. Serve immediately or cover and chill for up to 4 hours. *NM*

Crispy Vanilla-Coconut Shrimp

After arriving in NYC at 17 years old to fufil my dream of dancing with the American Ballet Theatre, I rented a room in a Soho loft. The owner 'volunteered' me to make tempura for the famous scarf designer Vera Neumann and her guests at a fund-raiser cocktail party he was hosting. I was a fine tempura-maker, but a little messy; often plastering the walls and stove in batter. Luckily the kitchen survived my 'Tempura Hurricane', and the guests were happy. However, many burnt their mouths – despite my warnings – from sampling shrimp just seconds out of the fryer. This easy but more sophisticated version leaves a lingering scent of coconut and vanilla in the room, and will prompt guests to circle back for more!

GF OPTION SERVES 6

large raw prawns/shrimp, tails on, chilled	about 18 pieces	750 g	1½ lb
white rice flour	¾ cup	85 g	3 oz
coconut flour*	¼ cup	30 g	1 oz
chilli powder, salt and sugar	big pinch of each		
egg, large	1		
vanilla cream soda or soda water, ice cold	⅔ cup	150 ml	5 fl oz
pure vanilla extract	2 tsp	10 ml	
tequila	1 Tbsp	15 ml	½ fl oz
lime juice	1 tsp		
shredded coconut, unsweetened	1 cup	90 g	3 oz
panko or GF breadcrumbs	1 cup	60 g	2 oz
coconut oil for frying	2 fl cups	475 ml	16 fl oz

* If coconut flour is unavailable use rice flour.

Remove prawn/shrimp heads, clean, and peel off the shells, leaving the tail intact. Pat dry, cover and chill.

Whisk together the flours with a big pinch each of salt, sugar and chilli powder.

In a separate bowl, whisk together the egg, cream soda, vanilla extract, tequila and lime juice. Whisk into the flours until smooth. You can use at this point, but resting the batter in the fridge for an hour is ideal.

In a large bowl, mix together the coconut and the panko. Set aside.

In a 1-L/1-qt saucepan/pot or deep fryer, heat the coconut oil to 150–160ºC/300–325ºF. Holding the tails, dip each prawn/shrimp in the batter then roll and pat to coat in the coconut panko. Lower 3 to 4 at a time into the hot oil and cook 2–6 minutes, depending on size, until golden brown. Lift prawn/shrimp from oil with slotted spoon and drain on paper towels until all have been cooked.

Arrange in paper-lined basket or dishes. Sprinkle with vanilla salt flakes (page 222) and serve with a lime wedge and chilli-vanilli sauce (page 56). *NM*

Party Pizzettas

with figs, grapes, feta and vanilla vincotto syrup

Indian summer. Harvest time. What better way to savour the season than with the seductive flavours of purple wine grapes, red-fleshed figs and pure white local feta over a crisp pizza crust? These grown-up mini pizzas, finished with lashings of vanilla vincotto syrup, add a 'wow' start to the evening.

MAKES 12 PIZZETTAS			
PIZZETTA DOUGH			
warm water (40–45°C/105–115°F)	1½ fl cups	350 ml	12 fl oz
runny honey	4 tsp	20 ml	⅔ fl oz
dry yeast, 1 packet	2½ tsp		
extra virgin olive oil	¼ fl cup	60 ml	2 fl oz
plain flour/all-purpose (plus extra for dusting)	4 cups + 2 Tbsp	480 g	17 oz
fine sea salt	2 tsp	10 g	½ oz
TO ASSEMBLE AND BAKE			
vanilla oil for brushing (page 222)	2 Tbsp	30 ml	1 fl oz
feta cheese, in small cubes	1 cup	115 g	4 oz
figs, dried or fresh, in wedges	4	200 g	7 oz
grapes, halved, preferably purple wine grapes	48	170 g	6 oz
thyme sprigs	6		
Parmesan, finely grated	2 Tbsp	15 g	½ oz
TO SERVE			
vanilla vincotto syrup (page 223)	2 Tbsp	30 ml	1 fl oz
lemon peel, threads	2 tsp		
cracked pepper			

Pizzetta dough

Pour warm water in the bowl of a stand-mixer with the paddle attachment or, if mixing by hand, use a large bowl and wooden spoon. Add honey and stir to combine. Sprinkle yeast over surface. Allow to foam, 10–15 minutes. Stir by hand or turn mixer on low speed and add oil, then pour in half the flour with all the salt. Add remaining flour a bit at a time until the dough pulls away from the sides of the bowl. Place dough on a lightly floured work surface. Knead until dough comes together into a smooth elastic ball. Place in an oiled bowl, cover with a towel and allow to rise 1 hour in a warm place.

To assemble and bake

Preheat oven to 240°C/475°F/gas mark 9.

Put a pizza stone in oven to heat or prepare a heavy foil-lined baking tray/cookie sheet brushed with grapeseed oil.

Punch down dough, knead a few times on work surface, using flour sparingly. Cut into 60 g/2 oz portions.

Roll out each pizzetta to a thin circle and place on pizza stone or prepared baking tray/cookie sheet. Brush tops with vanilla oil.

Arrange topping ingredients, finishing with a sprinkle of Parmesan. Bake for 10 minutes until edges are browned.

To serve

Drizzle pizzettas with vanilla vincotto syrup (page 223), scatter threads of lemon peel and sprinkle with cracked pepper. Serve with your favourite wine. *NM*

Rum & Vanilla Cured Salmon

DOUGLAS RODRIGUEZ

GF OPTION **MAKES 1½ KG/3 LB CURED SALMON**

side of salmon, skin on, all scales & bones removed, keep belly	1	1.5 kg	3 lb
dark rum, such as Meyer's, Gosling's or Stolen Rum	1 bottle	720 ml	25 fl oz
kosher or sea salt	2 cups	200 g	7 oz
brown sugar	1 cup	225 g	8 oz
cracked black pepper	3 Tbsp	30 g	1 oz
anise seeds	1 Tbsp	10 g	
coriander seeds, toasted and ground	3 Tbsp	25 g	¾ oz
cumin seeds, lightly toasted	3 Tbsp	25 g	¾ oz
vanilla pods	4		
pure vanilla extract	2 Tbsp	30 ml	1 fl oz

In a large shallow container, marinate the side of salmon in dark rum at room temperature for 1½ to 2 hours. Massage the salmon every 20 minutes in the rum as it cures, which kills any microorganisms living on the flesh.

Mix together the salt, sugar, pepper, anise, coriander and cumin seeds in a small bowl. Split and scrape the vanilla pods and rub the vanilla seeds into the salt–sugar mixture until well combined. Add the pods and vanilla extract to the mixture, combining well.

Remove salmon from rum and pat dry.

In a large shallow dish, sprinkle about one-third of the vanilla salt mixture on the bottom. Place salmon on top of this, then cover the salmon evenly with the remaining salt mixture and press down with your hands.

Place in refrigerator for about 2 days, then remove all salt and rinse under cold water. Pat dry.

To serve, slice thinly onto serving platter and serve with crème fraîche, capers and microgreens.

My first vanilla story comes from an old lady name Rosario, who used to live in the same building as me in New York when I was 9 years old. She had vanilla perfume and I used to follow her round just to smell her. I was fascinated with the perfume… until she told me it was vanilla and I immediately thought, vanilla? That's what my mama adds to desserts, no wonder I like the scent.

Vanilla ice cream is one of my most guilty pleasures of all time, and I made sure I was the first one to give vanilla ice cream to my kids. I can never forget their faces. I remember exactly the date I gave Dario, my youngest, vanilla ice cream. He was 9 months old and, well, I wanted him to taste the most delicious flavour in the world. He loved it so much, that he ended up crying and having a temper tantrum because he wanted more. I realised then that we were going to share the same passion – vanilla ice cream! **DR**

Saturn Peach, Onion & Blue Cheese Pie

My devotion to peaches began at age 10 when I read James and the Giant Peach by Roald Dahl. I so wanted to taste the luscious, fragrant, drippy peach of the author's imagination, that even now peach season becomes a single-minded obsession. The fragrant vanilla and peaches dance playfully through the contrasting flavours and textures of this dish. Serve warm with an ice-cold amber ale.

SERVES 8			
plain/all-purpose flour	3 cups	385 g	13½ oz
white sugar	2 tsp	10 g	
fine sea salt	¼ tsp		
vanilla powder	2 tsp		
unsalted butter, chilled and cut into small pieces	1 cup	225 g	8 oz
ice-cold water	9–12 Tbsp	90–120 ml	3–4 fl oz
caramelised onions (page 223)	¾ cup	170 g	6 oz
Flatto*/Saturn peaches	4–6	450 g	1 lb
Danish blue cheese, crumbled	¼ cup	90 g	3 oz
fresh thyme sprigs	4		
sea salt and cracked pepper	to taste		
egg yolk + 1 tsp water	1	30 ml	1 fl oz
vanilla sugar/salt for sprinkling edges, 1½ tsp each	1 Tbsp	15 g	½ oz

* Ripe Saturn (aka Flatto) peaches cut in half horizontally are a perfect shape for topping this pie. If not available, use 2 medium-size ripe peaches of your choice.

In a medium bowl, whisk together flour, sugar, salt and vanilla powder. Blend in butter with your fingertips or pastry blender until butter is pea-sized. Drizzle in the ice water, tossing gently with a fork to combine. Test a small handful – if it doesn't hold together, add a bit more water. Do not overwork the dough.

Turn out onto a lightly floured work surface and divide in half. Working quickly, use the heel of your hand to smear each portion once or twice to help evenly distribute the butter. Gather dough together into a ball then flatten into a 15-cm/6-in disk. Wrap tightly in clingfilm/plastic wrap and chill for at least 1 hour. (You can freeze dough tightly wrapped for up to 3 months.)

Preheat oven to 190°C/375°F/gas mark 5.

Roll out chilled dough to about 33 cm/13 in in diameter on a lightly floured work surface. Fold about a 8-cm/3-in lip around the edge, shaping into a rectangle. Transfer to a lined baking tray/cookie sheet and chill for 30 minutes.

Spread a thin layer of caramelised onions, top with halved peaches and scatter with cheese and thyme sprigs. Season with salt and cracked pepper.

Beat egg yolk with water, brush on edges of dough, then sprinkle with the vanilla salt/sugar mixture.

Bake for 35 minutes until bubbly and golden brown.

Cool 10 minutes before slicing. *NM*

Dessert Plates

Mayan Chocolate Mousse

This easy dairy-free version of rich chocolate mousse combines two of the greatest food discoveries – vanilla and chocolate. Before the Aztecs, the Mayan Indians of what is now Mexico, created an usweetened spicy drink made with ground cocoa beans, chilli, spices, such as cinnamon and allspice, water and vanilla pods – served cold. The Mayans had created a healthful, flavourful but bitter drink – a little bit of Mayan honey, perhaps from the Melipona bee, the only pollinator of the vanilla orchid, would have made it palatable for today's chocoholics!

GF SERVES 4–6

dark chocolate/semi-sweet (60%), finely chopped	1¼ cup	150 g	5 oz
pure Mexican vanilla extract*	1 Tbsp	15 ml	½ fl oz
coffee extract	½ tsp		
runny honey	1 Tbsp	15 ml	½ fl oz
egg whites, large, at room temperature	5	150 ml	5 fl oz
cream of tartar**	½ tsp		
caster/superfine sugar	1 Tbsp	15 g	½ oz
cinnamon	¼ tsp		
chipotle or smoked chilli powder	¼ tsp		
TO SERVE			
vanilla whipped cream	1 fl cup	240 ml	8 fl oz
cocoa nibs	1–2 Tbsp		
vanilla pod	1		

* If available, use Mexican vanilla – I use Nielsen-Massey.
** Substitute a few drops of lemon juice in place of cream of tartar if not available.

Melt chocolate in microwave or over double-boiler, gently stirring with a rubber spatula until smooth and silky. Be careful not to overheat chocolate. When just melted and smooth set aside on counter until just warm. Gently stir in vanilla, coffee extract, honey and a pinch of sea salt. Set aside.

In a clean, dry stand-mixer or large stainless bowl, whip egg whites on low speed until frothy. Sprinkle in cream of tartar and whip on medium–high for 2 minutes. Sprinkle in sugar and continue to whip until whites are thick, glossy, medium-stiff peaks. Turn to low speed and sprinkle in cinnamon and chilli powder, mixing to combine.

Fold 2 large spoonfuls of whites into chocolate, then fold chocolate in 3 stages back into whites until incorporated.*

To serve
Spoon mousse into serving glasses, cover and chill until ready to serve. Top each with a dollop of vanilla-scented whipped cream, a sprinkling of cocoa nibs and a sliver of vanilla pod. *NM*

* For a bit of creamy decadence, whip 240 ml/8 fl oz/1 fl cup whipping cream with 1 tsp honey and ½ tsp pure Mexican vanilla extract. Fold ¼ cream into mousse, then fold this back into the cream. Finish as above.

Zabaione di Vaniglia

GINA DEPALMA

GF SERVES 4 [MAKES ABOUT 2 CUPS]

egg yolks, large	4	120 ml	4 fl oz
white sugar	¼ cup	50 g	1¾ oz
Vin Santo*	¼ cup	60 ml	2 fl oz
Navan, or other vanilla liqueur	2 Tbsp	30 ml	1 fl oz
Heilala vanilla powder	⅛ tsp		
whipping cream, whipped (optional)	½ cup	120 ml	4 fl oz

* Vin Santo is a unique dessert wine that it is both acidic and sweet. A sweet dessert wine could be substituted, but add 2 tsp/10 ml of lemon juice along with it. Or you could use a medium-sweet Riesling.

Create a bain-marie from a saucepan and a large heatproof stainless steel or copper mixing bowl that will sit comfortably on top of it. The saucepan should be able to hold 8–15 cm/ 3–6 in of water, which, when simmering, should not touch the bottom of the bowl. Place the saucepan of water on medium heat to bring the water to a gentle boil.

Place the egg yolks in the bowl and add the sugar, whisking them together well with a large, balloon-shaped whisk. Slowly whisk in the Vin Santo and the Navan, then whisk until foamy.

Place the bowl on top of the saucepan; the water should be gently simmering. Immediately begin whisking at a steady, moderate pace. The zabaione will become frothy and thick. Continue whisking until the zabaione falls from the whisk and mounds on top of itself, keeping and holding its shape for a few seconds; this should take 4 to 6 minutes, depending on the heat of the bain-marie.

Remove the bowl from the saucepan/pot of water and whisk for a few more seconds. Whisk in the vanilla powder.

To serve hot
Immediately divide the zabaione among four dessert dishes, spooning it over berries, or cake, or serve with biscotti.

To serve cold
To hold/keep zabaione for several hours, continue whisking until it is completely cool, then cover and chill. Just before serving, gently fold in the whipped cream then spoon into dessert dishes over your choice of fruit, biscotti or cake, and serve immediately.

———— ⊗⊗⊗ ————

A vanilla bean is an investment that pays tenfold. You can scrape the seeds and use the pod to flavour two different recipes, pods can be reused to perfume sugar, or shoved in a jar with a neutral alcohol to make homemade vanilla extract. Spent pods from the extract can be reused to roast or sauté fruit. The uses go on and on, and absolutely nothing is wasted. I can't say that about any other ingredient in my sweet pantry. **GDP**

Vanilla-Spiced Pineapple Roast

with crispy coconut leaves & vanilla ice cream

DOMINIQUE & CINDY DUBY

SERVES 4

VANILLA ICE CREAM

vanilla pods, split lengthways	2		
milk	1¼ fl cups	300 ml	10 fl oz
whipping cream	½ fl cup	120 ml	4 fl oz
corn syrup or glucose	1 Tbsp	15 ml	
white sugar	⅓ cup	70 g	2½ oz
powdered pectin	½ tsp		
egg yolks	5	100 ml	3½ fl oz

CRISPY COCONUT LEAVES

vanilla pod powder, to taste	¼–½ tsp		
salted butter, melted	⅓ fl cup	90 ml	3 fl oz
feuille de brick sheets*	4		
medium shredded coconut	½ cup	50 g	1¾ oz

VANILLA-SPICED PINEAPPLE ROAST

fresh pineapple	1	1 kg	34 oz
banana, 1 large, peeled and puréed or mashed	⅓ cup	125 g	4½ oz
fresh mango, 1 medium, peeled, pitted and puréed or mashed	1 cup	200 g	7 oz
fresh ginger	3 slices	15 g	½ oz
white sugar	¼ cup	50 g	1¾ oz
dark rum	1 Tbsp	15 ml	½ fl oz
water	½ fl cup	120 ml	4 fl oz
Szechwan pepper, ground	1 pinch		
lemon zest and juice	1		
salted butter, melted	1 Tbsp	15 ml	½ fl oz
vanilla pods	2		

* Available in North African and Asian specialty stores, or substitute filo/phyllo pastry, but it will produce a different texture and appearance.

** Serving option: Decorate with microgreens, such as coriander/ cilantro or mint.

Vanilla ice cream

Scrape vanilla seeds out of split pods and combine seeds with milk, cream and syrup in a saucepan. Bring to the boil.

In a stainless steel bowl, combine sugar and pectin. Add egg yolks; whisk lightly until well mixed.

Pour the milk mixture into the egg mixture a little at a time, whisking constantly. Place the bowl over a saucepan of simmering but not boiling water on medium heat and whisk until the mixture reaches 85°C/185°F, or until the mixture coats the back of a spoon. Cool, transfer to a clean container with a lid, and refrigerate overnight. Churn using an ice cream machine. Cover and freeze until ready to use.

Crispy coconut leaves

Preheat the oven to 180°C/350°F/gas mark 4. Line a baking tray/cookie sheet with a silicone mat or baking paper. Mix vanilla powder with butter and brush evenly over a feuille de brick sheet. Place next sheet on top, brush with butter mixture, repeating until you have a stack of 4 sheets. Then fold sheets over to get 8 layers. Sprinkle top with coconut. Using a cookie cutter, cut into rounds and place on the lined tray. Bake for 5 minutes, or until golden brown. Cool, then store in an airtight container for up to 2 days.

Vanilla-spiced pineapple roast

Preheat oven to 180°C/350°F/gas mark 4. Peel, core and cut pineapple into quarters and place them in a pan 15 x 20 cm/ 5 x 7 in. In a bowl, combine banana, mango, ginger, sugar, rum, water, pepper, lemon zest and juice and butter. Split vanilla pods in half lengthways, scrape out seeds, and add seeds and pod to the banana mixture. Pour over pineapple. Bake for about 50 minutes. Cool.

With a slotted spoon, transfer pineapple to a bowl. Set aside, but keep warm. Strain roasting juice through a fine mesh sieve/strainer into a saucepan/pot; discard solids. Place on stove to reduce liquid by ⅓. Keep warm.

Assembly

Cut pineapple roast into thin slices and arrange loosely in the centre of a dish. Drizzle with a few spoonfuls of reserved sauce. Place 2 or 3 disks of coconut leaves over pineapple and top with a scoop or quenelle of ice cream. Serve at once.

Anton's Bread & Butter Pudding

ANTON MOSIMANN

SERVES 4

butter, unsalted	2 Tbsp	35 g	1¼ oz
small bread rolls/or a small brioche loaf, thinly sliced*	3	180 g	6½ oz
milk	1 fl cup	240 ml	8 fl oz
double/heavy cream	1 fl cup	240 ml	8 fl oz
fine sea salt	a pinch		
vanilla pod, split	1		
eggs, large	3		
white sugar	½ cup + 1 tsp	125 g	4½ oz
sultanas/golden raisins, soaked in water & drained	2 Tbsp	15 g	½ oz
apricot jam	1 heaped	20 g	¾ oz
sieved icing/powdered sugar to dust	Tbsp		

It is easier to thinly slice bread if you freeze it first.

Preheat oven to 160°C/325°F/gas mark 3.

Lightly butter a 14 x 23-cm/5 x 9-in ovenproof dish

Use the rest of the butter to spread over the bread slices. Arrange the bread slices in the base of the dish.

In a 1 L/ 1 qt saucepan/pot, bring the milk, cream, salt and vanilla pod gently to the boil. Turn off the heat and allow the vanilla to infuse in the liquid.

In a small bowl, whisk together the eggs and sugar until pale. Gradually add the milk and cream mixture to the eggs, stirring well to amalgamate. Strain into a clean saucepan/pot.

Sprinkle the drained sultanas/golden raisins over the bread in the dish, then pour in the milk mixture. The bread will float to the top.

Place a folded newspaper inside a bain-marie and place prepared dish on top. Pour in enough hot water to come halfway up the outside of the dish.

Bake carefully in the preheated oven for 45–50 minutes. When the pudding is ready, it should wobble very slightly in the middle. Remove from the oven and cool a little.

Gently heat the jam, thinning with a little water if necessary. Lightly brush a thin coat of the warm glaze over the top of the pudding and then dust with icing/powdered sugar. Serve slightly warm.

———— ❧ ————

Making bread and butter pudding is always a great treat for me; it is a dessert that has many wonderful associations, as I have cooked it for presidents and royalty throughout the world. Always, when I reach for the vanilla pod and slide the knife blade along the brown skin to reveal the precious seeds – and the aroma floods the room – it is a moment that I treasure. **AM**

Quince Tarte Tatin

'The quantity of dough is suitable for any pan from 20–26 cm (8 to 10 in). If using a mould at the larger end of that spectrum, simply increase the quantity of quince liquid by about 25%. If quinces aren't your thing, poached pears work just as well. And don't worry if the quince syrup gels after it sits for a bit in the pan. Heat it with a bit more liquid, stirring until it's smooth again. Extra syrup that collects from the finished tart should be saved to drizzle or brush over wedges of the tart, giving them a brilliant sheen.'

DAVID LEBOVITZ

8 SERVINGS

POACHED QUINCE

water	7 fl cups	1¾ L	1¾ qt
white sugar	1 cup	200 g	7 oz
honey	½ fl cup	120 ml	4 fl oz
lemon (preferably unsprayed), cut in half	1		
vanilla pod, split lengthways	1		
quince*	6 large, or 8 med	2 kg	4 lb

DOUGH

plain/all-purpose flour	1 cup + 4 tsp	140 g	5 oz
white sugar	2 tsp	10 g	
fine sea salt	¼ tsp		
unsalted butter, chilled & cut into 3-cm/1-in cubes	6 Tbsp	85 g	3 oz
ice water	3 Tbsp	45 ml	1½ fl oz

* Some recipes advise soaking the peeled quince slices in lemon-tinged water to avoid browning. I've never done that, I simply slip them into the warm poaching liquid and any trace of discolouring soon disappears. **DL**

Poached quince

Mix water, sugar, honey, lemon and vanilla pod in a large non-reactive saucepan/pot and turn it on to medium–high heat. Add any additional spices or seasonings, if you wish.

While liquid is heating, quarter, peel and remove cores of the quinces. Make sure to remove anything tough or fibrous.

As you peel and prepare the quince quarters, slip each one into the simmering liquid. Once they're all done, cover the surface with a round of baking paper with a walnut-sized hole cut in the centre.

Simmer quince (do not boil) for at least an hour, until fork-tender. Cooking time will vary, depending on the quince, and it's not unusual for them to take up to 2 hours, or more.

Pour the quince and their liquid into a storage container and refrigerate until needed, or for up to one week.

Dough

In the bowl of a stand-mixer, or food processor, blitz together the flour, sugar, salt and butter, until the butter is in small but discernible pieces, about the size of large peas.

Add water and mix (or pulse) until the dough just begins to hold together. If it looks too dry, add a sprinkle more water.

Use your hands to knead the dough for a couple of seconds, just until it comes together, and shape it into a flat disk. Wrap in clingfilm/plastic wrap and chill for at least 30 minutes.

To assemble

Pour 300 ml/10 fl oz/1¼ fl cup of strained quince poaching liquid into a tarte tatin pan or cast-iron frying pan/skillet.

Cook over moderate heat until the liquid is thick and syrupy (the consistency of honey), then remove from heat. The amount should be about 60 ml/2 fl oz/¼ fl cup.

Preheat oven to 190°C/375°F/gas mark 5. Place rack in lower half of oven.

Lay poached quince quarters, which have been patted dry, snugly against each other, rounded side down, in the pan. Pack them in tightly as they'll settle down once baked.

On a lightly floured surface, roll dough into a circle a few inches bigger than the pan you're using. Drape dough over the quince, tucking in edges, and bake for approximately 45 minutes. The tart is done when the dough is deep golden brown.

Remove from the oven and leave to rest on a cooling rack for a few minutes to settle, then place a rimmed serving platter over the tart and turn the tart out onto the platter. Serve warm with crème fraîche or vanilla ice cream.

Chocolate Cadeaux Entremet

'Dark chocolate mousse layered with vanilla crème brûlée, rum-soaked sultanas and chocolate "biscuit", the entremet, a classic French dessert with layers of mousse, crémeux, cake and a touch of crunch, is impressive for its elegance as much as its taste. Read through the recipe carefully before you begin, and soak sultanas a day ahead of making.'

WILLIAM CURLEY

GF MAKES 8			
RUM-SOAKED SULTANAS			
sultanas/golden raisins	¾ cup	125 g	4½ oz
dark rum	5 Tbsp	75 ml	2½ fl oz
VANILLA CRÈME BRÛLÉE			
double/heavy cream	7 Tbsp	100 ml	3½ fl oz
whipping cream	½ fl cup	120 ml	4 fl oz
vanilla pod, split and scraped	1		
egg yolks, large	2	60 ml	2 fl oz
caster/superfine sugar	5 Tbsp	40 g	1½ oz
BISCUIT CHOCOLAT SANS FARINE			
egg whites, large	2	60 ml	2 fl oz
caster/superfine sugar	3 Tbsp	45 g	1½ oz
egg yolk, large, lightly whisked	1	30 ml	1 fl oz
cocoa powder	1 Tbsp	15 g	½ oz
CHOCOLATE CADEAUX SHELLS			
dark chocolate, chopped	4 cups	500 g	18 oz
DARK CHOCOLATE MOUSSE			
dark chocolate, chopped	1¾ cup	225 g	8 oz
egg yolks, large	4	120 ml	4 fl oz
water	2 Tbsp	30 ml	1 fl oz
caster/superfine sugar	¼ cup	60 g	2 oz
whipping cream	1¼ fl cup	300 ml	10 fl oz
EQUIPMENT (SEE NEXT PAGE)			

Rum-soaked sultanas
Wash and drain the sultanas/golden raisins. Place in small container and add the rum. Cover and marinate overnight.

Vanilla crème brûlée
Preheat the oven to 140°C/275°F/gas mark 1. Place silicone muffin moulds on a baking tray/cookie sheet and set aside.

In a small saucepan/pot, combine creams with vanilla pod and seeds and bring to a simmer for 1 minute. Remove from heat and bring to room temperature, about 15 minutes.

In a small bowl, whisk together the yolks and sugar until thick and lightly coloured.

Pour the vanilla–cream mixture into the yolks and whisk vigorously until well combined. Pour the mixture through a fine sieve/strainer into a jug/pitcher, then pour equal amounts into the silicone forms. Bake for 20–25 minutes or until the custard has set.

Remove from oven, cool, cover the moulds and freeze.

Biscuit chocolat sans farine
Preheat oven to 200°C/400°F/gas mark 6. Line a baking tray/cookie sheet with a silicone baking mat or silicone paper.

Whisk whites in a bowl until foamy. While whisking, slowly stream in sugar. Continue whisking until soft peaks form. Whisk in yolk until incorporated. Sift cocoa powder over mixture and fold in until blended. Spread batter onto prepared baking tray/cookie sheet and smooth the top.

Bake for 12 minutes. Allow to cool. Using two ring cutters, one just smaller than the size of the cone mould, and one 2 sizes smaller, cut 8 circles of biscuit chocolat of each size. Cover with a tea towel and set aside.

Chocolate cadeaux shells
Temper (see Black Pepper Chai Truffles, page 200, for technique) the chopped chocolate and pour into a small jug/pitcher for forming the chocolate cone shells.

EQUIPMENT

8 x 5-cm x 3-cm/4-oz silicone muffin moulds* ● 8 x C-shaped acetate sheets to fit inside cone forms* ● 8 x cone-shaped plastic chocolate moulds* or martini glasses ● a set of ring cutters ● silicone baking mat or silicone baking paper to fit in a 30 x 20 cm/8 x 12 in baking tray/cookie sheet ● palette knife measuring jug with spout ● paintbrush ● cooking thermometer

Available from PCB in France, Mafter and JB Prince in USA, and ask your local cake shop about acetate sheets as well.

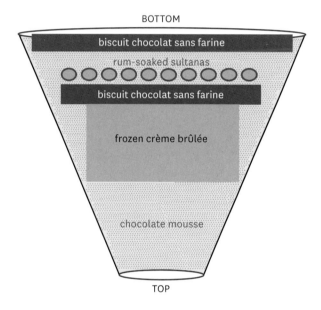

BOTTOM

biscuit chocolat sans farine

rum-soaked sultanas

biscuit chocolat sans farine

frozen crème brûlée

chocolate mousse

TOP

My grandmother was a great cook and regularly made Millionaire's Shortbread using vanilla in her caramel. We now do our own version of this Scottish classic, using only the best ingredients and Madagascan vanilla pods, which are my favourite. **WC**

Place 8 acetate 'C' forms on a flat surface, such as a piece of marble. Have the 8 cone forms or martini glasses ready. Spoon 2 Tbsp of melted chocolate onto the first piece of acetate and gently spread into an even layer with the back of the palette knife. As the chocolate begins to harden, carefully lift the acetate by one edge with the tip of a knife and finger and place the acetate in the mould with the chocolate side facing inwards, the acetate touching the mould. With a paintbrush, seal the edges with a bit of melted chocolate. You will have what looks like an upside down volcano with an opening at the tip. Repeat process with remaining acetate pieces. Set aside. The chocolate shells should be kept cool and dry at around 18°C/65°F.

Dark chocolate mousse

Melt the chocolate in a bowl set over barely simmering water, making sure the bowl does not touch the surface of the water, and heat to 45°C/110°F. With a spatula, gently stir until melted and smooth. Remove from the heat and set aside. In the bowl of a stand-mixer with the whip attachment, whip the yolks until thick and pale.

Simultaneously, in a small clean saucepan/pot boil the water and sugar to 120°C/250°F. With the mixer on low speed pour the hot sugar syrup down the inside of the bowl into the yolks, whisking to a light foamy custard known as a sabayon. Turn mixer to medium–high speed and continue whipping until cool.

While sabayon is cooling, whisk the cream until you can make a figure of 8 on the surface. Gently fold cream into the sabayon. Then fold one-third of the sabayon cream into the melted, cooled chocolate. Gently fold the rest into the chocolate mixture, folding until no streaks are showing. The amount will make more than needed, so save extra for another use.

To assemble chocolate cadeaux entremet
(see diagram)

Spoon the chocolate mousse into the tip and around the sides of the chocolate shell. Unmould the frozen crème brûlée and place in the centre of the mousse. Place the smaller disk of biscuit chocolat on top of the crème brûlée. Drain the sultanas/golden raisins, reserving liquid. Sprinkle a spoonful of sultanas/golden raisins on top.

Spoon additional mousse to cover, making sure to leave enough space for a final layer of biscuit chocolat. Brush these 8 larger disks with the rum sultana/golden raisin liquid if wished and place on the last mousse layer. Remove excess mousse and allow to set in fridge.

To serve

Using the palette knife, de-mould cadeaux from the cone forms to the serving plates. Use the palette knife to carefully level the tip of each cone, then lightly dust the top with cocoa powder. Carefully remove the acetate from around the cadeaux. Decorate if wished with chocolate disks and gold leaf.

The Plum Study

Plums are found in hundreds of shapes, colours and flavours in virtually all reaches of the world. The 'Black Doris' plum, considered New Zealand's backyard summer fruit favourite, grows readily in the Bay of Islands where I live, and yields a beautifully balanced combination of sweet and tart. Its dramatic purple flesh makes for a stunning dessert trio. Choose what is in season and look for varieties such as 'Elephant Heart' and 'Black Beauty' grown in the US, or the UK's 'Merryweather Damson' and 'President'. Whatever you choose, make sure the fruit is ripe, firm and full of flavour. The brown butter plum tart, originally created for Union Restaurant in Santa Monica, is still one of my favourite ways to enjoy the simple yet versatile plum.

SERVES 6

PLUM COBBLER

plain/all-purpose flour	1½ cups	185 g	6½ oz
fine sea salt	½ tsp		
white sugar	4 tsp	20 g	¾ oz
baking powder	1½ tsp		
lime zest	2 tsp		
unsalted butter, cold	¼ cup	60 g	2 oz
buttermilk	⅔ fl cup	150 ml	5 fl oz
purple plums, pitted and cut into rustic-shaped pieces	6	600 g	20 oz
white sugar	4 tsp	20 g	¾ oz
cornflour/cornstarch	1 Tbsp	10 g	
vanilla paste	¼ tsp		
egg yolk	1	30 ml	1 fl oz
whipping cream	2 tsp	10 ml	
vanilla sugar for sprinkling	4 tsp	20 g	¾ oz

BROWN BUTTER PLUM TART

VANILLA TART SHELLS [MAKES 6–8]

unsalted butter, softened	½ cup + 2 Tbsp	140 g	5 oz
vanilla sugar (page 222)	½ cup less 1 Tbsp	85 g	3 oz
egg, large	1		
plain/all-purpose flour, sifted	1¾ cups	225 g	8 oz

BROWN BUTTER BATTER

medium-sized dark red or purple plums	6	600 g	20 oz
unsalted butter	½ cup	110 g	4 oz
large eggs	2		
brown sugar, packed	⅔ cup	170 g	6 oz
plain/all-purpose flour	¼ cup	30 g	1 oz
vanilla paste	1 tsp		
brandy or dark rum	1 tsp		

Plum Cobbler

Mix dry ingredients in a medium bowl. Add zest and cut in butter with a pastry blender until mixture has butter-coated bits the size of small peas.

Pour in buttermilk, then fold in with a fork until well combined. You may have to add additional buttermilk if the dough is too flaky and won't come together.

Turn dough onto a floured cutting board and fold over twice. Roll to 1-cm/½-in thick and cut with a floured knife or ring cutter into 6 biscuit shapes. Place on baking tray/cookie sheet, cover and chill until needed.

In a small bowl, place plums, sugar, cornflour/cornstarch and vanilla paste. Stir to combine. Divide into six 8-cm/3-in ramekins.

Preheat oven to 190°C/375°F/gas mark 5.

Whisk together egg yolk and cream.

Place biscuit lids on filling, leaving a 1-cm/½-in space around the edge. Brush lids with egg yolk–cream glaze.

Sprinkle vanilla sugar on top and bake for 16–20 minutes until bubbly and golden brown. Remove from oven and allow to cool 10 minutes before serving.

Brown Butter Plum Tart

Vanilla tart shells
In a stand-mixer, beat butter on medium speed until smooth but not whipped. With mixer on low, stream sugar into butter until well combined. Add egg until mixed. Add flour in three stages, until just incorporated. Don't overwork dough. Turn out onto a board and work with a plastic dough scraper or spatula until smooth. It should feel like 'play dough'. Shape into 2 disks, wrap tightly in clingfilm/plastic wrap and chill until ready to bake.

Remove dough from plastic and press into pans, smoothing dough with your hands. If it gets too soft, place in fridge

The first time I made vanilla ice cream was under the apricot tree in the backyard at Rickety Ranch, Aunt Elaine and Uncle John's home in the hills above Santa Barbara, California. Well... actually, Elaine made the ice cream; my job was to turn the hand-crank on the ice-cream maker until my arms ached while staring into the salt and ice barrel just wishing the ice cream to freeze. When the delectable vanilla cream was softly set, I called out to Elaine, who appeared with a huge bag of chocolate chips and poured them all into 'my' ice cream! This was going to be the best vanilla chocolate chip ice cream in the whole world! She then lifted out the ice cream pail and carried it into the house. I was close behind. The ice cream was scooped into a loaf pan to harden in the freezer. Handed my reward of a spoon and the frozen pail, blissfully I scooped and devoured the few remaining spoonfuls of the vanilla chocolate chip treat!

---

* If a recipe needs tart shells to be fully baked, return to oven and bake until just lightly browned.

and chill until firm and then rework the dough. You may also roll chilled dough into rounds between layers of clingfilm/plastic wrap. Peel off bottom layer of plastic and place in tart tin/pan shaping sides to fit snugly (remove top layer of plastic before baking). Cover and chill until firm.

Preheat oven to 190°C/375°F/gas mark 5 (180°C/350°F fan).

Place a sheet of baking paper inside tartlet shells and fill with baking beans/pie weights.

Bake about 13 minutes, until edges are browned. Carefully remove baking paper and baking beans/pie weights.*

Brown butter batter
Pit and cut plums into 2-cm/1-in slices.

Brown butter in a small sauté pan over medium–high heat. Strain for large flakes of milk solids; small flecks are okay. Cool to room temperature.

Beat eggs and brown sugar together in a stand-mixer with paddle attachment on medium speed or whisk by hand until smooth. Sift in flour and a pinch of sea salt and continue mixing until well combined with no lumps – about 3 minutes. With mixer running on low speed, or whisking by hand, stream the butter into the mixture, combining well. Add the vanilla paste and brandy.

Just before baking, gently fold plums into the batter and spoon into par-baked tart shells, filling about ⅔ full. Bake 12–15 minutes until filling is golden and puffed.

(GF) PURPLE PLUM SHERBET [MAKES 1 L/1 QT]			
purple flesh plums	5	500 g	1 lb
vanilla syrup (page 223)	1 fl cup	240 ml	8 fl oz
golden syrup or corn syrup	2 Tbsp	30 ml	1 fl oz
milk, warmed	1 fl cup	240 ml	8 fl oz
lime juice and zest	2 Tbsp	30 ml	1 fl oz
vanilla vodka	1 Tbsp	15 ml	½ fl oz
pure vanilla extract	2 tsp	10 ml	

---

* If you don't have an ice-cream maker, pour sherbet mixture into a shallow glass or metal dish and freeze solid. Break up in a blender or food processor until smooth. Seal tightly and return to freezer until ready to enjoy.

Purple Plum Sherbet

Wash and quarter the plums and place in a medium-sized saucepan. Add vanilla syrup, golden syrup and pinch of sea salt. Simmer over medium–low heat until plums are soft. Allow to cool slightly, then using a spatula push purée through a sieve/strainer or wire colander to strain out pits and skin.

Whisk together plum purée, warmed milk and remaining ingredients. Cover and chill 2–8 hours. Spin in ice-cream maker according to manufacturer's instructions* until smooth and creamy. Gently spoon the sherbet into a storage container, top with a circle of baking paper and seal with a tight-fitting lid. Freeze immediately until firm. *NM*

Opposite, from top: Plum Cobbler, Brown Butter Plum Tart and Purple Plum Sherbet.

Raspberry Meringue 'Martinis'

Scribbling notes and making lists while sitting at chefs' conference, I wandered into a whimsical dessert daydream. Visualising a cocktail, I imagined a dessert disguised as a 'Martini'. Sketching the rough idea, I pitched it to executive chef Anne Conness, then of Napa Valley Grille in Los Angeles, for whom I was consulting. She LOL'd (laughed out loud) and said 'go make it!'

MAKES 6–8

MARTINI PIE TOPS

plain/all-purpose flour	1½ cup	180 g	6⅓ oz
cake/fine sponge flour*	⅓ cup	40 g	1⅓ oz
white sugar	2 Tbsp	25 g	1 oz
fine sea salt	¼ tsp		
lime, zest of	1	115 g	4 oz
unsalted butter, chilled, hard and cut in small cubes	½ cup		
vanilla pod, seeds or paste	½ ½ tsp		
egg yolk	1	30 ml	1 fl oz
water, chilled	¼ fl cup	60 ml	2 fl oz
raspberry vinegar (page 223)	½ tsp		
vanilla sugar for topping	2 Tbsp	25 g	1 oz

ITALIAN MERINGUE

caster/superfine sugar	1 cup	200 g	7 oz
glucose or corn syrup	½ tsp		
egg whites	4	120 ml	4 fl oz
cream of tartar**	¼ tsp		

RASPBERRY CURD [PAGE 224]

EQUIPMENT

2 plastic drinking straws cut into 5-cm/2-in pieces ● 6–8 sturdy martini glasses ● a sugar/candy thermometer ● a grease-free pastry brush ● a piping/pastry bag with open star tip ● a blowtorch or crème brûlée flame

---

* If cake flour isn't available, replace the plain/all-purpose flour and cake flour measures with 220 g/7⅔ oz/scant 2 cups plain/ all-purpose flour + 1 Tbsp/10 g cornstarch/cornflour.

** If you don't have cream of tartar use a few drops of lemon juice; the acid strengthens the egg white bubbles.

† If you have more meringue than you need, pipe into decorative shapes on a baking tray/cookie sheet lined with baking paper and cook at 95°C/200°F/lowest setting for an hour until set. Turn off oven and leave to cool for several hours.

Martini pie tops

Set aside a cookie cutter that fits inside the martini glass.

In a large bowl, sift flours, sugar, salt and zest. Cut in chilled butter with a pastry cutter or 2 forks to pea-sized butter bits. Whisk yolk, water and vinegar together and drizzle into the dry mixture, using a fork to toss and incorporate. Shape into a pad, wrap and chill for 1–2 hours.

On a lightly floured surface, roll out dough 1½-cm/½-in thick. Fold over twice and roll out again to 1½-cm/½-in thick, being careful not to overwork dough. Cut into rounds. Space on lined cookie sheet/baking tray and chill until cold.

Preheat oven to 190°C/375°F/gas mark 5 (180°C/350°F fan).

Lightly sprinkle rounds with vanilla sugar, then press a piece of plastic straw just off centre into each pie top. Bake for 8–12 minutes until golden brown. Remove and discard straws.

Italian meringue

In a clean small saucepan, mix sugar, glucose and enough water to make mixture like wet sand. Clip a thermometer to side of pan/pot and turn heat to medium. While sugar simmers, pour whites into a clean stand-mixer bowl with whip attachment or in bowl with hand-mixer at the ready. When sugar reaches 95°C/200°F, turn mixer to low and whip whites until foamy. Sprinkle in cream of tartar and turn to medium–high, whipping ⅔ of the way, slightly less than soft peaks. When sugar reaches 115°C/240°F, take off heat and let sugar bubbles subside. Return whites to low speed then pour sugar syrup in a thin stream down between the side of the bowl and beaters. Turn speed to high and continue whipping until meringue is glossy. Turn speed to medium–low and continue beating until bowl feels about room temperature. Set aside until ready to serve.†

To serve

Spoon raspberry curd into martini glasses until ¾ full. Pipe meringue on top of curd in a decorative swirl or zig-zag, covering top entirely. Use a blowtorch or brûlée flame, slowly waving the flame just above meringue until browned, being careful not to put the flame on edge of glass for too long. Place pie top on meringue. Garnish your 'martini' with raspberry 'olives' skewered on a sugar toothpick inserted into the straw hole. Serve within an hour of making as the meringue will begin to liquefy. *NM*

Vanilla Panna Cotta

with mixed berry compote & belli e brutti

'Nothing smells better than butter browning with a vanilla bean!'

NANCY SILVERTON

GF SERVES 4

PANNA COTTA			
cold water	1 Tbsp	15 ml	½ fl oz
unflavoured powdered gelatin	1½ tsp		
whipping cream	3 fl cups	700 ml	24 fl oz
white sugar	7 Tbsp	105 g	3¾ oz
vanilla pod, halved lengthways, pulp scraped	2-in piece	5-cm piece	
COMPOTE			
water	¼ fl cup	60 ml	2 fl oz
white sugar	½ cup	100 g	3½ oz
vanilla pod, halved lengthways, pulp scraped	1		
fresh mixed berries (raspberries, blueberries, blackberries)	3 cups	450 g	16 oz
brandy	½ fl cup	120 ml	4 fl oz
cornflour/cornstarch	2 Tbsp	20 g	¾ oz
BELLI E BRUTTI			
flaked/slivered almonds, toasted	1 cup	90 g	3 oz
hazelnuts, blanched, toasted	1 cup	140 g	5 oz
baking powder	¼ tsp		
pure vanilla extract	½ tsp		
honey	¾ fl cup	180 ml	6 fl oz
orange flower water	¼ tsp		
egg white	1	30 ml	1 fl oz
white sugar	¼ cup	50 g	1¾ oz
kosher salt or sea salt flakes	¼ tsp		

Panna cotta

Place water in a small bowl and sprinkle with the gelatin. Leave the gelatin to soften for 5 minutes.

Meanwhile, in a saucepan over medium–high heat, warm the cream with sugar and vanilla and pulp, stirring until sugar is dissolved. Turn off heat and add softened gelatin. Stir until it dissolves. Strain mixture through a fine sieve/strainer into a measuring cup with a spout, then pour it into four 240-ml/8-fl oz ramekins. Chill until firm, about 3 hours.

Compote

In a large heavy-duty frying pan/skillet, stir together the water and sugar, add the scrapings and the vanilla pod. Over medium–high heat, bring the mixture to the boil without stirring. Using a pasty brush dipped in water, brush down the sides of the pan and remove any undissolved sugar granules. When the sugar begins to colour, after about 3–4 minutes, tilt and swirl the pan to cook evenly. When the sugar reaches an even medium caramel colour, remove from the heat.

Add the fruit, tossing in the pan to coat. Be careful as mixture may spatter and the caramel may seize and harden. Add brandy, and return pan to low heat, carefully cooking the fruit until the sugar melts, about a minute.

Place a large sieve/strainer over a bowl and pour in fruit compote, straining the liquid into the bowl. Remove vanilla pod and transfer the fruit to a serving dish. Reserve the liquid.

Whisk cornflour/cornstarch into the reserved liquid. Return the liquid to the frying pan/skillet and over medium heat bring the liquid to the boil, whisking constantly. Remove from the heat and pour the thickened juice over the cooked berries. Set aside to cool.

Belli e Brutti

Adjust the oven racks to the middle–lower positions and preheat the oven to 180°C/350°F/gas mark 4.

Add all the ingredients to a medium metal bowl and gently mix together with your hands, being careful not to break the almond pieces.

Drop teaspoonful-mounds of mixture onto lightly sprayed, lined baking trays/cookie sheets.

Bake for about 15–20 minutes, until nicely browned and chewy, rotating baking trays/cookie sheets halfway through to ensure even baking.

To serve

Quickly dip each panna cotta mould in hot water to loosen sides, or alternatively run a small knife around the edges to loosen. Unmould on serving plates and spoon the compote mixture over the top. Serve immediately with pieces of Belli e Brutti.

Creamy Butterscotch Pudding

with Tash's English toffee

One day, after a busy lunch service at Union in Santa Monica, California, Chuck Craig, the manager, wandered into the pastry kitchen (as he usually did) craving something sweet but comforting. 'Pudding!' he shouted (as one must do to be heard above the din of the big extractor fan). 'I want pudding! Can you make pudding?' He looked as innocent as he could and I shouted back, 'Of course Chuck, I can make pudding.' 'Chocolate, with lots of whipped cream too?' 'Of course Chuck, come back in an hour.' As I had two chocolate desserts already on the menu, I went with butterscotch. The secrets to this creamy comfort food are a dash of apple cider vinegar, which cuts through the sugar, and vanilla that enhances the caramelly flavour. An hour later to the minute Chuck returned but could not wait for the pudding to cool so had his warm, freshly ladled from the pot. Spooning a generous dollop of vanilla whipped cream on the top, he plucked a toffee shard from the tray and quickly exited my kitchen! It remained on the menu from that day on.

GF 6 SERVINGS

whipping cream	2 fl cups	475 ml	16 fl oz
unsalted butter, softened	6 Tbsp	70 g	2½ oz
dark brown sugar, packed	1 cup + 2 Tbsp	225 g	8 oz
cornflour/cornstarch, sifted	4½ Tbsp	45 g	1½ oz
fine sea salt	¼ tsp		
milk	2 fl cups	480 ml	16 fl oz
egg yolks, lightly beaten	3	90 ml	3 fl oz
pure vanilla extract	1 Tbsp	15 ml	½ fl oz
dark rum (optional)	1 tsp		
apple cider vinegar	1½ tsp		

In a small saucepan, heat 300 ml/10 fl oz/1¼ fl cups cream until warm (or microwave in a small pitcher/jug until warmed). Remove from heat and set aside.

Combine butter and brown sugar in a medium stainless steel saucepan/pot over low heat. Simmer 2 minutes, stirring with a spatula until bubbly. Add warmed cream and stir until smooth.

Combine cornflour/cornstarch and salt in a small bowl. Slowly whisk in ¼ of the cold milk until cornflour/cornstarch dissolves. Add this mixture to pan/pot with remaining milk. Bring to a simmer over medium heat, stirring constantly to prevent burning. Stir about 2 minutes, until you see steam rise from surface and the pudding thickens. Slowly stream in egg yolks, whisking constantly.

Switch to spatula and continue to gently stir until bubbles form on top of pudding.

Remove from heat and stir in 2½ tsp vanilla, rum (if using) and the vinegar. Quickly strain into a jug/pitcher, to make pouring easier, and then immediately pour into 6 individual serving dishes or glasses.

Tightly cover each one with a piece of clingfilm/plastic wrap to keep a skin from forming. Chill 3 hours or until softly set. Can be made a day in advance.

To serve
Whip remaining cream with the ½ tsp vanilla until soft peaks form. Place a dollop of the whipped cream on top of each pudding. Garnish with a toffee shard (page 224). *NM*

Tin Roof Gooey Scooter Pies

Scooter pies or moon pies (depending on where you grew up) are vanilla marshmallow squished between digestive biscuits/graham crackers dipped in chocolate coating – an American childhood treat. My nostalgic remix with a 'Tin Roof' twist has peanuts, caramel and Mexican vanilla, adding a little spice to the richness of this decadent treat. When ready to assemble, it is a great party project for kids and grown-up kids alike! Yum!

MAKES 12–15 PIES

SCOOTER PASTRY CASE/PIE SHELLS, PAGE 225

PEANUT BUTTER CUP LAYER			
smooth peanut butter	½ cup	140 g	5 oz
unsalted butter	⅓ cup	85 g	3 oz
Mexican pure vanilla extract*	½ tsp		
icing/powdered sugar	⅔ cup	80 g	3 oz
GOOEY CARAMEL			
white sugar	1 cup	200 g	7 oz
corn or golden syrup	2 Tbsp	30 ml	1 fl oz
water	¼ fl cup	60 ml	2 fl oz
cream, slightly warmed	¼ fl cup	60 ml	2 fl oz
unsalted butter	¼ cup	60 g	2 oz
crème fraîche	1 Tbsp	15 g	½ oz
Mexican pure vanilla extract*	½ tsp		
GANACHE GLAZE			
dark chocolate,** chopped	1 cup	125 g	4 oz
whipping cream	⅓ fl cup + 1 Tbsp	90 ml	3 fl oz
glucose or corn syrup	1 tsp		
CHEWY MARSHMALLOW LAYER			
gelatin powder, 3 envelopes	3 Tbsp	30 g	1 oz
cold water	½ fl cup	120 ml	4 fl oz
white sugar	2 cups	400 g	14 oz
corn or golden syrup	⅔ fl cup	180 ml	6 fl oz
water	¼ fl cup	60 ml	2 fl oz
fine sea salt	¼ tsp		
pure vanilla extract	1 Tbsp	15 ml	½ fl oz
TO ASSEMBLE			
toasted peanuts	½ cup	60 g	2 oz

* I prefer Mexican vanilla for this dessert, if available, but it's fine to use other pure vanilla.

** I prefer Guittard, Sharffen Berger and Callebaut.

Peanut butter cup layer
In a small pan, melt peanut butter and butter over low heat. Stir in vanilla, sugar and a big pinch of sea salt. Set aside.

Gooey caramel
Gently stir sugar, syrup and water in a stainless saucepan/pot. Bring to a simmer over medium–high heat, washing any sugar crystals down sides of pan/pot with a clean water-dipped brush. Cook until the colour turns a dark golden brown. Slowly and carefully whisk in the cream, then whisk in the butter, crème fraîche and vanilla. Cool and cover. Do not refrigerate.

Ganache glaze
Put chopped chocolate in a medium bowl. In a small saucepan, heat cream until steamy. Pour over chocolate and leave to stand 1 minute then slowly stir until chocolate is melted. Do not refrigerate but set aside until ready to assemble.

Chewy marshmallow layer
In the bowl of a stand-mixer or mixing bowl with a hand-mixer, sprinkle the gelatin over the cold water, give a quick stir and soak for 15 minutes. Combine sugar, syrup and water in a grease-free small saucepan/pot. Give a gentle stir to dissolve sugar into water, clip on a thermometer and bring to the boil over high heat (115°C/240°F) – 5 minutes. Turn mixer on low and pour boiling syrup into gelatin in a thin stream between side of bowl and beaters. Once all syrup is in, turn mixer to high and beat for 15 minutes. Turn to medium, add salt and vanilla then turn back to high and beat another 5 minutes.

To assemble
Using an oiled tablespoon, quickly scoop marshmallow into each scooter pastry case/pie shell. Smooth flat with a wet finger and leave to stand 2 hours. Top with a spoonful of gooey caramel, let flow to edges. Top with spoonful of warmed chocolate and smooth top. Sprinkle with peanuts and salt flakes. Leave to set – about 1 hour, if they last that long! *NM*

Vanilla & Hazelnut Bavarois

'Heavenly, light as a feather but full of vanilla and hazelnut flavour.'

GALTON BLACKISTON

GF SERVES 6			
egg yolks	4	120 ml	4 fl oz
caster/superfine sugar	½ cup	100 g	3½ oz
milk	1 fl cup	240 ml	8 fl oz
vanilla pod, split	1		
Frangelico liqueur	6 Tbsp	90 ml	3 fl oz
gelatin leaves, softened in cold water	3		
whipping cream	1 fl cup	240 ml	8 fl oz

In a medium bowl, beat together the egg yolks and sugar until pale.

In a saucepan, warm the milk with the vanilla pod over low heat just until steam begins to rise from the pan. Don't let it boil. Remove from the heat and allow the vanilla to infuse into the milk.

Prepare an ice bath by filling a large metal bowl with equal amounts of water and ice. Have a sieve/strainer ready and resting on another bowl that fits snugly inside the ice bath bowl.

Add the milk mixture to the egg yolks and sugar and then return the mixture to the pan. Warm the mixture, stirring constantly over a moderate heat to produce a custard consistency.

In another saucepan, warm the Frangelico, add the drained softened gelatin to dissolve, then mix into the custard. Strain into the prepared bowl. Gently stir occasionally until just beginning to set.

While mixture is cooling, semi-whip the cream, then fold into the custard, gently combining until fully incorporated. Pour into serving dishes or into a 720-ml/3-cup capacity lightly oiled jelly mould. Refrigerate until set.

To serve
Dip the mould quickly into hot water to loosen sides, place serving plate tightly over mould and immediately flip over onto plate. Garnish as desired.

Vanilla is undoubtedly my favourite spice. My earliest vanilla memory has to be tasting a vanilla-pod ice cream that had lots of seeds throughout – it was just mind-blowing! Vanilla has, since then, remained a firm favourite in my kitchen and is used on a daily basis, whether it be for sweet or savoury dishes. Quality vanilla pods are fruits from nature's gods. **GB**

Author's note: I plated Galton's delicious bavarois on a bed of toasted ground hazelnuts with whole hazelnuts dipped in caramelised sugar quickly lifted to create the elegant sugar spikes.

Rhubarb Ginger Gazpacho & Buttermilk Panna Cotta

The gazpacho in this light, chilled spring-time dessert was inspired by US pastry chef Claudia Fleming, whom I had the unforgettable pleasure of working with at 'Cuisines of the Sun' in 2000 on Big Island, Hawaii.

GF SERVES 6

GAZPACHO			
rhubarb, washed, trimmed and chopped	10 stalks	1 kg	2 lb
fresh ginger	6 slices	30 g	1 oz
vanilla syrup (page 222)	1½ fl cups	350 ml	12 fl oz
lime juice (keep lime zest for garnish)	1 Tbsp	30 ml	1 fl oz
fine sea salt	¼ tsp		
PANNA COTTA			
gelatin leaves (or 2 tsp powdered gelatin)	2½		
whipping cream	1¼ fl cups	300 ml	10 fl oz
vanilla pod, split and scraped	1		
brown sugar	2 Tbsp	30 g	1 oz
honey	2 Tbsp	30 ml	1 fl oz
lime juice	1 tsp		
buttermilk	1 fl cup	240 ml	8 fl oz
Greek yogurt	½ cup	125 g	4 oz
TO SERVE			
small pineapple	½	285 g	10 oz
mango	½	100 g	3½ oz

Gazpacho
Combine the rhubarb, ginger and vanilla syrup in a large saucepan. Bring to a simmer over medium heat. Simmer 10–15 minutes, stirring occasionally.

Peel lime with zester and reserve zest for garnish.

Force rhubarb through a medium sieve/strainer or food mill, discarding solids. Add salt and 1 Tbsp lime juice (reserving 1 tsp of lime juice for panna cotta). Cover and chill for 3 hours, or overnight.

Panna cotta
Place gelatin sheets in a bowl of cold water to soften. Lightly oil six 120-ml/4-fl oz ramekins (or 6 plastic cups or moulds) and set aside.

In a medium stainless steel saucepan/pot, bring the cream, vanilla pod, seeds, brown sugar and honey to a slight simmer, stirring continuously. Remove from heat, add a pinch of sea salt, lime juice and gelatin sheets (drained and squeezed dry), stirring to completely dissolve the gelatin. Whisk in the buttermilk and yogurt until smooth. Strain and pour into prepared moulds and chill until set, 2–3 hours.

To serve
Peel, core and dice the pineapple into small cubes. Peel and dice the mango into small cubes. Have flat-bottomed soup bowls ready. Quickly dip each panna cotta mould in hot water to loosen sides. Pat moulds dry and invert panna cotta into soup bowls. Ladle the gazpacho around the sides of the panna cotta. Garnish with small cubes of pineapple and mango and curls of reserved lime zest. Serve immediately. *NM*

Peach, Cardamom & Vanilla Sablé Breton

JIM DODGE

MAKES 12–16 TARTLETS			
PEACHES			
peaches, medium-sized, ripe, organic	3	500 g	18 oz
vanilla sugar, divided	2 Tbsp	30 g	1 oz
DOUGH			
unsalted butter	¾ cup	170 g	6 oz
white sugar	¾ cup	150 g	5½ oz
pure vanilla extract	1 tsp		
egg yolks, large	3	90 ml	3 fl oz
plain/all-purpose flour	1⅔ cup	215 g	7¾ oz
baking powder	1 Tbsp	15 g	½ oz
cardamom, ground	½ tsp		
sea salt	pinch		
TO ASSEMBLE AND BAKE			
sliced almonds with skin	¼ cup	30 g	1 oz

The extraordinary flavour nuances of fine vanilla have been an essential part of my culinary pantry. In about 1990 the manufacturer of vanilla I used changed from dark glass bottles to plastic. I was surprised and skeptical but tried it. At first it was fine, but after a few days the vanilla started to smell and taste like petroleum. This became a valuable lesson; when reaching for this soft bottle, I flexed the plastic which released the chemical odours of the bottle, completely overwhelming the vanilla treasure within. **JD**

Peaches

Fill a 2-L/2-qt bowl halfway with equal amounts of water and ice. Set aside. Boil 1.5 L/6 cups of water. Add peaches and reduce heat to a simmer. Use a spoon to keep peaches under the water. After 1 minute, remove peaches with a slotted spoon and put into ice-water. After 1–2 minutes, lift peaches and place on a towel to drain (chilling time will depend on the ripeness and succulence of the fruit).

Using a small thin knife, peel skin from peaches and discard. Starting from stem end, cut peaches into quarters. Retaining the shape of the wedge, slice each quarter into about 5 or 6 thin slices. Place peach slices in a bowl, sprinkle lightly with half the vanilla sugar and gently toss so sugar is evenly covering the fruit. Cover and chill until needed.

Dough

Using a hand-held or stand-mixer with paddle (or by hand), cream butter until light and creamy. Stream in sugar and continue to beat on medium speed, scraping bowl as needed, until mixture is light and fluffy. Add vanilla; continue to beat, scraping bowl as necessary, until the mixture is again light and fluffy. Add egg yolks one at time until fully incorporated, scraping between each addition.

Sift flour with baking powder, cardamom and salt. Turn speed to low and sprinkle dry mixture into bowl, mixing until just evenly blended. Take care not to overwork dough.

Shape into a thick log about 7½ cm/3 in in diameter and wrap tightly in plastic. Chill about 2 hours until firm.

To assemble and bake

Preheat oven to 180°C/350°F/gas mark 4. Place tartlet pans or ring-form moulds on a lined baking tray/cookie sheet.

Remove the chilled dough and cut the log into disks thick enough to fill the pans or ring-forms half full, shaping to fit. Keep dough lightly dusted with flour for easy handling.

On centre of each dough disk fan 3 or 4 slices of peach. Keep them away from the edge; I find it best to form them with a slight curve, similar to a flower petal. Sprinkle with a few sliced almonds and pinches of the reserved vanilla sugar.

Bake for about 15 minutes until golden brown.

Serve warm with remaining peaches if you wish.

The Anna Pavlova

Anna Pavlova. When I began ballet lessons at six years old, I remember borrowing books from the library as I wanted to learn all about the world-famous ballerina loved for her ethereal grace, tutus and pointe shoes. What I didn't know until decades later was the ethereal, delicious link to New Zealand created just for Anna's arrival! This version, composed of airy rich Tahitian vanilla cream, regal raspberries and showers of rose petals between delicate tutu-tiered meringue, is a tribute to my first idol, and my first love – ballet.

SERVES 6–8

MERINGUE TUTU TIERS

cornflour/cornstarch	3½ tsp		
caster/superfine sugar	1½ cups	300 g	10½ oz
pure Tahitian vanilla extract	1½ tsp		
raspberry vinegar (page 223)	1½ tsp		
white wine vinegar	½ tsp		
egg whites, room temperature	6	180 ml	6 fl oz

PRESERVED ROSE PETAL SAUCE

rosewater	¼ fl cup	60 ml	2 fl oz
raspberries frozen, thawed	1 cup	140 g	5 oz
grenadine	3½ Tbsp	50 ml	1¾ fl oz
white sugar	¼ cup	60 g	2 oz
raspberry vinegar (page 223)	¼ fl cup	60 ml	2 fl oz
lemon juice	1 tsp		
pink peppercorns, cracked	¼ tsp		
vanilla pod, split and scraped	½		
unsprayed pink roses,* petals separated (reserve some petals for garnish)	3 roses		

TAHITIAN VANILLA CREAM

whipping cream, chilled	1¼ fl cups	300 ml	10 fl oz
crème fraîche or sour cream, chilled	1 cup	225 g	8 oz
caster/superfine sugar	1 Tbsp	15 g	½ oz
Tahitian** vanilla extract	2 tsp	10 ml	

TO ASSEMBLE

raspberries, fresh	1¼ cup	170 g	6 oz
pink roses to decorate	1–2		

* Unsprayed fragrant roses from the home garden are perfect!

** Tahitian vanilla, with its pronounced flowery fragrance, balances 'en pointe' with the scent of rose petals.

† Baking time will vary depending on your oven.

Meringue tutu tiers

Preheat oven to 140ºC/275ºF/gas mark 1. Line 2 baking trays/cookie sheets with foil and trace 3 circles with the edge of a spoon: 20-cm/8-in on one tray/sheet; and 15-cm/6-in and 10-cm/4-in on the other. Set aside.

Whisk cornflour/cornstarch and sugar together. In another bowl, stir together vanilla and vinegars. In a clean dry bowl of a stand-mixer, or using an electric mixer, on medium speed whip the egg whites with a pinch of sea salt until they hold soft peaks. Add sugar mixture 1 Tbsp at a time. When all sugar is added, beat a minute longer. Add vinegar mixture and turn to high, beating until meringue is glossy and holds stiff peaks, about 3 minutes.

Spoon meringue inside circles, making a wide shallow bowl in the centre of each. Using the back of a spoon make wavy 'tutu' shapes on edges. Place trays in centre of oven, then turn down heat to 100ºC/210ºF/lowest setting. Bake until meringues have a crisp crust and feel dry to the touch (the insides will remain chewy), about 1 hour.† Keeping door closed, turn oven off, cooling meringues in oven for an hour. As meringues cool, they will crack slightly.

Preserved rose petal sauce

Place all ingredients (except petals) with a pinch of sea salt in a small pan/pot. Bring to a simmer and stir until sugar is dissolved. Strain into a jug/pitcher, returning vanilla pod to sauce. Rinse pan/pot, then fill with 5 cm/2 in of water. Bring to the boil, and add rose petals. Lower to a gentle simmer and poach for about 3 minutes, tasting a few petals to check they are no longer bitter, but softened and tender. Drain petals and stir into sauce. Cover and refrigerate until chilled. Will keep chilled for 2 weeks.

Tahitian vanilla cream

In a large mixing bowl, whip cream to soft peaks, then fold in crème fraîche. Add sugar and vanilla, whipping until light and thick.

To assemble and serve

Spoon a dollop of cream in centre of serving plate to hold first meringue layer in place. Spread with a layer of cream, dot with raspberries and drizzle rose petal sauce on top. Repeat with remaining layers, drizzling extra sauce down sides. Garnish with fresh petals and serve immediately. *NM*

Scottish Shortbread Sundae

with blueberry ice cream

DUFF GOLDMAN

SERVES 4–6

BLUEBERRY ICE CREAM			
blueberries (fresh or frozen and thawed, fresh is better)	3 cups	425 g	15 oz
white sugar	1 cup	200 g	7 oz
water (you might need more, but start with this)	½ fl cup	120 ml	4 fl oz
lemon juice	2 tsp	10 ml	
half amount of cream and half of milk or half'n'half	2 fl cups	475 ml	16 fl oz
vanilla paste	3 Tbsp	45 g	1½ oz
SCOTTISH SHORTBREAD			
unsalted butter	1 cup	225 g	8 oz
icing/powdered sugar	¾ cup	85 g	3 oz
vanilla paste	1 tsp		
plain/all-purpose flour	2½ cups	285 g	10 oz
sea salt	hefty pinch		
CRÈME CHANTILLY			
whipping cream	½ fl cup	120 ml	4 fl oz
maple syrup	1 Tbsp	15 ml	½ fl oz
wildflower honey	1 Tbsp	15 ml	½ fl oz
vanilla pod seeds	½ a pod		
CRÈME FRAÎCHE SAUCE			
crème fraîche	1 cup	250 g	9 oz
vanilla pod, seeds scraped out; save pod for another use	1		
white sugar	3 Tbsp	45 g	1½ oz
TO SERVE			
cherries*	4–6		
chiffonade of lemon verbena leaves or edible flower petals	1 Tbsp		

* If in season, fresh cherries are ideal but you can use 'cocktail' cherries.

Blueberry ice cream

Put the blueberries, sugar and water in saucepan. Simmer for about 5 minutes while keeping an eye on the water. Don't let it get too dry and burn, but don't leave too much water either. Add lemon juice and purée in a blender until smooth. Chill in the fridge overnight.

Stir in the half cream and half milk/half'n'half and vanilla paste. Freeze in an ice-cream maker until it looks like soft-serve, then scoop out and put in the freezer until set and frozen.

Scottish shortbread

Preheat oven to 190°C/375°F/gas mark 5.

Cream butter, sugar and vanilla paste. Beat until smooth. Sift dry ingredients together, then GENTLY fold into the butter until the mixture is homogeneous.

Press dough evenly into an 20 x 30 cm/8 x 12 in square tin/pan. Mark into smaller squares by pushing the tines of a fork about ¾ of the way through the dough.

Bake in preheated oven 23–28 minutes. Cut along markings while still hot but let it cool in the tin/pan. Turn out and store in an airtight container.

Crème Chantilly

Heat the cream with syrup, honey and vanilla seeds until hot. DO NOT BOIL.

Chill in the fridge 3 hours or up to overnight. Whip to soft peaks when you are ready to serve.

Crème fraîche sauce

Combine all ingredients in a bowl, whisk together until smooth. Leave to sit for at least an hour, chilled, before serving. Give a quick whisk right before serving.

To serve

Pool the crème fraîche sauce on the plate and place one square of shortbread on top. Scoop a small sphere of blueberry ice cream and place on the shortbread. Spoon on a dollop of crème Chantilly and put the cherry on top. Lightly scatter the lemon verbena or flower petals.

Cake Plates

Banana Polenta Upside Down Cake

Simple to make, and not too sweet, this make-ahead vanilla banana cake is perfect for dessert or brunch.

GF OPTION SERVES 8

unsalted butter	¼ cup	60 g	2 oz
brown sugar, packed	½ cup	100 g	3½ oz
vanilla pods, split and scraped	2		
lime, zest of	1		
lime juice	2 Tbsp	30 ml	1 fl oz
dark rum (optional)	1 Tbsp	15 ml	½ fl oz
bananas, large, ripe with green tips	4	450 g	1 lb
plain or gluten-free flour	⅓ cup	50 g	1¾ oz
polenta, medium grind	1 cup	160 g	5½ oz
baking powder*	¼ tsp		
sea salt	¼ tsp		
eggs, large, separated	3		
caster/superfine sugar	⅓ cup	75 g	2½ oz
pure vanilla extract	½ tsp		
skim or soy milk	¼ fl cup + 2 Tbsp	90 ml	3 fl oz
corn or vegetable oil	¼ fl cup	60 ml	2 fl oz

* Most baking powders are gluten free, but check label to be sure.

❧

My most fragrant vanilla memory is quite recent. Returning from the Heilala plantation party in Tonga, our group leaned on luggage carts by the baggage carousel while the contraband-sniffing beagles wound in and out of the array of passengers. Suddenly, in unison, all eyes and noses turned towards two brown boxes emerging from behind the rubber flap of the carousel curtain. The beagles strained on their leads to get closer as Jennifer and Garth Boggiss, our Tongan hosts, lifted the boxes and went over to the inspection tables. The scent of hundreds of perfectly cured vanilla beans wafted through airport arrivals and except for the dogs, all who sniffed the air were smiling.

Line a 20-cm/9-inch cake or pie tin/pan with foil and butter the foil. Set aside. Preheat oven to 180°C/350°F/gas mark 4.

Melt butter in a frying pan over medium–low heat. Add brown sugar and stir with a heat-resistant or wooden spatula until the mixture begins to bubble. Add vanilla seeds and pods stirring well for 1 minute. Add lime zest, juice and rum – the mixture will sizzle – and stir until blended. Remove from heat and pour sugar glaze into prepared cake tin/pan with vanilla pods.

Arrange pods in centre of cake tin/pan. Peel, then slice bananas lengthways into ½-cm/¼-in thick slices. Carefully place in a single layer and drizzle with any remaining glaze. Set aside.

Whisk the flour, polenta, baking powder and salt in a small bowl.

In a large grease-free bowl, and using a hand-mixer or stand-mixer, whisk the egg whites until frothy. Slowly stream in half the sugar and whip the whites to glossy, soft peaks, tripled in volume.

In a large bowl, whisk the yolks with remaining sugar until well blended. Add the vanilla, milk and oil, whisking well.

Fold dry ingredients into yolks, using a spatula to combine. Fold in the whites in 3 stages until just blended. Gently pour or spoon batter on top of banana mixture, smoothing the top. Place in centre of oven and bake for 23–25 minutes until cake is set and springs back when touched in centre.

Cool for 10 minutes then invert onto a serving plate, carefully peeling foil off the top. Serve warmed or at room temperature with a spoonful of Greek yogurt or ice cream. *NM*

Pure Vanilla Layer Cake

with golden syrup buttercream

As a third generation Californian, I had never heard of golden syrup until I visited Ye Old King's Head in Santa Monica where one can indulge in authentic 'English Cream Teas' and peruse the shelves for British groceries. 'Tate and Lyles' classic golden syrup has a heavenly vanilla caramel taste. Add more vanilla, butter and a pinch of salt, then slather on layers of vanilla cake and watch it vanish!

SERVES 8

VANILLA LAYER CAKE

whole milk	1 fl cup + 1 Tbsp	250 ml	8½ fl oz
vanilla pod, split and scraped	1		
egg yolks, large	4	120 ml	4 fl oz
pure vanilla extract	1 tsp		
cake flour	3 cups	300 g	10½ oz
(or plain/all-purpose flour, + 1 Tbsp/10 g cornflour/cornstarch)	2¾ cups	340 g	12 oz
white sugar	1½ cups	300 g	10½ oz
baking powder	4 tsp	20 g	¾ oz
fine sea salt	¼ tsp		
unsalted butter	⅓ cup	155 g	5½ oz

GOLDEN SYRUP BUTTERCREAM

egg yolks, large, room temperature	5	150 ml	5 fl oz
white sugar	¼ cup	50 g	1¾ oz
golden or corn syrup	½ fl cup	120 ml	4 fl oz
sea salt	¼ tsp		
unsalted butter, softened	2 cups	450 g	16 oz
pure vanilla extract	2 Tbsp	30 ml	1 fl oz

Vanilla layer cake

Make sure all ingredients are at room temperature. Preheat oven to 180°C/350°F/gas mark 4 (170°C/325°F fan).

In a small saucepan, warm milk with vanilla pod and seeds until steam rises. Turn off heat to infuse 20 minutes. Rinse and dry pod to save for another use.

Butter and flour three 20–22-cm/8–9-in cake tins/pans. Line bottoms with oiled baking paper. Set aside. In a small bowl, whisk together 60 ml/2 fl oz/¼ fl cup cooled vanilla milk, yolks and vanilla extract. Set aside, reserving the remaining milk.

Sift the dry ingredients into bowl of a stand-mixer with paddle (or use a hand-held mixer). On low speed, add butter and reserved milk in alternating stages to combine. Turn speed to medium and beat 1½ minutes until batter is aerated and nearly white. Return to low and add egg mixture in 3 stages to combine. Scrape down sides of bowl after each addition. Do not overmix.

Divide into cake tins/pans, smoothing tops. Bake for 25–35 minutes or until centre springs back when touched. Cool cakes 20 minutes in tins/pans. Turn out onto cake racks, tops facing up. Cool completely before icing.

Golden syrup buttercream

Whip yolks on medium speed in bowl of a stand-mixer with whip attachment, or with a hand-held mixer, for 2 minutes. Turn off and scrape down sides. Turn to high and whip yolks until pale yellow and doubled in volume.

While yolks are whipping, in a small dry heavy saucepan/pot combine sugar, golden syrup and salt. Bring to a rolling boil. Stir occasionally until sugar is dissolved and surface is covered with large bubbles. This should take only a few minutes.

Turn off mixer and pour about a ¼ of the syrup into the yolks. Stop pouring and immediately whip on highest speed for 5 seconds to temper yolks. Turn speed to medium and slowly stream in the remaining syrup down the inside of the bowl being careful not to pour on the beaters. Turn speed to high and beat until completely cool.

Turn to medium–low speed and drop fingerfuls of butter a little at a time into the mixture until completely incorporated. Add vanilla and whip on high speed to fluff up the buttercream. Ice completely cooled cake layers. Decorate as wished or with coloured white chocolate curls, shown here.

Buttercream will keep up to one week or frozen, tightly covered, for up to a month. Allow to come to room temperature before whipping to aerate. *NM*

Inspired by Rose Levy Beranbaum.

Caramelised Pineapple Carrot Cake

Inspired by the endless array of pineapples, from white to golden, on Big Island, Hawaii, I adapted my carrot cake recipe and crammed it full of pineapple goodness. Caramelising the pineapple intensifies the flavour and reduces the overall liquid in the recipe. Adding toasted ground oatmeal – my secret ingredient – gives the cake a nutty flavour without adding any nuts.

MAKES ONE 2- OR 3-LAYER CAKE

pineapple, peeled, cored and diced small	scant 3 cups	565 g	20 oz
brown sugar (for caramelising pineapple)	¼ cup	55 g	2 oz
crystallised ginger, chopped	⅓ cup	65 g	2¼ oz
sultanas/golden raisins	1 cup	150 g	5¼ oz
vanilla paste	2 tsp	10 g	
corn or vegetable oil	¾ fl cup	180 ml	6 fl oz
brown sugar, packed	1 cup	225 g	8 oz
white sugar	⅔ cup	135 g	4½ oz
eggs, large, lightly beaten	4		
plain/all-purpose flour	2 cups	240 g	8½ oz
fine sea salt	¾ tsp		
baking powder	2 tsp		
bicarb of soda/baking soda	2 tsp		
cinnamon	1 Tbsp		
nutmeg, fresh grated	½ tsp		
ground allspice	½ tsp		
oats or multigrain flakes, toasted and ground in spice grinder	½ cup	50 g	1¾ oz
carrots, grated	3 cups	285 g	10 oz

CARDAMOM CREAM CHEESE FROSTING

cream cheese, at room temperature, cool and firm	2 cups	485 g	1 lb
unsalted butter, at room temperature, cool and firm	1 cup	225 g	8 oz
icing/powdered sugar, sifted	1 cup	140 g	5 oz
ground cardamom	1 tsp		
lime juice	1 tsp		
pure vanilla extract	2 tsp	10 ml	

Preheat oven to 160°C/325°F/gas mark 3 (150°C/300°F fan).

Lightly oil two 20-cm/8-in cake tins/pans, line with baking paper circles and set on a baking tray/cookie sheet.

Sauté diced pineapple in a large sauté pan with first measure of brown sugar over medium–high heat until caramelised and juices have evaporated. Add ginger and sultanas/golden raisins, then leave to cool. Stir in vanilla paste and set aside.

Mix oil, sugars and eggs together in a large bowl with a wooden spoon or spatula until well combined.

In a large bowl, sift flour, salt, baking powder, bicarb of soda/baking soda, cinnamon, nutmeg and allspice. Whisk in ground toasted oatmeal to dry ingredients, combining well.

Pour egg mixture into dry ingredients, mixing well with spatula. Add grated carrot, then pineapple mixture, combining well. Divide batter equally into cake tins/pans.

Bake for 45–50 minutes until cake springs back when softly pressed. Turn out on racks when completely cool.

Cardamom cream cheese frosting

Make sure cream cheese and butter are at room temperature, but cool and solid. In a small bowl, sift the sugar, cardamom, and a big pinch of sea salt. Set aside.

In bowl of a stand-mixer using paddle, or a hand-held mixer and a bowl, beat butter on low speed until it is smooth and free of lumps. Add cream cheese, beating until creamy, then add lime juice and vanilla. Add sugar mixture on low speed until just combined. (Overbeating the frosting will make it soupy. If this happens, chill in refrigerator until hard, then beat until spreadable.)

Ice cakes with frosting and, if wished, garnish with flash-fried candied carrots and oven-dried pineapple slices. *NM*

Aunt Helen's Victory Garden Bundt Cakes

When we were little, Great Aunt Helen would often come visit my sister, brother and I. We would race to the car as she pulled to a stop in the driveway, her big green 1960 four-door Chevy dwarfing her tiny figure. She would emerge like royalty, carefully placing her hankie-filled black purse firmly on her wrist. Then, with white-gloved hands, she would take her large wicker basket from the trunk and patiently follow our puppy-like skipping and jumping into the house. We would stare excitedly at her 'wicked witch of Oz'-like basket as she removed the Bullock's French-milled soap bars – four in a box and wrapped in crunchy pink tissue paper – for my mother, six egg raisin custards, the skin tops crusted with fresh ground nutmeg and, lastly, her cinnamon sugar-iced Victory Garden Cakes, which we all agreed were the very best way to eat your vegetables!

MAKES 8–10 BABY BUNDT RING CAKES

VICTORY CAKES

eggs, large	3		
corn or vegetable oil	1 fl cup	240 ml	8 fl oz
white sugar	1½ cups	300 g	10½ oz
brown sugar	½ cup	100 g	3½ oz
pure vanilla extract	1 Tbsp	15 ml	½ fl oz
walnuts, lightly toasted and chopped	⅔ cup	100 g	3½ oz
courgette/zucchini, grated	1¼ cups	180 g	6½ oz
parsnip, peeled and grated	1 cup	70 g	2½ oz
plain/all-purpose flour	3 cups	380 g	13½ oz
sea salt	1 tsp		
bicarb of soda/baking soda	1 tsp		
baking powder	½ tsp		
cinnamon	2 tsp		
nutmeg, fresh grated	½ tsp		

VANILLA SPICE ICING

icing/powdered sugar	1½ cups	170 g	6 oz
pure vanilla extract	1 tsp		
milk	2 Tbsp	30 ml	1 fl oz
salted butter, melted	2 Tbsp	30 ml	1 fl oz
cinnamon	1 tsp		

Preheat the oven to 180°C/350°F/gas mark 4 (160°C/325°F fan). Lightly oil 8 small Bundt-style* tins/pans and set on a baking tray/cookie sheet.

In a large bowl, whisk the eggs until smooth. Add the oil, sugars and vanilla, whisking well. Using a wooden spoon, fold in the walnuts, courgette/zucchini and parsnip and set aside.

In another bowl, sift together the flour, salt, bicarb of soda/baking soda, baking powder and spices. Add the dry mixture to the wet in 2 stages and mix until just combined.

Scoop into prepared tins/pans, filling ⅔ up, and bake for 28 minutes, or until cakes spring back when pressed lightly with a finger. Place on cooling rack and cool for 15 minutes, then gently shake to release and turn out onto a rack to cool completely.

Vanilla spice icing
Whisk the icing ingredients, with a big pinch of sea salt, until smooth. Drizzle tops of the cooled cakes with icing, letting icing run down the sides. *NM*

*Alternatively, use 2 dozen muffin cups, baking time about 15 minutes, or if using a large Bundt-style tin/tube, or 2 loaf or cake tins/pans, increase baking time to 1 hour.

Knotweed Vanilla Crumble Cakes

'In many parts of the world Japanese knotweed is an invasive thug of a creeping rhizome. It grows up to 1.5 m/5 ft tall and spreads its tendrils beneath our garden soil in an unrelenting onslaught, having gone so far as to slither its way in between the tightly fitted stones of our 200-year-old well. And while eradicating this pestilence is nigh impossible, one way of controlling it is to eat the tender shoots as they pop their ruby heads from the ground. The taste is lovely: part lemon, part herbaceous lightness. Think of lovely, non-invasive goodies like rhubarb and sorrel for a taste comparison. By infusing the cake batter with vanilla, the herbaceousness becomes lush and elegant.'

GESINE BULLOCK-PRADO

MAKES APPROXIMATELY 2 DOZEN			
CRUMBLE			
plain/all-purpose flour	1¼ cups	155 g	5½ oz
unsalted butter, melted	½ cup	110 g	4 oz
white sugar	¼ cup	60 g	2 oz
brown sugar	¼ cup	60 g	2 oz
sea salt	pinch		
CAKE BATTER			
unsalted butter	1 cup	220 g	8 oz
white sugar	1½ cups	250 g	9 oz
large eggs, room temperature	5		
vanilla paste*	1 Tbsp	15 g	½ oz
semolina flour	1 cup	150 g	5¼ oz
plain/all-purpose flour	2 cups	240 g	8½ oz
sea salt	1 tsp		
baking powder	1 Tbsp	15 g	½ oz
buttermilk	1¼ fl cup	300 ml	10 fl oz
cranberries, dried (or substitute dried currants)	½ cup	60 g	2 oz
knotweed, diced (or, if unavailable, rhubarb is a good substitute)	1 cup	120 g	4 oz

* *I use Nielsen-Massey.*

Crumble
Stir together all ingredients until the mixture comes together in small clumps.

Cake batter
Preheat oven to 180°C/350°F/gas mark 4. Grease muffin tins/pans or line tins/pans with baking paper cases/cups.

In the bowl of a stand-mixer with paddle attachment, cream together the butter and sugar until very light and fluffy.

Add eggs, one at a time, scraping the bowl after each addition, until well combined. Add the vanilla paste.

In a large bowl, whisk together the semolina flour, plain/all-purpose flour, salt and baking powder.

With the mixer running, add ⅓ of flour mixture to creamed mixture, and add ½ of the buttermilk. Continue alternating between the flour and buttermilk mixture until completely combined. Fold in the dried cranberries and diced knotweed.

Divide batter evenly among muffin cases/cups, filling just a little more than halfway.

Sprinkle the top of each cake with about 1 Tbsp of crumble.

Bake for 30 minutes, or until the cakes spring back when gently poked.

Vanilla Vanilla Vanilla!

50 bean vanilla ice cream, not-so-angel food cake, & vanilla mascarpone cream

'Start this amazingly rich vanilla experience a day ahead for maximum enjoyment.'

SHERRY YARD

SERVES 6

50 BEAN VANILLA ICE CREAM [MAKES 1 L/1 QT]

VANILLA INFUSION [12 HOURS IN ADVANCE]

whipping cream	2 fl cups	475 ml	16 fl oz
milk	2 fl cups	475 ml	16 fl oz
vanilla sugar (see page 222)	½ cup less 1 Tbsp	90 g	3 oz
Tahitian vanilla pods, split and scraped	5		
12 HOURS LATER			
yolks, large*	7	210 ml	7 fl oz
white sugar	½ cup	120 g	4 oz

* 'Easy yolks' (pasteurised yolks sold in a carton) are OK to use.

Once you have used vanilla pods in a recipe, wash them in a colander under cold water until clean. Place in dehydrator or on a sheet/tray atop the oven and dry out. You can then use for vanilla sugar. SY

Vanilla infusion (12 hours in advance)
In a 2-L/2-qt container add cream, milk and vanilla sugar.

With scissors, split vanilla pods in half. Scrape out the seeds, then add seeds and pods into the cream mixture. Whisk well, tightly cover and refrigerate for 12 hours or overnight.

50 Bean Vanilla Ice Cream

In a 2-L/2-qt stainless steel saucepan/pot, bring vanilla infusion to the boil, turn heat off and leave to infuse for 1 hour.

Prepare ice bath. Grab thermometer and whisk.

Over a medium heat, return the vanilla infusion to the boil, then turn off heat.

In a medium bowl, whisk together the yolks and white sugar.

Whisking constantly, ladle ¼ of the steaming vanilla infusion into the yolks. Yolks are now tempered. Still whisking, pour yolk mixture back into pan/pot and with a heatproof spatula stir constantly, scraping the bottom of the pan/pot, and heat to 80°C/175°F, or until the mixture coats the spatula. DO NOT STRAIN!

With immersion hand-held stick-blender, emulsify the ice-cream base until thick and creamy.

Cool *immediately* in the ice bath to below 4°C/40°F. Whisk constantly until cold then cover and refrigerate overnight.

The next day strain through chinois, pressing firmly to release the flavour from the vanilla pods. Freeze in an ice cream maker according to manufacturer's instructions.

NOT-SO-ANGEL FOOD CAKE [MAKES SIX 7½-CM/3-IN RING MOULDS]			
unsalted butter	¾ cup	200 g	7 oz
vanilla pod, split and scraped	1		
pastry flour*	1¾ cups	200 g	7 oz
baking powder	½ tsp		
egg whites	12	360 ml	12 fl oz
cream of tartar	½ tsp		
white sugar	2 cups	400 g	14 oz

* Pastry flour measures lighter than plain/all-purpose flour, so if you are using plain/all-purpose flour use 215 g/7¾ oz/1½ cups measure.

VANILLA MASCARPONE CREAM			
mascarpone	½ cup	115 g	4 oz
white sugar	1 Tbsp	15 g	½ oz
pure vanilla extract	¼ tsp		
whipping cream	1 fl cup	240 ml	8 fl oz

Not-so-angel Food Cake

Preheat the oven to 190°C/375°F/gas mark 5 (180°C/350°F fan).

Line a baking tray/cookie sheet with baking paper and top with ring moulds (DO NOT GREASE).

In a small saucepan, melt the butter with the vanilla seeds and pod, whisking until combined. Reserve HOT.

Sift together the pastry flour and baking powder. Reserve.

In a stand-mixer with whip attachment, on medium speed whip the egg whites to foamy then add the cream of tartar. Slowly stream in the sugar, whip to medium stiff peaks. Turn down to low speed and sprinkle in the sifted dry ingredients. Continue on low speed and stream in the butter.

Fill each mould with the batter, smoothing tops.

Bake 12 minutes or until a toothpick inserted into the centre of the cake comes out clean and the top is slightly firm to touch and deep golden brown. Allow to cool while making the vanilla mascarpone cream.

———

Vanilla Mascarpone Cream

In a stand-mixer with whip attachment, on low speed, whip the mascarpone, sugar and vanilla extract for 1 minute, until smooth. Scrape down sides.

Continue on low speed and slowly stream in the cream. Once all the cream is incorporated, turn speed to medium and continue to whip for 3 minutes until soft peaks.

Fill a piping/pastry bag with cream and reserve in refrigerator. Keep in mind that after whipping the mascarpone cream hardens in the refrigerator, so 30 minutes before serving, take the mascarpone piping/pastry bag from the fridge and allow it to come to room temperature.

To serve
Carefully unmould cakes using a paring knife to loosen the sides. Place on individual plates. Serve with a scoop of 50 bean vanilla ice cream and a swirl of vanilla mascarpone. To 'gild the lily', finish with a tiny piece of edible gold leaf.

Glorious Victoria Cake

'Based on a classic Victoria sponge, the key to this cake's success is using the best quality ingredients. For added flavour and moisture, soak the sponge layers in vanilla sugar syrup. The design is inspired by the era of the cake's origin, decorated using a Victorian-style scroll and shell piping technique.'

PEGGY PORSCHEN

MAKES 1 x 15-CM/6-IN ROUND 3-LAYER CAKE, SERVING 8–12 SLICES

SPONGES

unsalted butter, softened	1 cup less 2 Tbsp	200 g	7 oz
caster/superfine sugar	1 cup	200 g	7 oz
salt	pinch		
vanilla pod seeds (save pod for vanilla sugar)	½ a pod		
eggs, medium	4		
self-raising flour	1½ cups	200 g	7 oz

SUGAR SYRUP

water	scant ⅔ fl cup	150 ml	5 fl oz
caster/superfine sugar	⅔ cup	150 g	5¼ oz
vanilla pod, split and scraped	1		

BUTTERCREAM FILLING

unsalted butter, softened	1⅓ cups	300 g	10½ oz
icing/powdered sugar, sifted	2½ cups	300g	10½ oz
salt	pinch		
vanilla pod seeds	½ a pod		
pink food paste, small amount, as desired			
good-quality raspberry jam	¼ cup	85 g	3 oz

EQUIPMENT

3 x 15-cm/6-in round sandwich tins/pans ● cake leveller or large serrated knife ● non-slip turntable ● flat disk to place on top of the turntable(I use the loose base of a 30-cm/12-in springform cake tin/pan) ● 15-cm/6-in round cake circle/card ● metal side scraper ● 2 plastic piping/pastry bags ● medium star piping nozzle/tip ● plain round 4-mm/¼-in piping nozzle/tip

One day ahead

Bake the sponges one day ahead of serving. Make the sugar syrup while baking the sponges. Prepare the buttercream filling and assemble and decorate the cake on the day of serving.

Sponges

Preheat the oven to 180°C/350°F/gas mark 4.

Prepare three 15-cm/6-in round sandwich tins/pans by greasing and lining them with greaseproof paper.

Place the butter, sugar, salt and vanilla seeds in a stand-mixer bowl with paddle attachment (or by hand) and cream together until pale and fluffy.

Beat the eggs lightly in another bowl and slowly add to the butter mixture while whisking quickly. If the mixture starts to separate or curdle, stop adding the egg and beat in 2–3 tablespoons of the flour. This will rebind the batter. Once all the egg has been added and combined with the butter mixture, sift in the flour and stir until the batter is just combined. This will ensure the sponges stay light and fluffy.

Divide the batter evenly between the sandwich tins/pans. If you find it difficult to measure by eye, use your kitchen scales to weigh out the amount of sponge mixture for each tin.

Bake for 15–20 minutes, depending on your oven. (If you are using deeper cake tins/pans, the sponges will take longer to cook.) The sponges are cooked when the sides are beginning to shrink away from the edges of the tins and the tops are golden brown and spring back to the touch. If in doubt, insert a clean knife or wooden skewer into the centre of each sponge; it should come out clean.

Sugar syrup

While the sponges are baking, prepare the sugar syrup for soaking. Place the water, sugar and vanilla pod and seeds into a saucepan and bring to the boil. Simmer until all the sugar crystals have dissolved. Set aside to cool down slightly. Discard the vanilla pod.

Once the sponges are baked, remove from oven and leave to rest for about 10 minutes still in the tins. Using a pastry brush, soak the tops of the sponges with vanilla sugar syrup while they are still warm; this allows the syrup to be absorbed faster.

When cakes are just warm, run a knife all the way round the sides of the tins, remove cakes and leave to cool completely on a wire cooling rack.

Once cool, wrap the sponges in clingfilm/plastic wrap and then rest them overnight at room temperature. This will ensure that all the moisture is sealed in and the sponges firm up to the perfect texture for trimming and layering. If they are trimmed too soon after baking, the sponges tend to crumble and may even break into pieces.

Buttercream filling
Place the butter, icing/powdered sugar, salt and vanilla seeds into a mixing bowl and cream together until very pale and fluffy.

Add a small amount of pink food paste to the mixture and stir through until combined and the buttercream is a pastel shade.

To assemble the cake
With a long serrated knife, trim the tops to level cakes, then sandwich together the three layers using one layer of buttercream filling and one layer of raspberry jam, and the vanilla sugar soaking syrup. Crumb coat or mask the top and sides of the cake with remaining buttercream filling, reserving some for decoration.

To decorate
Place the cake either onto a cakestand or on top of a turntable covered with a piece of baking paper or cake circle/card.

Place a star nozzle/tip into a plastic piping/pastry bag and fill bag with a generous amount of the remaining buttercream. Place a round nozzle/tip into another plastic piping/pastry bag and fill with a small amount of the remaining buttercream.

Divide the top of the cake into eight equal segments. Using the star nozzle/tip, pipe a ring of C-scrolls around the circumference, revolving the turntable as necessary. Next, pipe a shell from the middle of each C-scroll towards the centre. Where all eight shells meet, pipe a rosette on top at the centre of the cake top. Using the plain round nozzle/tip, pipe a small dot between each shell.

Using the star nozzle/tip, pipe eight fleur de lys evenly around the sides at the top edge, with a single upside-down shell underneath each at the bottom edge. To finish, pipe a small dot between the fleur de lys and shell. If the cake has been placed on greaseproof paper, chill until the piped dots are set before transferring to a cakestand.

Serve the cake at room temperature. This cake is best enjoyed within 3 days of baking, but it will last for up to 1 week.

Two-Tone Chocolate Malt Cake

This cake boasts an unusual source of inspiration: my two-toned black-and-white saddle shoes. But it's more than a slice of nostalgia: it celebrates the flavour of vanilla at both ends of the chocolate spectrum.

MAKES ONE DOUBLE-LAYER CAKE

CHOCOLATE MALT CAKE			
plain/all-purpose flour	3¼ cups	400 g	14 oz
bicarb of soda/baking soda	1½ tsp		
fine sea salt	1 tsp		
white sugar	1¼ cups	225 g	9 oz
filtered water	2 fl cups	475 ml	16 fl oz
unsweetened cocoa powder	⅔ cup	60 g	2 oz
chocolate malt powder, e.g. Ovaltine, Milo or Horlicks	½ cup	70 g	2½ oz
corn or vegetable oil	½ fl cup + 2 Tbsp	150 ml	5 fl oz
pure vanilla extract	1 Tbsp	15 ml	½ fl oz
white balsamic vinegar or strained lemon juice	2 Tbsp	30 ml	1 fl oz

WHITE CHOCOLATE BUTTERCREAM			
white chocolate, chopped, melted* and cooled	1⅓ cup	170 g	6 oz
white sugar	1¼ cup	225 g	8 oz
egg whites	4	120 ml	4 fl oz
cream of tartar**	⅛ tsp		
unsalted butter, softened and cut into small cubes	1 cup	225 g	8 oz

TO ASSEMBLE			
chocolate-covered malt balls	1½ cups	150 g	5½ oz

* Use a good quality white chocolate that's not overly sweet such as Lindt, El Rey, E. Guittard or Valrhona. Easy chocolate melting guide, page 120.

** If not available, substitute a few drops of lemon juice.

Chocolate malt cake
Preheat oven to 160°C/325°F/gas mark 3 (150°C/300°F fan).

Butter two 22-cm/9-in cake tins/pans. Press 2 circles of baking paper inside each pan, then turn over. Lightly dust pans with cocoa powder. Set aside.

Sift together flour, bicarb of soda/baking soda, salt and sugar. In a small saucepan, heat water to a simmer. Whisk in cocoa and chocolate malt powder until smooth. Set aside to cool.

In a separate bowl, mix together oil, vanilla and vinegar. Whisk cocoa liquid into oil mixture until smooth. Add to dry mixture, stirring until smooth. Divide evenly into cake tins/pans. Tap sides of pans against the edge of the counter, or drop from waist height onto a towel-covered counter to pop air bubbles. Swirl a skewer through the batter to pop any remaining bubbles. Bake for 30–45 minutes, until a toothpick inserted in the centre comes out clean.

White chocolate buttercream
Place sugar in a clean, heavy-bottomed saucepan/pot. Add just enough water to create 'wet sand' consistency. Bring sugar to a simmer and simultaneously begin whipping the egg whites in a stand-mixer with the whip attachment or with a hand-held mixer on low speed. When whites froth, sprinkle in cream of tartar and whip to just soft peaks. Continue cooking the sugar until it reaches the soft-ball stage (118–120°C/235–240°F).

Slowly stream sugar syrup into whites, pouring down inside of bowl (to avoid beaters) while whipping on low speed. Turn to high and whip until white and glossy, and the outside of bowl when touched is lukewarm not hot. When it is, turn to low then add cubes of butter a little at a time, alternating with the melted white chocolate. When butter and chocolate are in, turn speed back to high. It may look like it's separating but don't worry; keep whipping and it will come back!

To assemble
Place one cake layer in centre of cake plate. Spread a layer of buttercream on top all the way to edges. Place second layer on top, then frost top and sides with remaining buttercream. Cut malt balls in random shapes. Just before slicing, take one handful of malt balls at a time and press into sides of cake until completely covered. *NM*

Inspired by Margaret Fox.

Beekeeper's Elderflower Cheesecake

Smooth, creamy delicious. This is a classic New York cheesecake scented with flavours designed by the planet's pollinators: our precious bees.

GF SERVES 6–8

CHEESECAKE

cream cheese*	1¾ cups	400 g	14 oz
cornflour/cornstarch	2 Tbsp	20 g	¾ oz
fine sea salt	¼ tsp		
mascarpone	¾ cup	170 g	6 oz
runny honey, mild flavoured	⅓ fl cup	80 ml	2½ fl oz
vanilla paste	1 Tbsp	15 ml	½ fl oz
elderflower liqueur**	2 Tbsp	30 ml	1 fl oz
eggs, large, beaten	2		

TOPPING

sour cream or crème fraîche	1 cup	250 g	8 oz
white sugar	1 Tbsp	15 g	½ oz
egg white, beaten to frothy	1	30 ml	1 fl oz
pure vanilla extract	1 tsp		
orange blossom water (optional)	½ tsp		

* Philadelphia Cream Cheese is ideal.

** I used St Germain or you can use elderflower syrup.

† If using a springform tin/pan, bake at 150°C/300°F/ gas mark 2 for 45–50 minutes. Spread with topping as directed, but cool in unopened oven for 1 hour before removing.

Cheesecake

Have all ingredients at room temperature. Prepare six to eight 8-cm/3-in ring forms or one 20-cm/8-in springform tin/pan. Wrap bottom and sides to make watertight with a double layer of foil and arrange forms in a roasting or baking dish. Set aside.

Preheat oven to 160°C/325°F/gas mark 3 (150°C/300°F fan).

Beat cream cheese with hand-held mixer or in a stand-mixer with whip attachment and beat on medium speed until completely smooth. Stop and scrape down sides with spatula and continue to beat and scrape until velvety smooth. Sift in cornflour/cornstarch and salt. Whip well and scrape down sides with spatula.

Add mascarpone and beat until incorporated. Add honey, vanilla and liqueur, beating until smooth, about 1 minute. Add eggs last, mixing until well combined.

Scoop cheesecake batter into moulds, filling to ⅔ full. Place dish in oven and pour boiling water a quarter of the way up sides of forms to create a water bath. Bake 35–40 minutes, until cheesecake is jiggly in the middle with semi-set sides.†

While cheesecake is baking make the topping.

Topping

Whisk all ingredients together in a small bowl, beating until smooth. When baked, remove cheesecake from oven and carefully spread topping 1½–2 cm/½–¾ in thick. Smooth tops and return to oven. Turn OFF oven and leave to sit for 30 minutes (do NOT open oven during this time). Lift forms out of water bath onto a cooling rack for 1 hour. Transfer to a flat tray, cover tops with a piece of baking paper and refrigerate for at least 8 hours or overnight.

To serve

Scatter a handful of shortbread or biscuit crumbs in the centre of each plate. Run a small knife around the inside of the form. Turn form upside down and peel away foil. Place the ring mould on crumbs and lift mould up and away. Decorate cheesecakes with seasonal fruit and micro herbs if wished. *NM*

Bittersweet Chocolate Torte

Rich, simple, deep dark chocolate enhanced with coffee and vanilla. The key to this flourless fallen soufflé torte is gently folding the whites into the chocolate batter.

GF ABOUT 12 SERVINGS			
unsalted butter	1 cup	225 g	8 oz
70% dark/bittersweet chocolate, finely chopped	1⅔ cup	225 g	8 oz
fine sea salt	¼ tsp		
strong espresso, cooled or 1 tsp espresso powder dissolved in 2 tsp water	2 tsp	10 ml	
pure vanilla extract	1 Tbsp	15 ml	½ fl oz
eggs, large, separated, at room temperature	7		
cream of tartar	¼ tsp		
caster/superfine sugar	1 cup	200 g	7 oz
icing/powdered sugar, to serve	2 tsp		
cocoa powder, to serve	2 tsp		

Melt butter with chocolate in a bowl set over barely simmering water, stirring occasionally until smooth. Remove from heat, stir in salt, coffee and vanilla and set aside.

Butter inside of an 20-cm/8-in springform tin/pan and line the bottom with a buttered baking paper circle. (You can also make individual sized cakes; simply reduce the baking time to 10–15 minutes.)

Preheat oven to 160°C/325°F/gas mark 3 (150°C/300°F fan).

In a clean, dry stand-mixer bowl with whip attachment or using a hand-held mixer with clean, dry beaters, beat whites until frothy. Sprinkle in cream of tartar and whip another 30 seconds. On low speed, slowly stream in half the amount of sugar then turn speed to high and whip until glossy soft peaks form. (Do not overbeat or whites will be dry and separate.) Transfer from mixing bowl into a large dry bowl and set aside.

Return the mixer bowl to the machine. Add yolks and remaining sugar. Whip on high speed 3–4 minutes until yolks are pale yellow and tripled in volume. Turn speed to low and fold in cooled melted chocolate until just mixed.

Turn off mixer and fold whites into chocolate mixture in 3 stages, not over-mixing but without leaving white streaks.

Pour into prepared tin/pan and lightly smooth top. Place on baking tray/cookie sheet and bake 25–30 minutes until the top is lightly cracked and the centre is set but still a little jiggly.

Cool for 20 minutes then run a knife around inside of tin/pan. Gently release metal ring and transfer torte to a serving plate to cool completely.

To serve
Dust with icing/powdered sugar and/or cocoa powder. Serve at room temperature or slightly warmed with salted almonds and fleur de lait amande (page 224), as shown here. A snifter of Cognac, bourbon or a steamy espresso are also great accompaniments. *NM*

Vanilla Sugar Shortcakes

A Bay of Islands take on my signature classic dessert from Union Restaurant that showcased heavenly McGrath organic strawberries from Arturo at the Santa Monica Farmers Market. My New Zealand favourite is to pair rhubarb and strawberries from my garden, layered with spoonfuls of passion lime curd. Frozen rhubarb is OK, but strawberries are best fresh from the garden or the local farmers market!

MAKES 6–8 LARGER OR 12–16 MINI			
VANILLA-ROASTED RHUBARB			
rhubarb, cleaned and cut into 3-cm/1-in pieces	4 stalks	400 g	14 oz
brown sugar, packed	2 Tbsp	30 g	1 oz
vanilla sugar	2 Tbsp	30 g	1 oz
vanilla paste	1 tsp		
lemon juice	1 Tbsp	15 ml	½ fl oz
PASSION LIME CURD			
lime juice	⅓ fl cup	80 ml	2½ fl oz
passionfruit purée or 6 ripe passionfruit	½ fl cup	120 ml	4 fl oz
orange zest	1		
vanilla pod, split and scraped	½		
eggs, large	5		
white sugar	1⅔ cup	280 g	10 oz
unsalted butter	¾ cup	170 g	6 oz
SHORTCAKES*			
plain/all-purpose flour	2 cups	240 g	8½ oz
brown sugar, packed	¼ cup	55 g	2 oz
baking powder	1 Tbsp		
sea salt	½ tsp		
poppy seeds	4 tsp		
lemon zest	1		
unsalted butter, chilled and cut in small pieces	½ cup	115 g	4 oz
egg, large, and 1 yolk, beaten (save white for glaze)	1 + yolk		
cream, chilled	¾ fl cup	180 ml	6 fl oz
vanilla sugar to sprinkle on top	2 Tbsp	30 g	1 oz
TO SERVE			
strawberries, small, preferably organic	3 cups	350 g	12½ oz
vanilla whipped cream	1 fl cup	240 ml	8 fl oz
pure vanilla extract	1 tsp		

* This recipe may yield extra shortcakes, which freeze beautifully for unexpected teatime guests. Take directly from the freezer, wrap loosely in foil and heat 10 minutes in a 180°C/350°F/gas mark 4 oven.

Vanilla-roasted rhubarb
Preheat oven to 160°C/325°F/gas mark 3 (150°C/300°F fan). Brush a baking tray/cookie sheet with oil or butter and set aside. Toss rhubarb with remaining ingredients and a pinch of sea salt until evenly coated. Scatter onto baking tray/cookie sheet and roast for 30 minutes, until rhubarb is softened but still holds its shape. Cool, then gently transfer to a small plate.

Passion lime curd
Combine lime juice, passionfruit, orange zest and vanilla pod and seeds in a small bowl.

Prepare an ice and water bath in a large bowl, setting a smaller bowl inside with a sieve/strainer set on top. Beat eggs and sugar in a 1-L/1-qt stainless steel saucepan/pot over low heat. Add juice mixture, butter and pinch of sea salt. Whisk constantly over medium–low heat. Replace whisk with a spatula and continue stirring until curd thickens, about 5 minutes.Remove from heat and strain quickly into prepared bowl, stirring to cool the mixture. When cool, cover tightly and chill until ready to use (will keep 2 weeks).

Shortcakes
Whisk together flour, brown sugar, baking powder, salt, poppy seeds and zest. Chop in chilled butter with a pastry blender or two forks until the mixture resembles coarse breadcrumbs.

Whisk eggs into cream, then drizzle over flour. Stir quickly and lightly with a fork until incorporated. Gently gather in a ball then turn out onto a lightly floured surface and pat or gently roll into an 3½-cm/1½-in high pad, using additional flour sparingly. Cut with a floured round cutter or knife into desired shapes and place on baking paper or mat-lined baking tray/cookie sheet. Chill until ready to bake.

Preheat oven to 190°C/375°F/gas mark 5 (180°C/350°F fan).

Brush shortcakes with whisked egg white and sprinkle with vanilla sugar. Bake for 12–15 minutes until tops are golden brown. Cool for 10–15 minutes to make slicing easier.

To serve
Rinse, hull and quarter strawberries. Using a serrated knife, gently split shortcakes in half. Spoon curd on bottom half, top with a handful of strawberries, vanilla-roasted rhubarb and a dollop of cream. Spoon more curd on cut side of top half and place on top of cream layer. Serve immediately! *NM*

The Cookie Plate

Tamarillo Melting Moments

I had never seen – let alone tasted – a tamarillo until I arrived in New Zealand's Bay of Islands. Also known as tree tomatoes, tamarillos originate from South America, but they flourish in New Zealand. The red ones are tart, flavourful and my favourite. To roast, cut in half lengthways, put on a baking tray/cookie sheet cut-side up, sprinkle with sugar and roast in a 180°C/350°F/gas mark 4 oven for 30–45 minutes until the fruit is a deep, dark red. Scoop out the pulp into a food-mill or sieve/strainer to remove the seeds, and purée. Tightly covered, the pulp will keep refrigerated for two weeks. If tamarillos are not available where you live, roast and purée firm red plums – an excellent choice!

MAKES ABOUT 36			
DOUGH			
unsalted butter, softened	1¾ cups	400 g	14 oz
icing/powdered sugar	2 cups less 1 Tbsp	225 g	8 oz
pure vanilla extract	2 tsp	10 ml	
cornflour/cornstarch	1⅔ cup	260 g	9 oz
plain/all-purpose flour	2 cups	270 g	9½ oz
baking powder	1 tsp		
fine sea salt	¼ tsp		
TAMARILLO FILLING			
unsalted butter, softened	½ cup	120 g	4¼ oz
icing/powdered sugar, sifted	2 cups	250 g	8¾ oz
roasted tamarillo or plum purée	3 Tbsp	75 g	2½ oz
vanilla paste	2 tsp		

Dough

Preheat oven to 180°C/350°F/gas mark 4. Line two baking trays/cookie sheets with non-stick baking paper or mat.

Cream butter, sugar and vanilla in a stand-mixer with paddle attachment on medium–high speed until creamy and pale. Scrape down sides of bowl.

In a separate bowl, sift cornflour/cornstarch, flour, baking powder and salt, combining well.

With mixer on low, add the dry mixture to the butter blend in 4 stages until fully combined, pausing to scrape down sides of bowl as needed.

Using a teaspoon or melon baller, scoop dough into balls and roll with your hands into smooth shapes. Evenly space on a baking tray/cookie sheet and lightly press down each with the tines of a small fork or decorative kitchen tool. Bake 12–15 minutes, until cookies are barely set, with no colour. Cool on tray for 5 minutes then carefully transfer to a rack to cool completely.

When cool, frost with roasted tamarillo filling.

Tamarillo filling

In a small bowl with a hand-held mixer or in a stand-mixer with whip attachment, combine butter, icing/powdered sugar and a pinch of sea salt. Whip on high speed until light and fluffy. Scrape down sides of bowl.

Turn speed to low and spoon in the tamarillo purée and vanilla paste. Return speed to high and beat until well combined.

Pipe or spoon a coin-sized bit of filling in the centre of one cookie. Top with second cookie and press together gently. Repeat until all cookies are sandwiched together. *NM*

Opposite, from top, clockwise: Tamarillo Melting Moments, Chocolate 'Sticky Bits', Izzy's GDF Lime Coolers, Palm Sugar Penuche, Espresso Brownie Bites, Pistachio Chocolate 'Biscotti'.

Chocolate 'Sticky Bits'

This chocolate-vanilla caramel treat - inspired by a New York Times article from March 6, 1881 entitled 'Receipts' - got its updated name from my Danish photographer Manja Wachsmuth as she arranged the 'sticky bits' for the photo. The addition of vanilla paste finishes each 'bit' with a 'vanilla caviar' pop!

MAKES 60 PIECES			
unsalted butter	3 Tbsp	45 g	1½ oz
dark/bittersweet chocolate, chopped	1 cup	125 g	4½ oz
whole milk	1 fl cup	240 ml	8 fl oz
dark muscovado sugar	½ cup	115 g	4 oz
white sugar	1 cup	200 g	7 oz
runny honey	½ fl cup	120 ml	4 fl oz
vanilla paste	1 Tbsp	15 ml	½ fl oz
sea salt flakes for sprinkling on caramels	2 Tbsp		
toasted sliced almonds for sprinkling (optional)			

Butter an 20 x 30 cm/8 x 12 in tin/pan and set aside.

Attach a sugar/candy thermometer to the inside of a 2-L/2-qt heavy-bottomed saucepan. Add butter, chocolate, milk, sugars and honey and cook over medium–low heat, stirring slowly but continuously with a silicone or wooden spatula until mixture reaches 120°C/250°F. (This may take up to 30 minutes.) Remove pan from heat and stir vanilla paste into the chocolate. (Be careful as the mixture may spatter when vanilla is added.) Pour mixture into prepared tin/pan.

As soon as the caramel is cool enough to handle, lift out onto a cutting board. Using a buttered chef's knife or scissors, cut caramel into 1-cm/½-in long strips, then crosswise into 1-cm/½-in bits. Sprinkle tops with a few sea salt flakes.

Wrap the sticky bits in waxed paper squares or layer on non-stick baking paper. Store tightly covered. 'Sticky Bits' will keep in a cool dry place for a month. *NM*

Izzy's GFDF Lime Coolers

'Sweet sixteen' Isabelle loves to bake and is always searching for yummy gluten/dairy-free recipes. At a rented beach house in Queensland, Australia, she and I unearthed a few stray cups and spoons, a very large salad bowl and a 'much loved' rolling pin. We made lime coolers that passed her younger siblings' taste-test with big smiles and happy tummies! The citric acid (vitamin C tablets) adds a citrus kick without adding additional liquid.

GF MAKES 48			
gluten-free flour blend*	1½ cups	250 g	9 oz
cornflour/cornstarch	⅓ cup	50 g	1¾ oz
citric acid or powdered vitamin C	½ tsp		
lime, 1, juice and zest	1 Tbsp	30 ml	1 fl oz
fine sea salt	¼ tsp		
vegetable shortening** or margarine, softened	¾ cup	170 g	6 oz
icing/powdered sugar	1 cup	125 g	4½ oz
pure vanilla extract	1 Tbsp	15 ml	½ fl oz

* King Arthur in the US, Doves Farm, UK, and Orgran NZ/Aus.

** I used Trex (UK), Fairy (Aus), Kremelta (NZ) and Crisco (US).

Whisk together flours, citric acid, lime zest and salt. Cream shortening with sugar using your biceps – like we did – or in stand-mixer on low speed with paddle, until just combined. Add vanilla and lime juice. On low speed, add flour mixture in 2 stages until just mixed. Dough will be sticky.

Turn out onto a work surface, divide in half and shape dough into 2 logs. Roll each log tightly in clingfilm/plastic wrap. Freeze until firm, about 2 hours.

Preheat oven 160°C/325°F/gas mark 3.

Slice cookies 1 cm/¼ in thick. Evenly space on baking trays/cookie sheets lined with baking paper or mats. Gently press tines of a fork dusted with powdered sugar onto tops. Bake 12–14 minutes until barely set but pale. Transfer to cooling racks and, when cooled, dust with icing/powdered sugar or drizzle with lime icing (page 225) and store tightly covered. *NM*

Palm Sugar Penuche

Pure vanilla tropical bliss!

MAKES 48 TRIANGLES

white sugar	1¼ cup	260 g	9 oz
pale coconut palm sugar, grated	2 tablets	140 g	5 oz
golden syrup or corn syrup	⅓ fl cup	80 ml	2½ fl oz
unsalted butter	2 Tbsp	30 g	1 oz
fine sea salt	¼ tsp		
mascarpone	½ cup	115 g	4 oz
pure vanilla extract*	2 Tbsp	30 ml	1 fl oz
golden rum (optional)	1 tsp		

* For an intense vanilla flavour use double fold (2x) vanilla extract.

Combine sugars, syrup, butter, salt and mascarpone in a saucepan over low heat. Stir with a silicone or wooden spatula until sugars dissolve. Turn heat to medium, cover and cook an additional 4 minutes allowing steam to wash any remaining sugar crystals down sides of pan.

Remove lid and attach a sugar/candy thermometer to side of pan. Continue cooking without stirring over medium heat until temperature reaches 110°C/230°F (soft ball stage). Remove from heat, leaving to stand for 20 minutes.

Butter an 20 x 20 cm/8 x 8 in baking dish (or line with a silicone mat or non-stick baking paper).

Remove thermometer, then vigorously beat the vanilla and rum into the penuche until it thickens. Pour into prepared dish. Once set, unmould and cut into triangles. Will keep tightly covered for a week, if it lasts that long! *NM*

Espresso Brownie Bites

The perfect mocha blend. For a gluten-free option, replace the flour with an equal amount of GF flour.

OPTION **MAKES 48 BITES**

cocoa powder for coating baking tray/cookie sheet	1 Tbsp		
dark good-quality chocolate such as Sharffen Berger, Lindt or Callebaut, chopped	2½ cups	425 g	15 oz
unsalted butter	1 cup	225 g	8 oz
eggs, large, lightly beaten	4		
white sugar	1 cup + 2 Tbsp	225 g	8 oz
pure vanilla extract	2 Tbsp	30 ml	1 fl oz
coffee extract	1 Tbsp	15 ml	½ fl oz
plain/all-purpose flour	¾ cup	100 g	3½ oz
fine sea salt	½ tsp		
baking powder	1½ tsp		
cocoa powder	¼ cup	25 g	1 oz
cocoa nibs to finish	⅓ cup	40 g	1½ oz

Preheat oven to 180°C/350°F/gas mark 4 (160°C/325°F fan). Butter a 20 x 30 cm/8 x 12 in baking tin/pan and dust with sifted cocoa powder.

In a small bowl set over barely simmering water, melt chocolate and butter. Place bowl on a towel (to catch water droplets), stir chocolate until smooth, then cool to lukewarm.

Whisk eggs, sugar, vanilla and coffee extract in a large bowl.

In another bowl, sift together flour, salt, baking powder and cocoa powder.

Fold egg mixture into chocolate, combining well. Add dry ingredients last and mix well. Pour into prepared tin/pan, smoothing the top. Sprinkle cocoa nibs over top. Bake for 15 minutes. Remove tin/pan from oven, hold level at waist height above countertop and drop on the counter about 5 times to release any air bubbles. Bake an additional 8 minutes. Cool completely before cutting into bite-sized squares. *NM*

Pistachio Chocolate 'Biscotti'

MAKES ABOUT 24			
unsalted butter, softened	1¼ cups	240 g	10 oz
plain/all-purpose flour	3¼ cups	400 g	14 oz
icing/powdered sugar	1½ cups	200 g	7 oz
eggs, large (save 1 white for finishing)	2		
pure vanilla extract	1 Tbsp	15 ml	½ fl oz
orange zest	1		
fine sea salt	¼ tsp		
bittersweet chocolate chips	1 cup	170 g	6 oz
pistachios whole, unsalted	1 cup	130 g	4½ oz
crystal or white sugar for sprinkling	⅓ cup	75 g	2½ oz

In a mixing bowl fitted with the paddle attachment, beat butter with flour and sugar until crumbly. Add egg, egg yolk, vanilla, zest and salt and mix until well combined. Add in chocolate chips and nuts.

Divide in half, flatten into rectangular blocks and wrap tightly in clingfilm/plastic wrap. Chill until firm.

Preheat oven to 180°C/350°F/gas mark 4 (160°C/325°F fan).

Line two baking trays/cookie sheets with baking paper or silicone mats. When oven is hot, slice the chilled dough into ½- cm/¼-in thick, long biscotti shapes and arrange on baking trays/cookie sheets spaced 2½ cm/1 in apart. Brush with lightly beaten egg white, sprinkle generously with sugar and bake 7–10 minutes until edges and tops are lightly browned.

Cool on trays 5 minutes, then transfer to cooling rack. Store in an airtight container. *NM*

Kentucky Bourbon Balls

My Kentucky-born Nana, Dorothy, spent her early childhood in the American South before the family settled in Los Angeles in the 1910s. I lived with Nana when I joined the cast of LA's Phantom of the Opera in the 1990s. Her daily pre-dinner ritual was to sit in the lounger on her red porch with a bourbon-on-the-rocks and a tiny bowl of Planter's cheese balls, while birds chirped with delight on the grapevine-covered patio. A Kentucky bourbon was Dorothy's afternoon treat until she was 99 and her timeless no-bake bourbon balls were a Christmas tradition. I treasure her perfectly penned recipe, though I have updated the ingredients a little.

MAKES ABOUT 60			
icing/powdered sugar, sifted	1 cup	125 g	4½ oz
cocoa powder	2 Tbsp	15 g	½ oz
bourbon (Makers Mark was Nana's choice)	¼ cup + 1 tbsp	75 ml	2½ fl oz
golden or dark corn syrup	2 Tbsp	30 ml	1 fl oz
pure vanilla extract	1 Tbsp	15 ml	½ fl oz
candied orange peel, chopped	1½ Tbsp	20 g	¾ oz
vanilla wafer or rich tea biscuit cookie crumbs	2½ cups	250 g	9 oz
ground almonds/almond meal	¾ cup	90 g	3 oz
extra icing/powdered sugar for coating, sifted	1½ cup	185 g	6½ oz
raisins or sultanas for garnish	¼ cup	45 g	1½ oz

Sift sugar, cocoa powder and a pinch of sea salt into a medium bowl.

Gently heat bourbon and syrup until blended. Remove from heat and add vanilla and candied orange peel. Pour into the cocoa mixture and whisk until combined.

Mix cookie crumbs with ground almonds/almond meal. Add to the cocoa mixture and stir until well mixed.

Scoop by teaspoonfuls, then use your hands to roll the dough into small balls. Roll in sifted icing/powdered sugar, and press a single raisin in the centre.

Cover and seal – like a fruit cake, they get better with time! Will keep tightly sealed for 6 weeks. *NM*

Opposite: Kentucky Bourbon Balls

After School Cookies & Milk

Butter. And Salt. An obsession. I was caught butter-handed many times when just tall enough to quietly extricate the pre-dinner treat from its plate on the dining table. That childhood craving resurfaces when I buy butter laced with sea salt flakes and spread it on a fresh baguette. Or, if in a mood for dark chocolate and vanilla, I will make a batch of a childhood favourite: chocolate chip cookies. In this recipe, the honey complements the vanilla, and the milk powder adds richness, making the cookies light, chewy and buttery delicious!

MAKES 36			
salted butter	1 cup	225 g	8 oz
caster/superfine sugar	⅔ cup	140 g	5 oz
brown sugar	¾ cup	170 g	6 oz
runny honey	1 Tbsp	15 ml	½ fl oz
eggs, large	2		
pure vanilla extract	1 Tbsp	15 ml	½ fl oz
high-grade/bread flour	3 cups	370 g	13 oz
milk powder	2 Tbsp	15 g	½ oz
flaked sea salt	½ tsp		
bicarb of soda/baking soda	1 tsp		
dark chocolate chips or chopped chocolate chunks	3 cups	340 g	12 oz
flaked sea salt for sprinkling on top			

In a stand-mixer or by hand, cream butter, sugars and honey together until light and fluffy.

Add eggs, one at a time, scraping down bowl between additions. Mix in vanilla.

Sift flour, milk powder, salt and bicarb of soda/baking soda together. On low speed, add to butter mixture in 3 additions, mixing well to combine. Stir in chocolate pieces.

Line a baking tray/cookie sheet with baking paper or a mat. Scoop large spoonfuls of cookie dough with a dessertspoon or ice-cream scoop into 35-g/1¼-oz balls (approx 3 cm in/1½ in diameter).* For best results, place on tray, cover dough and chill at least 2 hours or overnight.

Preheat oven to 180°C/350°F/gas mark 4 (160°C/325°F fan).

Spread cookies on lined baking trays/cookie sheets and sprinkle tops with a few flakes of sea salt. Bake until edges are golden and cookies are set but soft in the middle, 9–11 minutes. Serve with a big glass of frosty cold milk! *NM*

---

* Dough may be scooped and frozen, tightly wrapped, for up to a month.

Organic Walnut Shortbread Stars

Intrigued by a recipe for 'green walnut liqueur' from David Lebovitz, I was given some Nocino by a regular diner customer at Em Bistro and made all sorts of dessert specials, including these melt-in-your-mouth biscuits. Made with fresh toasted walnuts, Nocino and vanilla powder, these crumbly shortbread stars are delicious with an afternoon cuppa.

MAKES 48			
organic walnuts, shelled, broken and lightly toasted	1 cup	125 g	4½ oz
unsalted butter, softened	1 cup	225 g	8 oz
light brown sugar, packed	⅔ cup	125 g	4½ oz
Nocino (green walnut liqueur*)	2 tsp	10 ml	
plain/all-purpose flour	2 cups + 1 Tbsp	255 g	9 oz
vanilla powder	1 Tbsp		
sea salt	¼ tsp		
icing/powdered sugar for rolling			

* If unavailable, substitute walnut extract.

Chop walnuts finely and set aside.

In the bowl of a stand-mixer with paddle attachment, beat butter and sugar until well combined and smooth. Then scrape down sides of bowl.

Add Nocino, blending well, and scrape down sides of bowl.

Sift flour, vanilla powder and salt together. On low speed, add flour mixture until just combined. Fold in nuts. Scrape dough into a disk and wrap tightly in clingfilm/plastic wrap. Chill until firm.

Preheat the oven to 180°C/350°F/gas mark 4 (160°C/325°F fan). Line two baking trays/cookie sheets with silicone mats or baking paper.

Sprinkle a board with sifted sugar. Roll the dough to ½ cm/¼ in thick and cut with a star-shaped cookie cutter, dipping in icing/powdered sugar as needed.

Evenly space shortbread on trays and bake about 15 minutes, turning trays halfway through, until cookies are a light golden brown. Transfer to racks and cool completely. Store in an airtight container. *NM*

Vanilla Bean Biscotti, Two Ways

ROCHELLE HUPPIN

MAKES APPROXIMATELY 5 DOZEN BISCOTTI

plain/all-purpose flour	3¾ cups	380 g	13½ oz
fine sea salt	½ tsp		
bicarb of soda/baking soda	1½ tsp		
white sugar	1⅓ cups	280 g	10 oz
eggs large	3		
egg whites, large	16	480 ml	16 fl oz
Heilala pure vanilla extract	2 tsp	10 ml	
Heilala vanilla pod, split and scraped	1		
unsalted butter, melted	⅓ fl cup	80 ml	2½ fl oz
lightly toasted almond slices	2 cups	180 g	6½ oz
dried apricots, chopped into small pieces	2½ cups	250 g	9 oz
crystal sugar* or white sugar for sprinkling	⅓ cup	70 g	2½ oz

* Large-grained sugar, called crystal sugar, sanding sugar or German white rock sugar, adds sparkle and crunch. It's available at gourmet shops or online.

⊷⊶⊷

There's nothing I would rather dip into my cappuccino than one of Rochelle's delicious biscotti! **NM**

Almond/Apricot/Vanilla Bean Biscotti (#1 Way)

Preheat oven to 180°C/350°F/gas mark 4.

Butter two Swiss roll/jelly-roll tins/pans (25 x 40 cm/ 10½ x 15½ in) and set aside.

In a stand-mixer bowl with paddle attachment, or by hand with a large bowl and a wooden spoon, combine the flour, sea salt, bicarb of soda/baking soda and sugar on the lowest speed for 1 minute.

In a separate bowl, combine eggs, egg whites, vanilla extract, scraped seeds from the vanilla pod and melted butter. Add the wet ingredients all at once to the dry ingredients and mix on low speed for about 2 minutes or until well combined.

Stir in almonds and apricots.

Divide batter equally into the two prepared tins/pans and spread evenly. Lightly sprinkle the entire top with crystal or granulated sugar. Bake for approximately 25 minutes or until set and baked through. The edges will pull away slightly from the sides of the baking sheet and a toothpick inserted in the centre will come out clean.

Remove biscotti from oven. Turn oven down to 150°C/300°F/gas mark 2 while the biscotti cool.

Carefully slide biscotti out onto a cutting board. Slice very thinly with a long serrated knife. You may slice lengthways or widthways. Bake biscotti on wire racks placed on top of baking trays/cookie sheets for approximately 10 minutes, and then turn over and bake another 10 minutes until dry and golden.

MAKES APPROXIMATELY 5 DOZEN BISCOTTI			
plain/all-purpose flour	3 cups	360 g	12¾ oz
cocoa powder	¾ cup	70 g	2½ oz
fine sea salt	½ tsp		
bicarb of soda/baking soda	1½ tsp		
white sugar	2¾ cups	500 g	18 oz
eggs large	3		
egg whites, large	16	480 ml	16 fl oz
Heilala pure vanilla extract	1 tsp		
Heilala vanilla bean paste	1 tsp		
unsalted butter, melted	⅓ fl cup	80 ml	2½ fl oz
pecan halves, lightly toasted	2 cups	170 g	6 oz
dark chocolate, semi-sweet, chopped	1½ cups	250 g	9 oz
dried sour cherries	1½ cups	170 g	6 oz
crystal sugar or white sugar for sprinkling	⅓ cup	70 g	2½ oz

Chocolate Cherry Pecan Biscotti (#2 Way)

Preheat oven to 180°C/350°F/gas mark 4.

Butter two Swiss roll/jelly-roll tins/pans (25 x 40 cm/10½ x 15½ in) and set aside.

In a stand-mixer bowl with paddle attachment, or by hand with a large bowl and a wooden spoon, combine the flour, cocoa, salt, bicarb of soda/baking soda and sugar on lowest speed for 1 minute.

In a separate bowl, combine eggs, egg whites, vanilla extract, paste and melted butter. Add the wet ingredients to the dry ingredients all at once and mix on low speed for about 2 minutes or until well combined.

Stir in pecans, chocolate and cherries.

Divide batter equally into the two prepared tins/pans and spread evenly. Lightly sprinkle the entire top with granulated or crystal sugar. Bake for 20–25 minutes or until set and baked through. The edges will pull away slightly from the sides of the baking sheet and the centre will lightly spring back when touched in the middle.

Remove biscotti from the oven. Turn oven down to 150°C/300°F/gas mark 2 while the biscotti cool.

Carefully slide biscotti out onto a cutting board. Slice very thinly with a long serrated knife. You may slice lengthways or widthwise. Bake biscotti on wire racks placed on top of baking trays/cookie sheets for approximately 10 minutes and then turn over and bake another 10 minutes, or until dry.

Who doesn't love vanilla? Oftentimes I have thought that my life has been one grand pursuit of the perfect chocolate chip cookie, so I have definitely had my experience with vanilla extract. However, one vanilla incident stands out amongst the rest. The year was 1987 and I had just graduated from The Culinary Institute of America in Hyde Park, New York, and I was most fortunate that my first job out of culinary school was as a pastry apprentice for the legendary talented Michel Richard. He had just opened Citrus, his wildly popular restaurant on Melrose Avenue in West Hollywood. The stars were obviously lined up perfectly because he took me under his wing and shared his great knowledge of pastry with me. One of the biggest sellers on the dessert menu was crème brûlée. To make this dessert I had the enchanting experience of working with plump, moist Tahitian vanilla beans for the first time. I was spellbound with the ethereal fragrance... and the delicate teeny tiny crunch of the seeds against the supremely creamy custard was euphoric. My love for this miraculous fruit of the vanilla orchid will never wane. RH

Gold Ingots

*'These are the perfect melt-in-your-mouth financiers classiques. I consider
the financier, or ingot, to be the fingerprint of the pastry chef.'*

ROSE LEVY BERANBAUM

MAKES 16 7½ x 2½-CM/3 x 1-IN FINANCIERS*

almonds, sliced	⅔ cup	60 g	2 oz
unsalted butter**	11 Tbsp	155 g	5½ oz
vanilla pod	half		
white sugar	¾ cup	150 g	5¼ oz
pastry flour† sifted and levelled off	½ cup	50 g	1¾ oz
baking powder	¾ tsp		
egg whites, large	4	120 ml	4 fl oz
vanilla paste or pure vanilla extract	¼ tsp, rounded		

EQUIPMENT

financier mould, preferably silicone, 7½ x 2½-cm/3 x 1 x 1 in,
i.e. capacity 60 ml/2 fl oz/¼ fl cup ● piping/pastry bag fitted
with a round piping nozzle/tube (optional), ¾–1 cm/⅜–½ in

* The recipe can be multiplied and made in several batches.

** Sticks are used to measure butter in the USA:
1 stick = 8 Tbsp = ½ cup = 4 oz

† Pastry flour is lighter than plain/all-purpose flour, so if
using the latter use only 50 g/1¾ oz/ ½ cup minus 1 Tbsp.

Preheat the oven 20 minutes or longer before baking. Set
an oven rack in the middle of the oven and preheat to
190°C/375°F/gas mark 5.

Coat financier moulds with baking spray or shortening
then flour. If using silicone moulds, set on a rack and then
on a baking tray/cookie sheet.

Toast the almonds
Place the almonds on a baking tray/cookie sheet and toast
them, stirring occasionally, for 5–7 minutes or until very
lightly browned. Cool completely.

Clarify and brown part of the butter (beurre noisette)
Place a fine sieve/strainer, or sieve/strainer lined with
muslin/cheesecloth, into a heatproof cup.

Place 6 Tbsp/85 g/3 oz of the butter in a small heavy
saucepan. Cook, uncovered, over low heat until the butter
is melted. Continue cooking, stirring constantly and
watching carefully to prevent burning, until the milk
solids turn deep brown. Immediately pour the butter
through the fine strainer/sieve into the heatproof cup.

Measure 4 Tbsp/50 g/1¾ oz of the beurre noisette into a
microwave-proof cup with a spout and set it in a warm spot
(or reheat it when ready to add it to the batter). Store any
remaining beurre noisette in the refrigerator for future use.

Melt the remaining butter
Place the remaining 5 Tbsp/70 g/2½ oz of butter in a small
saucepan and melt over low heat. Pour the melted butter
into a microwave-proof cup with a spout and set it in a
warm spot (or reheat it when ready to add it to the batter).

Mix together the vanilla pod and sugar
With a small sharp knife, split the vanilla pod in half
lengthways, setting one half aside. Scrape the vanilla pod
seeds from the other half into the sugar. Rub the seeds
in with your fingers. Rinse and reserve vanilla pod for
another use.

My first vanilla memory was of my grandmother making whipped cream and adding some brown liquid from a little brown bottle that smelled like heaven. I asked her what it was and she said 'vanilla'. So I asked her if I could taste it and she said you won't like it, it tastes very bitter. But the smell was so compelling, I didn't believe her. When her back was turned, I took a sip and learned she was right. She let me lick the whipped cream from the beaters and I had an epiphany – it was one of the most delicious things I had ever tasted. Thus I discovered that when added to other things the vanilla tastes the way it smells – just perfect. I have loved vanilla ever since, but not sipped directly from the bottle! **RLB**

Grind the almonds

In a food processor, combine the toasted almonds and vanilla sugar mixture and process until very fine. Stop the motor and scrape the sides of the bowl a few times to ensure that all the almonds are processed to a fine powder.

Mix the batter

In the bowl of a stand-mixer fitted with flat beater, mix almond mixture, flour and baking powder on low speed for 30 seconds. Add egg whites and beat on medium speed for 30 seconds or until well mixed. Add vanilla and beat for a few seconds to incorporate evenly.

On medium–low speed, drizzle in the hot beurre noisette and then the hot melted butter. It should take about 5 minutes for the mixture to emulsify completely into a smooth golden cream.

Fill the moulds

Scrape the mixture into a bowl or cup with a spout and pour the batter to half-fill each mould (i.e. 30 g/1 oz in each). If you don't have enough moulds, you can pour the remaining mixture into a piping/pastry bag fitted with a ¾–1 cm/⅜ in–½ in round piping nozzle/tube or a freezer-weight zip-seal bag and refrigerate it for a minimum of 1 hour, or overnight. It will be soft enough to pipe into the moulds but if it was refrigerated for more than 1 hour, leave it to sit for 30 minutes in the moulds at room temperature before baking. (You can spoon the batter into the moulds, but piping is quicker and easier.)

Bake for 18–20 minutes or until golden brown and if pressed lightly with a fingertip they will spring back.

Cool and unmould the financiers

Leave the financiers on the rack to cool completely before unmoulding. If using a metal mould, set it on a wire cooling rack and cool 5 minutes before unmoulding. Run a small metal spatula between the sides of the pans and the cakes, pressing firmly against the pans. Invert cakes onto a wire rack and reinvert them onto a second rack to cool completely. If using silicone moulds, push each out with your finger pressed against the bottom of the mould.

Store wrapped airtight in clingfilm/plastic wrap and in an airtight container: 3 days at room temperature, 5 days refrigerated, or several months frozen.

Cranberry Tweed Cardigans

When the air turns crisp and autumn leaves enthrall, out comes my old friend, Dad's tweed cardigan. Far cuter than a well-worn sweater, these tiny toaster-style tarts are flecked with hazelnut and vanilla seed 'tweed' and sport vanilla-glaze buttons. Don't be surprised while decorating these cookies when you start giggling like a kid again.

MAKES 12 CARDIGANS

CRANBERRY FILLING [MAKES 400 G/14½ OZ/2 CUPS]			
cranberries, frozen	1¾ cups	170 g	6 oz
cranberries, dried	½ cup	60 g	2 oz
orange juice	¼ fl cup	60 ml	2 fl oz
orange zest	½		
cinnamon stick (quill)	½		
demerara/raw sugar	⅓ cup	60 g	2 oz
water	¼ fl cup	60 ml	2 fl oz
vanilla pod, split and scraped	½		
TWEED DOUGH			
unsalted butter	½ cup	120 g	4½ oz
white sugar	½ cup + 1 Tbsp	115 g	4 oz
egg white, large	1	30 ml	1 fl oz
lemon zest	½		
vanilla paste	1 tsp		
fine sea salt	¼ tsp		
plain/all-purpose flour, plus additional for dusting bench	1⅔ cup	215 g	7¾ oz
hazelnut flour	½ cup	50 g	1¾ oz
oat or barley flakes, lightly toasted	3 Tbsp	25 g	scant 1 oz
CARDIGAN GLAZE			
icing/powdered sugar	½ cup	60 g	2 oz
pure vanilla extract	¼ tsp		
milk	2 tsp	10 ml	

Cranberry filling

In a small pan/pot, add all ingredients with a pinch of sea salt and bring to a simmer. Cook 5–7 minutes, until liquid is reduced and mixture thickens. Turn off heat, remove cinnamon stick and discard. Leave the vanilla pod in until ready to fill the cardigans. (Then it can be rinsed and dried for another use.) Set filling aside until ready to use. May be covered and refrigerated at this point for up to 2 weeks.

Tweed dough

In the bowl of a stand-mixer with paddle attachment, cream together butter and sugar on low speed about 3 minutes, scraping down sides as needed. Add egg white, zest and vanilla seeds and beat to combine.

In a small bowl, sift salt with both flours and oat or barley flakes. Add to butter mixture in 2 stages, scraping down sides after each addition. Pat dough into a flat round, cover in plastic and chill at least 2 hours or overnight.

On a lightly floured counter top, roll out the dough into a rectangle about ½ cm/¼ in thick. Working quickly with the chilled dough, use a pastry wheel or sharp knife to cut into 24 rectangles 8 x 10 cm/3 x 4 in, rerolling and using a small amount of additional flour as needed. (If dough has become too soft, place rectangles on a tray and chill until firm.)

Cut a 'V' shape into half the rectangles to make the cardigan 'fronts', discarding triangles. Place 2 tsp filling in the centre of each 'back', leaving a 1-cm/½-in edge around sides. Paint the edges with eggwash.* Lift the cardigan fronts and sandwich on top. Seal edges and crimp with a fork. Chill until firm.

To bake and glaze

Preheat oven to 190°C/375°F/gas mark 5 (180°C/350°F fan).

Brush tops of cardigans with eggwash.* Bake for 12–14 minutes until tops are lightly brown. Cool on racks.

To make the cardigan glaze, mix together icing/powdered sugar, vanilla and milk in a small bowl until smooth. Drizzle or pipe the glaze to decorate the cardigans. *NM*

---

* For eggwash, beat 1 egg with 1 tsp of water, a pinch of sea salt and 1 tsp caster/superfine sugar.

Black Pepper Chai Truffles

Pepper, spice and vanilla-infused cream with milk chocolate – a truffle for now, and one for later!

MAKES 30 TRUFFLES			
TRUFFLES			
whipping cream	⅔ fl cup	150 ml	5 fl oz
chai tea bag, 1	2 tsp		
black pepper, finely ground	¼ tsp		
runny honey	1 tsp		
vanilla pod, split and scraped	½		
milk chocolate,* finely chopped	2¼ cups	285 g	10 oz
fine sea salt	⅛ tsp		
COUVERTURE COATING			
cocoa powder,** sifted	3 Tbsp	20 g	¾ oz
dark chocolate, finely chopped	1¾ cups	225 g	8 oz

* I prefer El Rey, Callebaut or Guittard milk chocolate.

** Cacao Barry Extra Brute has the finest flavour for dusting truffles.

Ganache
Heat cream, tea, pepper, honey and vanilla pod just to a simmer. Turn off heat and infuse for 2 hours or chill overnight.

Warm infused cream until steamy, place a dry sieve/strainer over chocolate and pour cream over. Shake bowl to agitate chocolate, then wait 1 minute. Using a spatula upright, gently stir chocolate in a circular motion until completely melted and smooth. Scrape into a small container, then cover, or chill, until firm.

When ganache is set, scoop with a teaspoon or small ice-cream scoop and roll into balls. Place on lined pan, cover and chill until solid, about 3 hours.

Couverture
Roll truffles in sifted cocoa powder to coat and leave until just cool to the touch. Set aside a large lined tray.

To temper chocolate in a microwave
Microwave chocolate pieces at half power for about 30 seconds. Stir pieces a bit to even out the heat then microwave again for 30 seconds. Stir and repeat a few more times using shorter intervals (10–15 seconds) until chocolate just begins to melt.

Taking time and care, microwave at half power for just a few seconds at a time until the pieces are about ⅔ melted.

Don't rush as the chocolate will overheat and then will not temper. The end temperature should be barely warm (32°C/90°F). To test this, dip your finger into the chocolate and touch it just under your bottom lip. If it feels like 'nothing', neither hot nor cold, it is the correct temperature.

Temper test: Tempered chocolate looks cohesive and will show a path if stirred. If it is ready to use, it will pass this simple test: a little dribble or dab on a clean plate will set within a minute or two with even consistency and a glossy appearance.*

As you use the chocolate it may become thick and cold. Rewarm carefully for just a few seconds at a time to keep it tempered and flowing, without going over 32°C/90°F.

To temper in a double boiler
Place ⅔ of the chocolate in a double boiler or in a bowl set over a pan/pot of steamy but not simmering water. Using a silicone spatula gently 'massage' the chocolate until fully melted. Remove bowl from heat and place on a dishtowel. Sprinkle in half the remaining chocolate and continue to massage with spatula until smooth and completely melted. Add remaining chocolate and repeat. Check your chocolate is ready using the 'temper test' (see above).

If the tempered chocolate begins to harden around the edges of the bowl, return to the double boiler for a few minutes and gently stir until it returns to a smooth liquid.

To cover the truffles
Place one of the truffles into the melted chocolate and quickly submerge. Fish out with a small fork or dipping tool, allow excess chocolate to drain for a few seconds then place the coated truffle on prepared tray to set. Repeat with remaining truffles. Drizzle with melted white chocolate if wished.

* If you end up with untempered chocolate, there is a back-up plan! Stir in 2 Tbsp/30 ml/1 fl oz of melted fat (any sort of shortening or oil will work). This is another way to give a cohesive quality and keep crystals from separating. You still need to gently warm and stir it as it is used. The downside is that the coating will not be as hard or durable as tempered chocolate, so take care to keep your finished truffles cool.

With many thanks to my pastry instructor Peggy Alter, creator of Pastry Pieces/www.pastrypieces.com, who taught me the best way to make truffles!

Ginger Fruit Squares

TUI FLOWER

MAKES ABOUT 24			
BASE			
salted butter, softened	½ cup + 1 tsp	125 g	4½ oz
white sugar	⅔ cup	140 g	5 oz
golden syrup or corn syrup	1 Tbsp	15 ml	½ fl oz
egg, large	1		
pure vanilla extract	1 tsp		
sultanas or raisins	½ cup	60 g	2 oz
crystallised ginger, chopped	¼ cup	30 g	1 oz
dried apricots or prunes, chopped	¼ cup	30 g	1 oz
plain/all-purpose flour	1¼ cups	120 g	4½ oz
ICING			
salted butter	3½ Tbsp	50 g	1¾ oz
golden syrup or corn syrup	1 Tbsp	15 ml	½ fl oz
ground ginger	1 tsp		
pure vanilla extract	1 tsp		
icing/powdered sugar	¾ cup	85 g	3 oz

Preheat oven to 180°C/350°F/gas mark 4 (160°C/325°F fan).

Lightly grease the base of an 20 x 30-cm/8 x 12-in sponge roll tin/pan.

Base
Cream butter and sugar, add golden syrup and beat well. Beat egg and vanilla and mix in. Stir in the dried fruits. Sift flour in and mix to combine.

Spread into prepared tin/pan.

Bake for about 30 minutes.

Remove from oven and leave to cool a little.

Ice while still warm.

Cut into squares when almost cold.

Icing
Melt together the butter, golden syrup, ginger and vanilla, then add sufficient icing/powdered sugar to make a spreadable consistency.

I recall back in the 1960s, when I was teaching, that one of my students returning from a visit back home brought me a most precious gift – a handful of vanilla pods. You see, she was from Tahiti. Actual vanilla pods were scarce in New Zealand back then, and we had to make do with vanilla essence or the dreaded imitation vanilla. A vanilla pod was used several times and never split open. A finished crème brûlée was silky white topped with crackly caramelised sugar; scraping the seeds from the pod and stirring into the dish is a relatively recent method. **TF**

Dad's Spiced Oatmeal Cookies

These are my take on Dad's favourite cookie. I think they were his Scottish dad's favourite too. Rolling the dough in vanilla-spiced sugar just before baking adds a delectable taste to the cookies and a gorgeous aroma to the kitchen as they cool! For best cookie goodness, make the dough a day ahead.

MAKES 4 DOZEN			
plain/all-purpose flour	2 cups	240 g	8½ oz
wholemeal/wholewheat flour	½ cup	70 g	2½ oz
fine sea salt	½ tsp		
bicarb of soda/baking soda	½ tsp		
baking powder	1 tsp		
cinnamon	1 tsp		
ginger	¼ tsp		
oat bran (optional)	¼ cup	25 g	1 oz
oats (not quick cooking)	2½ cups	280 g	9¾ oz
raisins, dried cherries, dried cranberries, or mixture	2 cups	130 g	4½ oz
unsalted butter, softened	1 cup + 2 Tbsp	225 g	9 oz
caster/superfine sugar	1 cup	200 g	7 oz
brown sugar, packed	1 cup	215 g	7¾ oz
eggs, large, room temperature	2		
water	2 Tbsp	30 ml	1 fl oz
pure vanilla extract	1 Tbsp	15 ml	½ fl oz
VANILLA SPICED SUGAR			
vanilla sugar	1 cup	200 g	7 oz
cinnamon, ground	2 Tbsp		
ginger, ground	1 Tbsp		
mixed spice or pumpkin pie spice, ground	1 Tbsp		
vanilla powder	1 tsp		

Measure the flours, salt, bicarb or soda/baking soda, baking powder and spices in a medium bowl and whisk well to combine. In a large bowl, mix in oat bran, oats and dried fruit. Set aside.

By hand or using a stand-mixer, combine butter with both sugars and cream well. Add eggs one at a time, scraping down bowl with each addition. Add water and vanilla, mixing well.

On low speed, add flour mixture into butter mixture in 3 stages, scraping down sides of bowl after each addition. Add oats and combine well.

Using a small ice-cream scoop or teaspoon, shape dough into balls. Cover and refrigerate dough overnight; this allows the oats to absorb liquid ingredients.

When ready to bake, preheat oven to 180°C/350°F/gas mark 4 (160ºC/325ºF fan).

Vanilla spiced sugar

Place all ingredients in jar with a screw-on lid and shake to combine.

Roll each cookie in spiced sugar then evenly space on ungreased baking trays/cookie sheets. Bake 9–12 minutes, until edges are golden brown and just set but still soft in the middle. Transfer to cooling rack. Once cooled, store in an airtight container. *NM*

Bevvies & Bar Snacks

Vava'u Wow Creamsicle   208

Salt & Pepper Vanilla Kettle Corn   208

The One Dollar Beach Bevvie   210

Toasty Coconut Chips & Nuts   210

Iced Cappuccino Fortuna   212

Carrot–Vanilla Gougères   214

Vanilla Passion Martini   214

Zazen Iced Tea Elixir   216

Pink Ginger Zinger   216

Spiced Lime Smoothie   218

Vava'u Wow Creamsicle

This combination of fresh coconut milk, blood orange juice, vanilla syrup and rum is my grown-up take on an orange and vanilla ice-lolly. Smooth and refreshing, it's perfect for sipping while watching a sunset. Or even just imagining one.

SERVES 4			
vanilla syrup (page 222)	½ fl cup	120 ml	4 fl oz
white rum*	½ fl cup	120 ml	4 fl oz
fresh or canned coconut milk	1 fl cup	240 ml	8 fl oz
fresh-squeezed tart blood orange juice**	½ fl cup	120 ml .	4 fl oz
fresh lime juice	¼ fl cup	60 ml	2 fl oz
vanilla pod, split in quarters	1		
Thai basil, fresh sprigs	4		

Pour all ingredients except vanilla pod and basil into a large cocktail shaker and add ice. Shake until well chilled, strain and pour immediately into coconut shells or high-ball glasses. Garnish with a sliver of vanilla pod and a stem of fresh Thai basil. *NM*

---

* I prefer using New Zealand's Stolen Rum.

** You can use Kerikeri or Valencia oranges, which aren't as colourful as blood oranges but are full of flavour.

Salt & Pepper Vanilla Kettle Corn

Who can resist kettle corn? A bowlful of salty-sweet vanilla-packed crunchy popcorn is so quick and simple that I can succumb to its temptations anytime!*

SERVES 4 [IN MY HOUSE 2... MAYBE]			
coconut or grapeseed oil	¼ fl cup	60 ml	2 fl oz
vanilla sugar (page 222)	3 Tbsp	45 g	1½ oz
unpopped popcorn kernels	½ cup	100 g	3½ oz
vanilla salt flakes (page 222)	2 tsp		
cracked black pepper	⅛–¼ tsp		

Mix 1 Tbsp oil with vanilla sugar and set aside.

Have a large bowl ready for tossing and serving kettle corn.

Heat 3 Tbsp oil with a few popcorn kernels in a heavy pan/pot or wok and cover with lid. When kernels have popped, add oil and sugar mixture, give a quick stir and add remaining popcorn. Cover with lid and shake pan to keep sugar from burning. Keep shaking pan until almost all of the popcorn has popped. Turn off the heat, and keep shaking pan until you no longer hear popping kernels.

Turn out into serving bowl, add vanilla salt and pepper, tossing to coat. Serve immediately; then sit on the sofa and enjoy the movie! *NM*

---

* Kettle corn dates back to the Dutch in the 1700s. Originally popped in black cast-iron kettles (or cauldrons), the aroma of kettle corn being swirled and stirred in enormous kettles can be enjoyed today at fairs and farmers markets around the world.

The One Dollar Beach Bevvie

As I daydreamed for a self-allotted 10 minutes in a hammock in Tonga, I gazed at the coconuts gently swaying in the palms above and the fragrant combination of this drink came to mind. I climbed out of my woven piece-of-paradise and scurried across the hot sand, arriving at the shaded bar where, along with brother chef and temporary Tongan resort mixologist Peter Gordon, the afternoon's refreshing tropical beverage was to be born. This tart aromatic cocktail was named after the entrepreneurial attempts of a local, who tries charging tourists one Tongan dollar to swim from their boats to a Vava'u beach!

SERVES 2			
kola limes* and juice, 4	½ fl cup	120 ml	4 fl oz
white rum**	4 shots	120 ml	4 fl oz
vanilla syrup (see page 222)	2 shots	60 ml	2 fl oz
sparkling water, to top			

* Tongan kola limes have orange flesh, a light green smooth skin and a fragrant tart flavour. If not available, use a blend of tart orange and smooth-skinned limes, juiced to taste.

** Peter Gordon and I prefer using New Zealand's Stolen Rum.

Quarter 2 limes and put 4 lime wedges in the bottom of each tall glass. Muddle (mash) to release the juice and oil. Squeeze remaining 2 limes and divide the juice into each glass. Add 2 shots rum and 1 shot vanilla syrup to each. Fill with ice, stirring to combine, and top with sparkling water. Give a quick stir, add a straw and serve immediately. *Malo 'aupito!* NM

Toasty Coconut Chips & Nuts

I must confess that I have a talent for burning nuts. The telltale bitter smell permeating the air is rather embarrassing to a pastry chef. This is why I purchased two kitchen timers and why I still hear chef Nancy Silverton's voice saying 'never toast nuts on the stovetop - use the oven.' Believe me, it's worth it.

MAKES 3 CUPS			
coconut flakes	1½ cups	125 g	4½ oz
whole almonds	½ cup	100 g	3½ oz
macadamia nuts	½ cup	75 g	2½ oz
brazil nut pieces	½ cup	75 g	2½ oz
coconut or nut oil	1 tsp		
vanilla sugar	¼ tsp		
ground chilli pepper	pinch		
vanilla salt flakes (page 222)	¾ tsp		

Preheat oven to 150°C/300°F/gas mark 2.

Spread coconut flakes on a baking tray/cookie sheet and bake for 6 minutes, until lightly toasted. Leave to cool. Turn oven up to 160°C/325°F/gas mark 3 and, on another baking tray/cookie sheet, toast remaining nuts for 10–12 minutes, just until you can smell them. Remove and transfer to a medium bowl and mix in coconut flakes.

Warm coconut oil in a small pan or microwave, add vanilla sugar and chilli powder. Drizzle over nut mix and toss to coat. Sprinkle vanilla salt flakes over nuts and spoon into serving bowls. NM

Iced Cappuccino Fortuna

with black & white ice

Back in the 1980s, when I lived on Manhattan's West Side, I would splurge once a week on an iced cappuccino at Café La Fortuna after ballet class. I would be met by opera music and an enormous glass case overflowing with exquisite Italian pastries. Finding a tiny table, I ordered my weekly treat, nursing it for hours while writing in my journal and never once given the eye to move along (a miracle in pre-internet-café days). Each time I've visited New York since, I returned to my memory-lane treat, but sadly now Café La Fortuna is gone. This is my re-creation of a NYC moment.

SERVES 8			
WHITE ICE MILK			
white sugar	⅓ cup	70 g	2½ oz
whole or low fat milk	2¼ fl cups	540 ml	18 fl oz
milk powder	2 Tbsp	15 g	½ oz
pure vanilla extract	2 tsp	10 ml	
BLACK ICE MILK			
water	½ fl cup	120 ml	4 fl oz
dark cocoa powder	½ cup	40 g	1½ oz
white sugar	⅓ cup	70 g	2½ oz
golden syrup or corn syrup	1 Tbsp	15 ml	½ fl oz
whole or low fat milk	1½ fl cups	350 ml	12 fl oz
pure vanilla extract or paste	1 Tbsp	15 ml	½ fl oz
TO SERVE			
milk, chilled, per person	⅓ fl cup	80 ml	2½ fl oz
espresso double shot, chilled, per person	⅓ fl cup	80 ml	2½ fl oz

White ice milk

Prepare an ice bath by filling a large metal bowl halfway with ice and cold water.

In a 1-L/1-qt stainless steel pan/pot, whisk sugar with milk. Heat to scald the milk until it is just steamy. Whisk in the milk powder, a big pinch of sea salt and the vanilla extract.

Stir and cool in ice bath, then pour into a deep tray or baking dish and put in freezer, stirring with fork every 30 minutes until frozen into ice crystals. Alternatively, spin in an ice-cream maker following the manufacturer's directions. Spoon loosely into small metal bowl or plastic container. Cover and keep frozen until ready to serve.

Black ice milk

In a 1-L/1-qt stainless steel pan/pot bring the water, cocoa powder, big pinch of sea salt and sugar to a simmer, whisking to a smooth liquid. Add syrup and milk, whisk and warm just until the surface becomes steamy. Strain, add vanilla and cool in refrigerator.

Follow instructions to freeze as for white ice milk above.

To serve

Pour the milk – low fat froths best – into a large bottle or jar with a tight-fitting lid and shake vigorously until foamy. In a tall glass, place a scoop of black ice followed by a scoop of white ice. Pour the chilled espresso over and top with frothy milk. Serve immediately. *NM*

Carrot-Vanilla Gougères

A two-bite savoury puff flecked with vanilla seeds – a perfect accompaniment for cocktails.

MAKES 4 DOZEN			
bread/high-grade flour*	½ cup	75 g	2½ oz
vanilla powder	1 tsp		
smoked paprika	⅛ tsp		
nutmeg and black pepper, freshly ground	a few grinds ea		
unsalted butter	2½ Tbsp	20 g	¾ oz
carrot, peeled and finely grated	3 Tbsp	30 g	1 oz
fine sea salt	¼ tsp		
caster/superfine sugar	1 tsp	15 g	½ oz
aged gouda or cheddar cheese,** finely grated	½ cup	35 g	1¼ oz
eggs, room temperature	2		

* High-gluten bread flour is best, but plain/all-purpose flour will work as well.

** I love New Zealand's Mahoe Aged Gouda. In the US I use Beecher's Flagship and in the UK it's Montgomery's Cheddar.

† Stand-mixer method: Scrape dough into mixing bowl and mix on medium speed with paddle attachment. Add beaten eggs in 2 stages and mix until dough is glossy, smooth and holds a 'V' shape when the paddle is lifted out of the bowl.

Preheat oven to 220°C/425°F/gas mark 7 (200°C/400°F fan). Line 2 trays with baking paper or mat.

Whisk flour with vanilla powder, paprika, nutmeg and pepper in a small bowl and set aside.

In a saucepan place butter, carrot, salt, sugar and 240 ml/8 fl oz/1 fl cup water. Over medium–high heat, simmer for 3 minutes to soften the carrots and reduce the liquid. Turn heat off and add flour mixture to pan all at once, stirring with a wooden spoon constantly until dough pulls away from sides.† Continue beating and sprinkle in cheese until melted. Beat, then add eggs in 2 stages to combine and continue to beat until dough is smooth, glossy and holds a 'V' shape when spoon is lifted vertically out of the dough.

Working quickly – the dough will thicken as it cools – drop tiny spoonfuls of batter 2½-cm/1-in apart onto lined baking trays/cookie sheets. (Or fill a piping/pastry bag with no nozzle/tip and pipe coin-sized buttons.) Use a wet finger to smooth the tip of each so they don't burn.

Bake 25 minutes until doubled in size, golden brown and light in weight. Remove from oven and pierce the side of each one with a small knife to release the steam. Serve warm or at room temperature. You can make ahead of time and freeze them in an airtight container for up to 1 month. *NM*

Vanilla Passion Martini

SERVES 2			
vanilla sugar (page 222)	1 Tbsp	15 g	½ oz
egg white, whisked to frothy	1	30 ml	1 fl oz
passionfruit vodka*	½ fl cup	120 ml	4 fl oz
lime juice, fresh	2 Tbsp	30 ml	1 fl oz
vanilla syrup (page 222)	2 tsp	10 ml	

* I use 42 Below passionfruit vodka.

Sprinkle vanilla sugar on a small dry saucer. Dip a clean finger in the egg white and run around rim of martini glass. Dip glass in the vanilla sugar and allow to dry.

Fill a martini shaker with ice. Add vodka, lime juice and vanilla syrup. Shake vigorously until well blended. Strain and pour into prepared martini glasses.

Serve immediately. *NM*

Zazen Iced Tea Elixir

This refreshing elixir, fragrant with the scent of passionfruit and vanilla, tart hibiscus tea, a hint of honey and ginseng herbal tonic, gives a burst of energy without the caffeine shakes!

MAKES 1 L/1 QT			
hibiscus tea, 4 bags	4 tsp		
manuka or local honey	2 Tbsp	30 ml	1 fl oz
vanilla pods, split and scraped	1½		
fresh ginger or galangal,* peeled and thinly sliced	2-in piece	20 g	¾ oz
filtered water	3 fl cups	700 ml	24 fl oz
lime juice	¼ fl cup	60 ml	2 fl oz
orange juice	1 fl cup	240 ml	8 fl oz
passionfruit, fresh, flesh and seeds scooped out	4		
limes, thinly sliced for garnish	2		
ginseng tonic**	2–3 tsp	10–15 ml	½ fl oz

* A tender white ginger popular in Thai cooking.

** Available at health food stores, ginseng has an earthy, slightly bitter flavour, so add a bit at a time to taste!

Combine hibiscus tea with honey, vanilla seeds and pods and ginger in a jug/pitcher of filtered boiling water. Steep for 10 minutes. Or, for the sun tea method, pour fresh cool filtered water into a glass jug/pitcher, add tea, honey, vanilla and ginger and let sit in a sunny window 1–4 hours, until steeped.

Strain or remove the tea, leaving the vanilla pods and ginger in the jug/pitcher. Add the lime juice, orange juice, passionfruit and slices of lime. Add additional lime juice to taste.

Add the ginseng tonic just before serving over ice or it will lose its punch. *NM*

Pink Ginger Zinger

Refreshing, fizzy and pink! For a bit of extra zing add a few drops of vanilla or Angostura bitters (see photo, page 237).

SERVES 2			
lemongrass,* piece chopped	1	5 cm	2½ in
ginger, freshly grated	1 tsp		
vanilla paste	¾ tsp		
vodka	2 shots	60 ml	2 fl oz
Campari	½ shot	15 ml	½ fl oz
vanilla bitters or Angostura bitters (optional), or to taste	10 drops		
pink grapefruit soda, to top up	1 bottle	340 ml	12 fl oz

* Plus lemongrass 'swizzle sticks' for garnish.

Muddle lemongrass, grated ginger and vanilla paste in the bottom of a martini shaker. Add vodka and Campari, and bitters if using, and top with ice. Shake until chilled.

Strain into ice-filled Collins glasses, top with pink grapefruit soda and swirl to blend with a stick of lemongrass. *NM*

Spiced Lime Smoothie

with Tami's granola

A quick, sweet-tart, refreshing breakfast-on-the-go that Tami enjoys before cycling the forested mountain passages near Lake Tahoe, California.

SERVES 6

TAMI'S GRANOLA

rolled oats	4 cups	400 g	14 oz
flax seed	½ cup	70 g	2½ oz
coconut, unsweetened threads	1½ cups	200 g	7 oz
coconut sugar or brown sugar	4 Tbsp	60 g	2 oz
runny honey	⅓ fl cup	80 ml	2½ fl oz
cinnamon	2 tsp		
vegetable or coconut oil	½ fl cup	120 ml	4 fl oz
pure vanilla extract or paste	2 Tbsp	30 ml	1 fl oz
dates, pitted and chopped	1 cup	200 g	7½ oz
crystallised ginger, chopped	⅓ cup	70 g	2½ oz
sea salt flakes	1 tsp		
unsalted almonds, chopped	1 cup	140 g	5 oz

MANGO PURÉE

ripe mangoes, 2 medium, or mango purée	2 cups	425 g	15 oz
lime juice	1 tsp		
caster/superfine sugar	3 Tbsp	45 g	1½ oz

SPICED LIME SMOOTHIE

plain Greek yogurt	3 cups	750 g	24 oz
buttermilk	1 fl cup	240 ml	8 fl oz
runny honey	2 Tbsp	30 ml	1 fl oz
vanilla syrup (page 222)	3 Tbsp	45 ml	1½ fl oz
lime juice, to taste, plus zest of 1 lime	2–4 Tbsp	30–60 ml	1–2 fl oz
ground cardamom	½–1 tsp		
fresh ginger, grated	2 tsp	15 g	½ oz

Tami's granola

Preheat oven to 135ºC/275ºF/gas mark 1. Oil 2 deep casserole dishes or baking pans and set aside.

In a large bowl mix all ingredients together. Divide equally in pans and spread evenly. Bake for 45 minutes, stirring every 15 minutes, until golden brown. Remove from oven and turn out onto a large tray to cool completely. Store in a container with a tight-fitting lid.

Mango purée

Peel and pit mangoes and place flesh in a blender with the lime juice, sugar and a pinch of sea salt. Purée on high speed until smooth, adding water as needed to thin. Cover and chill until ready to serve.

Spiced lime smoothie

Whisk all the ingredients together until smooth. Adjust lime juice to taste, then chill covered until ready to serve.

To serve

Using a funnel, pour the purée evenly into glasses or half-pint milk bottles. Rinse funnel, then use again to slowly and carefully pour the smoothie mixture on top of the mango purée to keep the layers separate. Serve granola in little bowls or sprinkle on top of your smoothie. *NM*

Vanilla Pantry

Vanilla Sugar

vanilla pod, split and scraped and cut into pieces	1		
white sugar	2 cups	400 g	14 oz

Put the vanilla pod and sugar in a jar with a tight-fitting lid. Shake the jar daily to infuse vanilla into sugar. It will be ready to use in 1 week. Add leftover pods to your vanilla sugar and top up with sugar as needed.

Vanilla Salt Flakes

sea salt flakes*	¼ cup	30 g	1 oz
vanilla powder or finely ground toasted vanilla pods	1 tsp		

* Maldon, Murray River Pink, Halen Môn Anglesey

Gently mix salt flakes and powder together. Store in a jar with a tight-fitting lid.

Vanilla Extract

vanilla pods	about 5	20 g	¾ oz
vodka (40% proof)	¾ cup	180 ml	6 fl oz

Put whole unsplit pods in a dark glass bottle with a tight-fitting lid. Pour in vodka, seal bottle and swirl the liquid once a day. Store in a cool dark place. The clear vanilla extract will be ready to use in 3 weeks.

Vanilla Syrup

water	1 fl cup	240 ml	8 fl oz
vanilla pod, split and scraped	1		
white sugar	2 cups	400 g	14 oz
pure vanilla extract	2 tsp	10 ml	

Heat water with vanilla pod to a simmer. Stream in the sugar and simmer until liquid is clear. Cool, then add vanilla extract. Remove pod and insert into a glass bottle with a tight-fitting lid. Pour in syrup, seal and store in refrigerator. Will keep chilled for a month.

Vanilla Oil

grapeseed oil	¾ fl cup	180 ml	6 fl oz
vanilla pods	2		

Gently warm oil in a saucepan/pot over low heat. Split and scrape vanilla pods and seeds into a dark glass jar with a screw-top lid. Once oil is just warmed through but not spatteringly hot, take off heat and pour over vanilla pods. Cool to room temperature then seal jar and leave to stand for 24 hours, swirling occasionally. Will keep in a cool dark place for two months. Strain out seeds if wished.

Vanilla Aioli

MAKES 240 ML/8 FL OZ/1 FL CUP

garlic head	1		
vanilla paste	1 tsp		
egg yolks, large	2	60 ml	2 fl oz
extra virgin olive oil, plus extra for roasting garlic	1 fl cup / 1 Tbsp	240 ml / 15 ml	8 fl oz / 1 fl oz
fresh lemon juice	1 Tbsp	15 ml	1 fl oz

Preheat oven to 200°C/400°F/gas mark 6.

Cut top off garlic to expose cloves. Peel away the outer layers of the garlic bulb skin, leaving skins of individual cloves. Wrap loosely in foil and drizzle reserved oil over cloves.

Bake in pan 30–35 minutes until soft, golden brown and caramelised. Squeeze 3–4 cloves into a small dish, add vanilla paste, mix well and set aside until cooled. (Save rest of caramelised garlic for another use.)

In a medium-sized bowl, whisk yolks with a big pinch of sea salt until well blended. Add the garlic–vanilla paste, and lemon juice, and whisk, combining well.

Make a tight ring with a kitchen towel and place bowl in centre of ring to hold bowl steady. Whisk egg mixture continuously and drizzle oil in a slow steady stream until sauce begins to come together and thicken. If too thick, whisk an additional teaspoon of water to thin. Cover and chill until ready to use.

Vanilla Caramelised Onions

MAKES 4 CUPS*			
grapeseed or sunflower oil	2 Tbsp	60 ml	2 fl oz
butter	½ cup	100 g	3½ oz
brown onions, peeled, halved and thinly sliced	8 med	1 kg	about 2 lbs
vanilla pods,** split	2		

* 1 cup caramelised onions = 230 g/8 oz
** Alternatively add 2 tsp vanilla paste at end.

Place oil and butter in large 2-L/2-qt pan/pot and heat over low heat until sizzling. Add sliced onions and sweat until translucent, stirring occasionally. Add split vanilla pods and continue to cook over low heat until onions are caramel coloured, continuing to stir occasionally. Cover, refrigerate until needed. Can be frozen up to 3 months.

Vanilla Vincotto

Short of sipping, this is the best way to use leftover red wine. The cherries and vanilla add great flavour layering and complement the pizzetta toppings of cheese, figs and dark wine grapes (page 112).

MAKES 240 ML/8 FL OZ/1 FL CUP			
red wine	3 fl cup	700 ml	24 fl oz
vanilla pods, split	2		
runny honey	¼ fl cup	60 ml	1½ fl oz
orange peel, 1 wide strip			
fresh cherries,* split	about 6	70 g	2½ oz

* or substitute 2 Tbsp/15 g/½ oz dried cherries

Place all ingredients in small saucepan. Slowly simmer until reduced by ⅔. Remove peel and cherries and discard. Remove vanilla pods and insert into a small sterilised bottle. Pour in vincotto and seal.

For vanilla vincotto syrup: Take 60 ml/2 fl oz/¼ fl cup of vincotto and slowly reduce in a shallow pan to a thick syrup, about 10 minutes. This makes 2 Tbsp, enough to drizzle on the pizzettas on page 112.

Vanilla Candied Bacon Bits

The ultimate bacon bit combo, perfect for devilish eggs (page 108) and Tonga Trifle (page 103).

vanilla sugar (page 222)	2 Tbsp	45 g	1½ oz
pink peppercorns, freshly ground	¼ tsp		
lightly smoked bacon	4 slices	125 g	4½ oz

Preheat oven to 180°C/350°F/gas mark 4. Mix sugar and peppercorns in a pie tin or small bowl. Dredge the bacon in the mixture and lay on lined baking tray/cookie sheet.

Cook 25–30 minutes, turning over halfway through baking. (Do not be tempted to increase oven temperature as bacon will burn.) Remove from oven and drain on a cooling rack. Chop into bacon bits. If not crispy enough, heat in a small dry sauté pan until crispy. Cool completely and store chilled in an airtight container.

Raspberry-Vanilla Vinegar

In writing Vanilla Table, I often discovered an ingredient that I 'knew' was on the shelf at the local market was indeed on the shelf… just in another country! I made this quick opaque raspberry-vanilla vinegar for just such an occasion while making the preserved rose petal vinegar on page 150. For best flavour, let stand 2 days before straining and bottling.

raspberries, fresh or frozen	2½ cups	300 g	1½ oz
white wine vinegar	1½ fl cups	350 ml	12 fl oz
vanilla pod, split and roughly chopped	½		
white sugar	2 Tbsp	30 g	1 oz

Put all ingredients except sugar in a blender and blitz to combine. Pour in a bowl, cover with a dry cloth and leave to sit on counter overnight, up to 2 days.

Pour liquid into a stainless steel pan/pot. Add sugar and bring to a gentle simmer. Cook for 5 minutes then strain through fine muslin/cheesecloth. Discard muslin/cheesecloth and fruit. Pour vinegar into sterilised bottles and seal. Will store in fridge for 3 months.

Adapted from Nigel Slater.

Tash's English Toffee

In the US 'English Toffee' is a sumptuous luxury. The 'English' bit is the addition of a thin chocolate layer scattered with toasted almonds.

MAKES A SHEET 30 x 45 CM/12 x 18 IN			
light brown sugar, packed	⅓ cup	80 g	3 oz
caster/superfine sugar	1 cup	200 g	7 oz
fine sea salt	½ tsp		
unsalted butter	1 cup	225 g	8 oz
pure vanilla extract	¼ fl cup	60 ml	2 fl oz
dark rum	2 Tbsp	30 ml	1 fl oz
bicarb of soda/baking soda	½ tsp		
dark/bittersweet chocolate, chopped, melted, kept warm	¾ cup	160 g	5½ oz
flaked/slivered almonds, lightly toasted	½ cup	50 g	1¾ oz

Grease a 30 x 45 cm/12 x 18 in baking tray/cookie sheet lined with oiled baking paper or mat.

Mix sugars and salt in a small bowl. In a clean saucepan, over medium–high heat, melt the butter, swirling to coat the sides. Add sugar mixture and stir continuously with a wooden spoon until the mixture begins to bubble. Attach a sugar/candy thermometer.

When to a gentle boil, add the vanilla. Keep stirring, but step back as the mixture will foam up! Cook until the mixture reads 286°F/141°C. Add sifted bicarb of soda/baking soda, stirring vigorously to combine then immediately pour into prepared pan, smoothing to ¾ cm/ ¼ in thick with a spatula.

When toffee is set pour melted chocolate over all and smooth top. Sprinkle with almonds and cool completely. Refrigerate on tray tightly sealed with clingfilm/plastic wrap. Break into shards as needed.

Raspberry Curd

MAKES 675 G/24 OZ/3 CUPS			
raspberries fresh or frozen, thawed with juices	¾ cup	225 g	8 oz
raspberry vinegar (page 223)	1 Tbsp	15 ml	½ fl oz
lemon, juice and zest	2 Tbsp	30 ml	1 fl oz
eggs large	5		
white sugar	1⅓ cup	225 g	10 oz
unsalted butter	¾ cup	170 g	6 oz
vanilla pod, split and scraped	½		

In a small bowl combine raspberries with juices, lemon juice, zest and vinegar, equaling about 240 ml/8 fl oz/1 fl cup. Have a bowl of ice water with another bowl that fits inside a sieve/strainer on top. Set aside.

In a 1-L/1-qt stainless steel pan/pot, whisk eggs with sugar until smooth. Place on medium–low heat then add the raspberry liquid, butter, vanilla pod and pinch of sea salt. Stir slowly but continuously with a spatula or spoon until thickened, about 5–8 minutes. Strain immediately into the bowl above ice bath. Stir to cool, cover tightly and chill until ready to use.

Note: Makes more than you need but will keep tightly covered 3 weeks in the refrigerator and is divine with yogurt, ice cream, scones or just by the spoonful!

Fleur de Lait Amande

Silky smooth and vegan!

MAKES 1 L/1 QT			
sliced almonds, skin on	1 cup	80 g	3 oz
almond milk, plain	2½ fl cups	600 ml	20 fl oz
cornflour/cornstarch	2 Tbsp	20 g	¾ oz
brown sugar, dark	¼ cup	50 g	1¾ oz
fine sea salt	¼ tsp		
pure vanilla extract	1 Tbsp	15 ml	½ fl oz
cider vinegar	¾ tsp		
almond liqueur (optional)	2 tsp	10 ml	

Preheat oven to 180°C/350°F/gas mark 4.

Toast almonds on baking tray/cookie sheet until dark golden brown. Roughly chop then add to almond milk, cover and soak overnight.

Blitz with hand-/stick-blender and strain through chinois or muslin/cheesecloth, discarding almonds. Pour 60ml/2 fl oz/¼ cup almond milk into cornflour/cornstarch, whisk to combine, then mix into rest of milk. Add sugar and salt then bring to a simmer, stirring to thicken for 2 minutes, until silky. Mix in remaining ingredients then chill well before spinning in an ice-cream maker according to manufacturer's directions.

Freeze until firm. *NM*

Inspired by David Lebovitz's addictive 'Fleur de Lait' recipe from The Perfect Scoop.

Feijoa Ice Cream

What is it about New Zealand and feijoas? Available fresh in the fall, Kiwis go crazy for all things feijoa, including feijoa muffins, yogurt, jam, cakes, salads and even feijoa vodka! When I arrived in New Zealand, I saw this six-letter word I simply could not pronounce: 'feijoa'. Tasting the New Zealand variety of a pineapple guava (pronounced 'FEE-joe-ahh'), all I could think of was gritty pink bubble-gum-flavoured toothpaste from childhood visits to the dentist – not a favourite memory. However, as neighbours brought brown papersacks heaped with the fresh green fruit to make feijoa treats, I began to enjoy the taste, especially as thinly sliced oven-dried chips and – my favourite feijoa treat – Feijoa Ice Cream.

MAKES 1 L/1 QT			
cream	2 fl cups	500 ml	17 fl oz
whole milk	1 fl cup	240 ml	8 fl oz
vanilla pod, split and scraped	1		
white sugar	1¼ cups	115 g	4 oz
egg yolks, large	6	180 ml	6 fl oz
feijoas, fresh	10–12	1 kg	2 lb
lemon juice	3 Tbsp	45 ml	1½ fl oz
feijoa vodka or light rum	1 Tbsp	15 ml	½ fl oz
pure vanilla extract	1 Tbsp	15 ml	½ fl oz

Make an ice bath by filling a large metal bowl halfway with ice and cold water. Nest a smaller metal bowl inside large enough to hold the cooked ice cream custard base. Place a sieve/strainer on top of bowl. Set aside.

Attach a thermometer to a large stainless steel pan/pot and over low heat scald cream and milk with scraped vanilla pod and half of the sugar. Stir, scraping pan/pot to keep from sticking.

Whisk yolks with remaining sugar until well beaten.

When temperature reaches 60°C/140°F, pour a little cream mixture into the egg mixture, whisking constantly, then add a little more, whisking again. Add this 'tempered' egg liquid back into the cream, whisking continuously. (This method keeps the eggs from scrambling and is often used for dishes that are custard-based.)

Switch to a spatula and stir until custard reaches 80°C/175°F. Strain at once into the prepared bowl. Continue stirring until mixture stops steaming.

While the custard base is cooling, halve and scoop out the feijoa pulp and squeeze in the lemon juice to keep pulp from oxidising. Mash or purée the pulp until smooth and

add to the cooled custard base. Whisk in feijoa vodka (or rum) and vanilla extract, returning pod to custard base.

Chill 4 hours, or preferably overnight, allowing the flavours to meld together. Remove the vanilla pod, rinse and dry. Freeze custard in an ice-cream maker according to the manufacturer's directions.

Scooter Pastry Cases/ Pie Shells

MAKES 12–15 PASTRY CASES/PIE SHELLS			
unsalted butter	½ cup	110 g	4 oz
brown sugar	2 Tbsp	30 g	1 oz
white sugar	2 Tbsp	30 g	1 oz
runny honey	2 Tbsp	30 ml	1 fl oz
plain/all-purpose flour	⅔ cup	90 g	3 oz
wholemeal/wholewheat flour	½ cup	60 g	2 oz
Mexican vanilla extract	1 tsp		
digestive biscuit/graham cracker crumbs	⅓ cup	60 g	2 oz
fine sea salt	½ tsp		
metal or silicone mini pie or tart shells	12–15	7–10 cm	3–4 in

Cream butter, sugars and honey in a stand-mixer on low speed, or by hand, until creamy and light.

In a medium bowl, whisk together remaining ingredients. Combine dry blend to butter in 2 stages, scraping down the sides of the bowl between additions, mixing well.

Portion dough into small 60-g/2-oz pieces and press into pie or tart shells. Freeze until firm, about 1 hour.

Preheat oven to 180°C/350°F/gas mark 4 (160°C/325°F fan).

Arrange on baking tray/cookie sheet and cover each tart with a little oiled piece of foil. Smooth foil onto dough and bake for 20 minutes. Carefully remove foil and return to oven until lightly golden brown and dry, an additional 3–5 minutes. Cool before filling. *NM*

Lime Icing

icing/powdered sugar	½ cup	70 g	2½ oz
pure vanilla extract	¼ tsp		
lime juice	2 tsp	10 ml	

Mix all together and drizzle on cooled GFDF lime biscuits (page 184).

Notes, Weights & Measures

I must admit, I created a monster of a challenge when I wanted readers to be able to use *Vanilla Table* wherever they might be in the world. Users of cookery books will know that certain ingredients have different names in different countries, they are measured differently and even things we think of as 'certain' such as cup measures and tablespoons vary in different countries. I have had to make some tough calls! Wherever you live and however you describe and measure your food, try to use the best quality ingredients you can and choose local and seasonal foods as much as possible.

Measurements

I have provided metric, avoirdupois (pounds and ounces used in the US) and cups and spoons in each recipe so you can double-check that measures are correct. I have had to round things up and down, but have endeavoured to be both accurate and realistic as to what the majority of home cooks (and chefs) can measure. The measures have been rounded up or down to the nearest 5 g/5 ml or ¼ oz to convert easily, depending on dish, and I have not converted any spoon measure that weighed less than 10 g.

For many of the savoury dishes this level of accuracy is not vital, but for those sweet dishes, especially desserts and pastry, where precision is critical, I have 'broken' my own rules to ensure you will have success when you try the recipe, and that you can make double quantities or more with confidence. For example, 1 fl cup (8 fl oz or ½ fl pint) is 236.58 ml but I have generally adjusted this to 240 ml (note that a standard fluid cup measure in many countries is rounded up further to 250 ml). However, for those recipes where the liquid measure is important, I have indicated 235 ml. Lesser liquid amounts, such as ½ cup and ¼ cup are 120 ml and 60 ml, respectively, which is the correct standard conversion in most countries (see table opposite.)

The addition of metric and avoirdupois weights for produce has been included because a medium shallot in one country, for example, can vary in weight considerably to that in another. Also, our perception of small, medium and large varies too. So do check the weight measure given as a guide.

The dairy aisle

I could write a graduate thesis on milk, cream and butter with the plethora of butterfat percentages, viscosity and flavour descriptors that there are around the world. But here are some global basics:

BUTTER: European Style Butter is 85% butterfat and is used throughout the book as this is the most commonly used worldwide. US butter at 80% has a higher water content which can vary the recipe balance, especially of baked goods and specifically pie, tart and cookie doughs. Brands such as Plugra, Anchor and the European-style Cabot, Challenge and Vermont have the higher % of butterfat and are readily available in the US. Salted or unsalted butter is indicated in each recipe.

CREAM: I have selected whipping cream for the global description of what is variously known as double/heavy/thickened cream. All have about the same butterfat content of 35%.

MILK: Unless otherwise specified, milk means whole milk, also known as full fat or blue top milk. Low fat milk, also known as half fat milk has approximately 2% fat content.

Other ingredients

EGGS: Unless otherwise noted, all eggs used are large, this is because large eggs (also known as No. 7 eggs) have the closest 50:50 ratio of yolk to white. This balance is important in baking and pastry recipes. For accuracy, I have also given the fluid measure when whites and yolks are used separately in recipes. A large egg is equal to 60 ml or 2 fl oz, so its yolk is 30 ml, as is the white. However, in Germany a medium-sized egg is this fluid measure.

PURE VANILLA EXTRACT: recipes use standard single fold unless otherwise indicated.

SALT: Sea salt has been used throughout the book. Kosher salt is also mentioned in some recipes. As it is not readily available in many countries, convert kosher to sea salt as follows: 1½ tsp Morton or 2¼ tsp Diamond (kosher salts) = 1 tsp fine sea salt (table salt is equal to fine sea salt, but not my ideal choice because of the anti-caking agents. For the same reason, I prefer to use aluminium-free baking powder). If you are using sea salt flakes, 1½ tsp of flakes = 1 tsp fine sea salt.

GOLDEN SYRUP: In general, corn syrup or dark corn syrup can be used as a replacement for golden syrup. However, in recipes where the key flavour ingredient is golden syrup, substituting with corn syrup won't give the same result. Luckily, golden syrup is available in most countries, including the United States.

I hope that most ingredients are described in a way that will be clear, even if it is not a word you would use first. Opposite is a table of the main ones, but there are others such as clingfilm vs plastic wrap, baking paper vs parchment paper vs silicone paper, aubergine vs eggplant, red bell pepper vs capsicum and cookies vs biscuits ... who would have thought we're all speaking the same language!

MEASUREMENTS			
1 fl cup (US)	240 ml (236 ml)	½ fl pint	8 fl oz
2 fl cups	475 ml (473 ml)	1 fl pint	16 fl oz
3 fl cups	700 ml (710 ml)	1½ fl pints	24 fl oz
1 Tbsp	15 ml	3 tsp	½ fl oz
1 Tbsp (Aust)	20 ml	4 tsp	
1 Tbsp (SA)	12.5 ml	2½ tsp	
1 tsp	5 ml		
PLAIN/ALL-PURPOSE FLOUR WEIGHT MEASURE			
1 cup	120 g		4¼ oz
PASTRY/CAKE/SPONGE FLOUR WEIGHT MEASURE			
1 cup	115 g		4 oz

ALTERNATIVE WORDS FOR INGREDIENTS		
plain flour	all-purpose flour	(ideally unbleached)
wholemeal flour	wholewheat flour	
bread flour	high-grade flour	
pastry flour	cake flour	sponge flour
baking soda	bicarbonate of soda	bicarb
caster sugar	superfine sugar	baker's sugar
cornflour	cornstarch	
icing sugar	powdered sugar (10x)	confectioners' sugar
white sugar	granulated sugar	
whipping cream	heavy or double cream	thickened cream
golden syrup*	corn syrup	dark corn syrup

All Sorts of Sources

A few of my favourite farmers markets:
BC Farmers Market, Vancouver, Canada/
www.bcfarmersmarket.org
Borough Market, London Bridge, UK/
www.boroughmarket.org.uk
Brockley Market, South East London, UK/
www.brockleymarket.co.uk
Bury Market, Manchester, UK/
www.burymarket.com
Cedar Park and Mueller Markets, Austin, Texas, USA/
www.texasfarmersmarket.org
Coconut Grove Saturday Organic Market, Miami, USA/
www.glaserorganicfarms.com
Green City Market, Chicago, USA/
www.greencitymarket.org
Ferry Plaza Farmers Market, San Francisco, USA/
www.cuesa.org
Portland Market, Oregon, USA/
www.portlandfarmersmarket.org
Santa Monica Wednesday Market*, California, USA/
www.smgov.net/farmersmarket (* The LA chef's secret!)
Union Square Greenmarket, New York, USA/
www.grownyc.org

Gourmet ingredients and equipment
Heilala Vanilla, NZ & worldwide/www.heilalavanilla.com
Callebaut Chocolate, worldwide/www.callebaut.com
Beanilla, Michigan, USA/www.beanilla.com
The Cheese Store of Beverly Hills, California, USA/
www.cheesestorebh.com
Chocosphere, Oregon, USA/www.chocosphere.com
Crate and Barrel, USA/www.crateandbarrel.com
King Arthur Flour, Vermont, USA/
www.kingarthurflour.com
The Meadow, OR and NYC, USA/www.atthemeadow.com
Nielsen-Massey Extracts, USA/www.nielsenmassey.com
Niman Ranch, California, USA/www.nimanranch.com

Santa Monica Seafood, California, USA/
www.santamonicaseafood.com
The Spice House, Milwaukee, USA/
www.thespicehouse.com
Sur la Table, USA/www.surlatable.com
Surfas, California, USA/www.culinarydistrict.com
Wailea Shipped Fresh Heart of Palm, Hawaii, USA/
www.waileaag.com
The Conran Shop, London, UK/www.conranshop.co.uk
Divertimenti, London, UK/www.divertimenti.co.uk
La Fromagerie, London UK/www.lafromagerie.co.uk
Padstow Farmshop, Cornwall, UK/
www.padstowfarmshop.co.uk
The Spice Shop London, UK/www.thespiceshop.co.uk
Vanilla Mart, UK/www.vanillamart.co.uk

Vanilla research: a selection of books, sites and blogs
Consider The Fork: A History of How We Cook and Eat, Bee Wilson (Basic Books, 2012)
The Essence of Chocolate: Recipes for Baking and Cooking with Fine Chocolate, John Sharffenberger & Robert Steinberg (Hyperion, 2006)
The Flavour Thesaurus: A Compendium of Pairings, Recipes and Ideas for the Creative Cook, Niki Segnit (Bloomsbury, 2012) www.flavourthesaurus.com
'Rose's Vanilla Bible', Rose Levy Beranbaum, in *Food Arts Magazine* (2006)
The Story of Vanilla, Chat Nielsen Jr (Nielsen-Massey, n.d.)
Vanilla Orchids Natural History and Cultivation, Ken Cameron (Timber Press, 2011)
Vanilla: Travels in Search of the Ice Cream Orchid, Tim Ecott (Grove Press, 2005)
www.davidlebovitz.com
www.food52.com
www.ginadepalma.net/blog
www.tastingtable.com
www.vanilla.com (Patricia Rain)

Contributing Chefs

In 1973, **Maggie Beer** and husband Colin settled in the Barossa Valley with the simple intention of breeding game birds and growing grapes. Their farm success led to the Pheasant Farm Restaurant, which was awarded the Gourmet Traveller Restaurant of the Year in 1991. In 1993 the closure of the restaurant saw Maggie free to pursue new ventures. Today her career spans food production, writing and television. ABC's *The Cook & The Chef*, and her superb line of products, reinforced her standing as one of Australia's best-loved food stars. Her honours of Senior Australian of the Year (2010) and South Australian of the Year (2011) are highlights of a truly busy life. In 2011 Maggie was thrilled to be appointed a Member of the Order of Australia for her service to tourism and hospitality. Being the South Australian Patron for the Stephanie Alexander Kitchen Garden Foundation led Maggie to begin her own Foundation For A Good Life, focusing on aged care.
www.maggiebeer.com.au

Rose has been called the 'Diva of Desserts' and 'the most meticulous cook who ever lived'. Her most recent accolade was: 'If ever there was a cookbook author who could place her hands on top of yours, putting you through the proper motions, helping you arrive at just the right touch, **Rose Levy Beranbaum** is the one.' Rose's first book, *The Cake Bible*, was the 1989 winner of the IACP Book of the Year and the NASFT Showcase Award for the cookbook that has contributed most to educating the consumer and professional chefs. Now in its 51st printing, it has been included in *101 Classic Cookbooks*. A luminary in the world of food writing, Rose is also an internationally known food expert and has been featured presenter in the Melbourne Food & Wine Festival and Oxford Food Symposium. She has also been inducted into the Beard Foundation's Who's Who of Food and Beverage in America. Her *Baking Bible* was released in 2014.
www.realbakingwithrose.com

'Creating fantastic food,' says **Galton Blackiston**, 'is a passion dating back to my teenage years.' As a cash-strapped 17-year-old Galton set up a market stall in Rye selling homemade baking and preserves. The range, known as 'Galton's Goodies', was constantly sold out and he soon realised cooking was his future. Never formally trained, Blackiston's knowledge was honed in the various kitchens in which he worked, including John Tovey's Miller Howe Hotel in the Lake District. Stints in New York, Canada, South Africa and London led Galton back to Norfolk where he opened his award-winning hotel and Michelin-starred restaurant Morston Hall. The menu there is built upon fresh, locally sourced ingredients. His other great passions are his family and Norwich City Football Club. Galton's three cookbooks include his latest *Summertime*.
www.galtonblackiston.com

British-born chef **Neil Brazier** learned his trade in the UK working in various Michelin star-rated restaurants and elite country house hotels. He travelled extensively and worked throughout Europe, America and Asia, ending up in New Zealand, where he became an executive chef for some of the finest eateries, including the award-winning Kauri Cliffs in the Bay of Islands. His quirky outlook is reflected in the very inventive but approachable menu that belies the level of training and experience he has attained. Neil draws inspiration from the various cultures he has experienced and combines them to create food that is as unique as it is elegant. In 2013 Neil became the Head Chef of The Sugar Club, Peter Gordon's restaurant in the Sky Tower, Auckland, New Zealand.
www.skycity.co.nz

Al Brown is a chef, restaurateur, writer and TV presenter. His approach to cooking is all about simplicity and generosity, and his dishes showcase the culinary landscape of New Zealand. In Al's opinion, food is the vehicle for conversation, fun and memorable occasions. His restaurant, Depot, opened in Auckland in 2011 and has been an unprecendented success. He is also the mind behind Auckland's newest bagel factory, Best Ugly Bagels, making Montreal-style wood-fired bagels, and the old-school NYC Jewish deli, Federal Delicatessen. Al is the author of *Go Fish: Recipes and Stories from the New Zealand Coast*, winner of the Best Single Subject at the International Association of Culinary Professionals Awards in the USA. Al spends his spare time with his family, walking his dogs, and fishing from his 'new' old boat, Nautilus.
www.albrown.co.nz

Gesine Bullock-Prado is a pastry chef, chef instructor at King Arthur Flour, author of the captivating baking memoir *My Life from Scratch* and cookbook author of *Sugar Baby, Pie It Forward* and *Bake It Like You Mean It*. She lives on an historic Vermont farm with her husband, three dogs, chickens, geese and ducks.
www.gesine.com

Francesco Carli was born in Asiago, Veneto, Italy. Working in several restaurants on the shores of the Adriatic, in 1981 he returned to Asiago to work at Vecchia Milano bakery, and opened the bakery's restaurant. He took on the kitchen of Hotel Europa, and cooked at the renowned restaurant, Lepre Bianca. Showing his art and skill, Francesco worked at both restaurants for a while, but remained at Lepre Bianca until 1993. In 1993 he began at the Hotel Cipriani in Venice and soon after accepted an invitation to visit Brazil, and never returned. After only three months in Rio de Janiero, he opened the Cipriani restaurant, at the world-famous Copacabana Palace, and then became the executive chef there. After 20 years at the Copa, Francesco now heads the kitchens of The Country Club of Ipanema, the oldest and most exclusive club in Brazil, celebrating its 100th anniversary in 2016.
www.rjcc.com.br

Josiah Citrin is the chef/owner of the highly respected two Michelin-starred Mélisse Restaurant in Santa Monica, California. His inventive cuisine focuses on laser-sharp presentation of California farm-to-table ingredients. It is highlighted by his French heritage and the influence of his years spent in Paris. A respected veteran of the Los Angeles' gourmet dining industry, Citrin's first cookbook, *In Pursuit of Excellence*, was released in 2011. It was named Best Cookbook by the Independent Book Publishing Professionals Group and was one of three finalists for a Benjamin Franklin Award.
www.melisse.com

Contributing chefs

Growing up in Fife, Scotland, **William Curley** began as an apprentice at the famous Gleneagles Hotel, then honed his skills at Michelin-starred kitchens in the UK and Paris. Joining the Savoy, working under Anton Edelman and leading a team of 21 pastry chefs, William was the youngest ever Chef Pâtissier. Here he met Suzue, a highly respected pâtissier, originally from Osaka, Japan, now his partner and wife. William and Suzue have represented Scotland at numerous culinary events, winning gold medals in Chicago and Basle, and at the Culinary Olympics. His book *Couture Chocolate* won Best Cookbook of the Year at the UK Food Writers Awards 2012, and his latest book, *Pâtisserie*, is an astonishing, innovative and delicious modern adaptation of classic pastry creations.
www.williamcurley.co.uk

Jason Dell is a multi-award winning international chef who first earned his stripes cooking across the breadth of New Zealand in the kitchens of leading restaurants and hotels, including the international luxury lodge Blanket Bay in Queenstown. The author of *Savvy: Fresh Inspired New Zealand Cuisine*, Jason is often engaged to promote his cuisine internationally. He has spent the best part of five years exploring Asia and sharing his passion for fine food and culinary excellence. Recently Jason headed up the kitchens for the all new Regent Bali in Sanur, before being lured to his current appointment, weaving his culinary magic at the luxurious five-star resort Velassaru in the Maldives. The Antipodean chef's modern eclectic repertoire seduces and tickles appetites with his delicious, healthy and colourful cuisine.
www.jason-dell.com

James Beard Award-winning Pastry Chef **Gina DePalma** credits her close-knit Italian family for instilling a love and understanding of good food simply prepared from the best of ingredients. Her training began at home in the kitchens of her mother and grandmother, and continued in the pastry kitchens of some of New York's top restaurants. In 1998, she signed on with Chef Mario Batali to open Babbo Ristorante and Enoteca, where her creativity shone forth through the marriage of seasonal regional ingredients with traditional Italian desserts. Her first cookbook, *Dolce Italiano: Desserts from the Babbo Kitchen,* was published in 2007. Gina is currently perfecting her latest book while inventing divine treats to post on her beautiful blog.
www.ginadepalma.net

Jim Dodge was born into a seventh-generation hotelier family. Leaving the family's New Hampshire resorts, he worked for Fritz Albicker, the Swiss chef responsible for his decision to become a chef instead of a hotelier. Jim learned to meld Swiss influence with his New England heritage, resulting in unique baking and pastry recipes. Jim is hailed by the James Beard Foundation as 'an award-winning pastry chef, author and educator and is included in almost everyone's short list of those who have had the greatest influence on American cuisine in the past 30 years'. Based in San Francisco, Jim is director of specialty culinary programs throughout the US for Bon Appétit Management.
www.bamco.com

Dominique & Cindy Duby are the chefs/owners of Wild Sweets®, a critically acclaimed science-based chocolate-making laboratory, art-based designer chocolate atelier and virtual boutique. They have won gold awards in world chocolate competitions including Best Chocolatiers & Confectioners in America. Dubbed 'Canada's most notable sweet chefs', they led Pastry Team Canada several times in the world's most prestigious team pastry events, including the World Pastry Cup in Lyon, France. Their exploits have been captured in documentaries and other TV appearances on The Food Network. Having authored and photographed five internationally acclaimed cookbooks, the couple also offer culinary training and consultation to companies worldwide in product development, food design and food photography.
www.dcduby.com

Elizabeth Falkner is an award-winning chef who founded two Michelin-recommended restaurants, Citizen Cake and Orson, both in San Francisco. In 2006 *Bon Appetit* named her 'Pastry Chef of the Year', just after being hailed as one of 'America's 10 Top Pastry Chefs'. In 2005 she was nominated for 'Pastry Chef of the Year' by the James Beard Foundation, named 'Best Pastry Chef' by *San Francisco* magazine and 'Rising Star Chef' by the *San Francisco Chronicle*. Author of two cookbooks, Elizabeth moved to New York in 2012 and launched two independent restaurants, quickly gaining accolades, including a two-star *New York Times* review for her pizza restaurant in Brooklyn. Elizabeth has competed in many events, including Food Network's *Next Iron Chef, Redemption, Iron Chef America* and *Next Iron Chef, Super Chefs*, where she was a finalist and runner-up. She is currently president of Women Chef and Restaurateurs.
www.elizabethfalkner.com

Tui Flower, QSM, has had a huge influence on a generation of New Zealand cooks. A home science graduate, she spent time in the US where she was exposed to food journalism and then became the first woman to study at the Jean Drouant École Hôtelière de Paris, sending her towards the food industry, rather than her original preference for clothing and textiles. She was appointed Food Editor of the *New Zealand Woman's Weekly* in 1965, with a brief to create the first magazine-based test kitchen in New Zealand. Soon Flower and her test kitchen team were producing articles for the *Weekly* and the daily paper, *The Auckland Star*. Her books include *New Zealand The Beautiful Cookbook*, which went to several editions, and her autobiography, *Self Raising Flower*. Now in her late 80s, she maintains a lively interest in her subject, particularly food history, and continues to mentor, advise and assist those who have followed her in food journalism.

A native Angeleno, chef **Neal Fraser** is the chef/owner of two of Los Angeles' best-loved restaurants: the former Grace and BLD. Redbird at Vibiana opened in 2014, along with a new BLD at LAX and ICDC, an ice-cream/doughnut/coffee shop. Chef Fraser, a graduate of the Culinary Institute of America in Hyde Park, New York, began his culinary career at age 20 and has worked with culinary luminaries throughout the country. Known for his take on New American cuisine, he has consistently garnered critical praise and is acknowledged as one of LA's premier chefs, showcasing ambitious flavours and artfully composed dishes. Accolades include 'Hot Tales', *Condé Nast Traveler*, 'LA's 25 Best Restaurants', *Los Angeles Magazine* and *Angeleno Magazine*'s 'Chef of the Year' in 2007. TV credits include *Iron Chef America*, *Top Chef Masters* and *Knife Fight*.
www.vibiana.com

Contributing chefs

Gale Gand is partner and founding executive pastry chef of Michelin-starred restaurant TRU in Chicago, and she recently opened a new restaurant, Spritzburger, with the Hearty Boys, featuring bubbles, burgers and brunch. She was named Pastry Chef of the Year by the James Beard Foundation and *Bon Appétit* magazine in 2001. Host of the long-running Food Network and Cooking Channel's *Sweet Dreams,* Gale has appeared on *Iron Chef America*, *Martha Stewart*, *Baking with Julia (Child)*, *Oprah*, and judged Bravo's *Top Chef* and *Top Chef Just Desserts*. In 2011, Gale created a special dessert for the President of China on his visit to Chicago. She has written eight cookbooks, the most recent being *Gale Gand's Lunch!* Gale also has her own root beer company producing 'Gale's Root Beer'. She is married to environmentalist, Jimmy Seidita, has an 18-year-old son, Gio, and 10-year-old twin daughters, Ella and Ruby.
www.galegand.com

Chef **Duff Goldman** is the owner/operator of the famed Baltimore-based bakery Charm City Cakes. After gaining national attention by pushing the boundaries of what a cake could be, The Food Network tapped Duff and his staff to star in *Ace of Cakes*. Ten seasons later, the show is still wildly popular in over 40 countries. In 2012, Duff opened Charm City Cakes West and Duff's Cakemix, a do-it-yourself cake shop in the heart of Hollywood, California. In addition to the new bakeries, Duff also stars in many Food Network series, including *The Best Thing I Ever Ate* and *Sugar High*, and has been featured in *Iron Chef America*, *Next Food Network Star*, *Diners, Drive-Ins and Drives*, *Cupcake Wars* and *Chopped*. A two-time James Beard Foundation nomimee for Best TV Food Personality/Host and Best TV Program, Duff and his brand currently partner with several companies including Gartner Studios, Dean & DeLuca and Godiva.
www.charmcitycakes.com

Known as the 'godfather of fusion cuisine', **Peter Gordon** is renowned for his unique culinary philosophy; he pushes the boundaries of where one national cuisine starts and another stops. Born in Whanganui, New Zealand, now living between Auckland and London, Peter has restaurants in both cities: The Sugar Club and Bellota in Auckland, and The Providores & Tapa Roon and Kopapa in London. He consults to other restaurants and food businesses around the world, including Istanbul's Changa and Müzedechanga, and designs menus for Air New Zealand. He is a co-founder of Crosstown Doughnuts, a London-based gourmet doughnut company that launched in 2014. Peter has written seven food books, the latest being *Peter Gordon Everyday*, and contributed to another dozen. In the 2009 New Year Honours List he was awarded an ONZM by HM The Queen for services to the food industry.
www.peter-gordon.net

Upon graduating from the Culinary Institute of America in Hyde Park, New York, with honours in 1987, **Rochelle Huppin** began her notable career in the culinary field. Her first job was making pastries with Michel Richard at his restaurant Citrus in Hollywood. After further training with Richard, she went on to be pastry chef at Hotel Bel-Air, The Lark Creek Inn in Northern California and at Wolfgang Puck's restaurants in Southern California: Spago, Chinos-on-Main, Eureka and Granita. Unhappy with the uniforms that were available for chefs to wear, Rochelle created better ones; there was an immediate demand for them and her company Chefwear was born. Rochelle's first pairs of pants went to distinguished chefs such as Jonathan Waxman, Wolfgang Puck and Bobby Flay. For 23 years she has continued to design chef apparel based on the needs of her colleagues.
www.rochellehuppin.com

Paul Jobin started his culinary trek wielding a Japanese cleaver and cooking with long chopsticks – not an ordinary start for a Kiwi lad entering a kitchen in Wellington, New Zealand. Paul has cooked in Sydney, New York and Slovakia, before returning to New Zealand, where he opened the highly regarded Pure Taste restaurant in the Bay of Islands. He has a love for Asian, Middle Eastern and South American food, using these influences to create layers of textures, lots of colour and bold, assertive flavours in his dishes. You will find him either cooking for guests at the breathtaking Annandale Coastal Farm Escape and Luxury Villa Collection on Banks Peninsula, South Island, or on YouTube, delivering recipe ideas and cool tips with organic products and rice bran oil.

www.pauljobin.co.nz

David Lebovitz began working in restaurants at the age of 16 until ending up at Chez Panisse in Berkeley, California, working with Alice Waters and co-owner, pastry chef Lindsey Shere, who he considers his mentor. David spent nearly 13 years in the kitchens at Chez Panisse before leaving in 1999. That same year, he launched his website to coincide with the release of his first book, *Room for Dessert*. David was named one of the Top Five Pastry Chefs in the Bay Area by the *San Francisco Chronicle* and has been featured in *Saveur*, *Food+Wine* and *Sunset* for his brilliant, balanced and addictive desserts. Author of eight books, including his latest, the highly acclaimed *My Paris Kitchen*, David lives in Paris, where he blogs, writes and gives market and chocolate tours.

www.davidlebovitz.com

Christine Manfield is one of Australia's most celebrated chefs. A curious cook and a perfectionist, inspired by the culinary melting pot of evocative flavours and textural nuance, she is also a writer whose successful books – *Tasting India*, *Fire, Spice, Stir, Paramount Cooking* and *Paramount Desserts* – have spiced up the lives of keen cooks everywhere. Her latest book, *Dessert Divas* (2014), is an anthology of desserts from her restaurant, Universal. Her professional culinary life as restaurateur has culminated in three award-winning restaurants: Paramount in Sydney from 1992 to 2000, East@West in London from 2003 to 2005, and Universal in Sydney from 2007 to 2013. An inveterate traveller, Christine continues to broaden her global interest working alongside chefs around the world and hosting frequent gastronomic tours to exotic destinations, including India, Spain, Morocco, Tunisia, Bhutan and France.

www.christinemanfield.com

Esteemed chef **Anton Mosimann**, OBE, is owner and chairman of Mosimann's, the private members' club, and Mosimann Academy in Battersea, which houses his valuable collection of over 6,000 cookery books. As owner of Mosimann's Party Service, he holds a Royal Warrant of appointment to HRH The Prince of Wales for catering services. The world of food and restaurants was different in 1963 when Anton entered his first professional kitchen as a young lad in Switzerland. By the age of 28, he was Maitre Chef des Cuisines at London's Dorchester Hotel. In 2004, Anton was awarded an OBE by Her Majesty, Queen Elizabeth II and in 2006 he was appointed Officer, National Ordre du Mérite Agricole (France). His philosophy of Cuisine Naturelle, letting the flavours of the food shine, will continue to inspire a generation of new chefs.

www.mosimann.com

Contributing chefs

KEIKO OIKAWA

GEORGIA GLYNN SMITH*

TOM CALTABIANO

Yotam Ottolenghi completed a master's degree in philosophy and literature while working on the news desk of an Israeli daily, before coming to London in 1997. He started as an assistant pastry chef at the Capital and then worked at Kensington Place, Launceston Place, Maison Blanc and Baker and Spice, before starting his own eponymous group of restaurants/food shops, with branches in Notting Hill, Islington and Belgravia. His books *Ottolenghi: The Cookbook*, *Plenty*, *Jerusalem* and the latest release *Plenty More* (all co-authored with Sami Tamimi) have been international bestsellers.
www.ottolenghi.com

Fascinated by baking and cake decorating from childhood, **Peggy Porschen** moved from Germany to London in 1998 to study at Le Cordon Bleu. Quickly developing her own style, Peggy set up her business in 2003 in Belgravia, London, with New Zealand husband Bryn Morrow, founding Peggy Porschen Cakes, a bespoke design company that creates irresistibly pretty, delicious cakes that reflect her lifelong love of baking. In autumn 2010, with her talented team of pastry artists, she opened the Peggy Porschen Parlour, where her previously made-to-order designs are enjoyed by all. Early 2011 marked the opening of Peggy's Cake Academy, London's first cookery school dedicated entirely to baking, cake decorating and sugar craft. Her many books include *Romantic Cakes*, *Pretty Party Cakes*, *Boutique Baking* and, her latest, *Cakes in Bloom*.
www.peggyporschen.com

Douglas Rodriguez, a son of Cuban immigrants, was raised in Miami. He grew up with the sights, smells and tastes of Cuban/American cuisine. His culinary creativity changed the image of Latino food in America when in 1994, at age 27, the twice-nominated James Beard rising chef moved to NYC and became the executive chef and co-owner of Patria, earning a three-star review in the *Times*; it was the laboratory for his new cuisine he calls 'Nuevo Latino'. Having opened three further ventures, including Alma de Cuba, rated the Best Cuban Restaurant in Philly, Doug missed his hometown so in 2004 he returned to Miami, eventually opening two award-winning restaurants. Douglas is the author of four books, including *Nuevo Latino*, *Latin Flavours on the Grill* and *The Great Ceviche Book*, first published in 2003.
www.drodriguezcuba.com

Throughout her celebrated career **Nancy Silverton** has received many accolades, including, in 2014, the James Beard Foundation's highest honour as 'Outstanding Chef'. In 2010 she was named one of *Food and Wine Magazine's* 'Best New Chefs' as well as 'Pastry Chef of the Year' and 'Who's Who of Cooking' by the James Beard Foundation. Author of four award-winning cookbooks, currently she is the co-owner of Pizzeria and Osteria Mozza, LA and Singapore, Mozza2Go and Chi Spacca. Silverton founded the world-renowned La Brea Bakery and Campanile Restaurant, an LA institution cherished for decades. Nancy has an amazing capacity for embracing the beauty of wonderful food and each loaf, pizza and mozzarella dish is a world of its own waiting to be discovered... she will never stop exploring.
www.osteriamozza.com

Norman Van Aken, chef and founder of Norman's at the Ritz–Carlton, Grande Lakes, Orlando, has been described as 'legendary, visionary and a trailblazer', and is the only Floridian to be inducted into the prestigious James Beard list of 'Who's Who in American Food and Beverage'. Known internationally for introducing the concept of 'Fusion' to the culinary world, he has been described as the 'founding father of New World Cuisine', a celebration of Latin, Caribbean, Asian, African and American flavours. His restaurant was nominated as a finalist for the James Beard Foundation's 'Best Restaurant in America', and he has been a James Beard Foudation semi-finalist for 'Best Chef in America'. In 2014 Norman was the first American to receive the AIG Grand Prix Gastronomic Culture Prize. He is the author of five cookbooks.

www.normanvanaken.com

Jonathan Waxman was raised in Berkeley, California, where his entire family fostered a love of food from an early age. He attended culinary school in San Francisco and Paris before he returned to the United States to work at several notable kitchens, including Domaine Chandon, Chez Panisse and Michael's restaurant in Santa Monica. Waxman then opened Jams New York and subsequent successful restaurants around the world. Today, Jonathan is chef and owner of Barbuto in Manhattan's West Village. He is a founding partner of Nashville's Music City Food+Wine Festival, and in 2014 opened Adele's by Jonathan Waxman in Nashville, as well as Montecito restaurant in Toronto, in partnership with Ivan Reitman. In late 2014, Jonathan opened a restaurant in 1 Hotels Central Park, a new brand from Starwood Capital Group.

www.jonathanwaxman.com

A 1996 James Beard Award Winner for 'Best Chef, Pacific Northwest' and a renowned master of Hawaii Regional Cuisine, chef **Alan Wong** has made a successful career marrying elements of the different ethnic flavours of Hawaii's immigrant past. Using the finest Island-grown ingredients, he enjoys taking something old and reinterpreting it with a contemporary twist, always giving his customers a taste of Hawaii. Chef Wong, author of *New Wave Luau* and *The Blue Tomato*, is chef/owner of Alan Wong's Restaurant on King Street and The Pineapple Room by Alan Wong in Macy's at Ala Moana Shopping Centre. His cuisine is exclusively featured at the Watabe Wedding Company's newest chapel and reception facility, Honu Kai Lani, in Ko'Olina. Chef Wong's latest concept is Alan Wong's Amasia at the Grand Wailea on Maui.

www.alanwongs.com

For nearly thirty years, renowned chef **Sherry Yard** has created savoury and sweet menus, crafted masterful breads and opened new restaurants, all while mentoring an entire generation of chefs in kitchens from Singapore to Santa Monica. Yard has earned the praise of critics and peers and her multiple accolades include the James Beard Awards 'Outstanding Pastry Chef of the Year', 'Best Baking Book', and the prestigious 'Who's Who of Food and Beverage in America' for her significant contributions to the culinary profession. Yard was born and bred in Brooklyn, New York, and began her culinary career at the venerable Rainbow Room. She established herself as a prominent pastry chef at the celebrated Campton Place before moving to Los Angeles to work with Wolfgang Puck. Sherry currently serves as VP of Culinary Development for iPic Entertainment and in 2015 will revive the iconic Helms Bakery.

www.helmsbakerydistrict.com

Acknowledgements

To those who helped along the way... I thank you.

To my amazing assistants: I couldn't have prepared and plated such beautiful dishes without you: Kathy Kordalis (London, United Kingdom), Abi Featherstone (Bay of Islands, New Zealand), Nagaraju Sunkara (Auckland, New Zealand).

To my recipe testers and tasters all over the globe: Anne Conness, Shirley Dellenbach, Tami MacAller, Sequanna Williams, Neil Brazier (still waiting for the pâté), Alexa Bell, Gillian (Giselle) O'Callaghan, Christina Musrey, Elaine Skeete, Jeffrey Mora, Bonnie Knight, DV Taylor, Vicki Anstey, Rex and Jennie Barnaby, Suzanne and Russell Callander, Roy Goodwin, Graham Dobson and C. & K. Bevan.

Special thanks to: Jacques Pépin, Bee Wilson, Jim Dodge, Rochelle Huppin, Elizabeth Falkner, Sherry Yard, Tui Flower, Peggy Alter, Rosalinda Monroy, Michael McGrath, Chuck Craig, Lyn Barnes, Wendy Dobson, Judith Patterson, Sarah Gumbley, Richard Xerri, Jason Burgess, Pam Reed,

Sue Knight, Paul & Lyndsay Jobin and the wonderful Heilala Vanilla Family.

Many thanks to my very patient editors Janice Wald Henderson and Bateman's Tracey Borgfeldt.

A big thank-you to my UK publisher Jacqui Small, her editors Fritha Saunders and Eszter Karpati, plus Jessica Axe, Jessica Atkins, Lisa Trudeau and Adrian Greenwood in the UK and USA sales, publicity and marketing team.

To the inspiring Peter Gordon for your friendship and support.

Huge thanks to Ryan Marx and Johnny McCormack for their stunning graphic design and to Manja Wachsmuth for her breathtaking photographs.

And finally, my enormous thanks to each of the 33 fabulous chefs who generously donated a vanilla dish for 'The Table'.

Thank you for your help and contributions

Heilala Vanilla, New Zealand/www.heilalavanilla.com

Russ Wilkinson, PAK'nSAVE, Botany Bay, New Zealand/ www.paknsave.co.nz

Roger Holmes, Stolen Rum, Auckland, New Zealand/ www.stolenrum.com

Churchills Butcher's, Kerikeri, New Zealand

Mighty Mushroom Microgreens, Kerikeri, New Zealand/ www.mightymushrooms.co.nz

Mahoe Farmhouse Cheese, Bay of Islands, New Zealand/ www.mahoecheese.co.nz

Bhana Bros Fruiterers, Ponsonby, Auckland, New Zealand

Nielsen-Massey Vanilla, USA/www.nielsenmassey.com

The Providores, London, UK/www.theprovidores.co.uk

Henry Harris, Racine Restaurant, London, UK/ www.racine-restaurant.com

John Lewis, Kauri Cliffs, Matauri Bay, NZ/www.kauricliffs.com

Props contributed by:

The Conran Shop/www.conranshop.co.uk – Porcelain Variopinte fork: pp. 25, 83, 115, 153. Roasting dish: p. 83. Mud salt dish: pp. 77, 83, 89. Plume dessert plate: pp. 125, 147, 175. Mud plate: p. 123. Wooden tray: p. 163. Mud platter: p. 187. Glasses: p. 213.

Country Road/www.countryroad.com.au – Teaspoon: pp. 21, 79. Spoon and glass: p. 59. Fork: pp. 43, 49, 57, 69. Brass servers: p. 105. Teaspoons and bowl: p. 101. Glass: pp. 209, 237. Bowl: p. 211.

Design Denmark/www.designdenmark.co.nz – Ego Whiskey Glasses: p. 15; Ego Cognac Glass: p. 53; Norman Cph Fork: p. 63; Ego Espresso Glass: p. 75; Ego Glass: pp. 91, 211; Norman Cph Bowl and Fork: p. 147.

Divertimenti/www.divertimenti.co.uk – Glass: pp. 25, 77, 205, 217.

Laguoile knives: p. 27, 117. Rack: pp. 85, 143. Cake stand: p. 172. Little basket: p. 197.

Everyday Needs/www.everyday-needs.com – Wooden Plate: p. 99. Japanese wine glass: p. 120. American modern platter: p. 161.

Flotsam & Jetsam/www.flotsamandjetsam.co.nz – Stilton plate: pp. 115, 179. Stilton plate and antique chiffon: p. 153. Vintage cake stand: p. 151. Tray and milk bottles: p. 219.

Fog Linen Work/www.shop-foglinen.com – Napkin: pp. 12, 16, 18, 24, 28, 34, 43, 57, 59, 65, 69, 75, 79, 89, 91, 106, 121, 129, 147, 165, 197, 215. Tray: pp. 77, 137, 143. Tea towel: pp. 81, 101, 141. Fabric coasters: p. 141

Freedom Furniture/www.freedomfurniture.co.nz – Lunch plate: pp. 13, 19. Bowl: p. 59. Plate: pp. 23, 37. Platter: pp. 129, 149.

Peggy Porschen – Cake stand: p. 171.

The Props Department, New Zealand – Rack: pp. 97, 73, 157, 205.

Shop @ Charles/www.shopatcharles.co.nz – Papaya plate: pp. 57, 75. Rockpool aqua plate: pp. 41, 49. Rockpool blue bowl: p. 61. Rockpool blue plate: p. 69.

Simon James Concept Store/store.simonjamesdesign.com – Alessi cups: pp. 21, 75. Alessi Beechwood plate: pp. 29, 43. Alessi jar and bowl: p. 53. Alessi water glass: pp. 49, 79. Alessi wine glass: p. 99. Alessi platter: p. 183. Alessi plate: p. 209.

Wonki Ware/www.wonkiware.co.za – Bowl: pp. 25, 35. Plate: pp. 27, 63, 65, 127, 129, 145. Plate and Platter: p. 177.

Photographer's own: Square plate and napkin: p. 21. Napkins and knife: p. 29. Napkins: pp. 23, 105, 129, 139, 151, 156, 203. Zara knife + fork and glass: p. 37. Slate: p. 53, 135. Vintage tablerunner: p. 49. Zara fork: p. 23. Fork: p. 65, 135, 175. Knives: pp. 73, 129, 156. Zara teaspoon: pp. 123, 141. Teatowel: p. 199.

Other props writer's own.

Chef jacket, aprons, trousers donated by Chefwear, Chicago USA/www.chefwear.com

Index

First published in New Zealand by David Bateman Ltd in 2013
30 Tarndale Grove, Albany, Auckland, New Zealand

First published in the UK and USA by Jacqui Small LLP in 2014
74–77 White Lion Street, London N1 9PF

Text © Natasha MacAller, 2013
Text © individual contributors
Typographical design © David Bateman Ltd, 2013
Photographs © Manja Wachsmuth, 2013 unless attributed otherwise

Photography: Manja Wachsmuth
Food styling: Natasha MacAller and Manja Wachsmuth
Art direction: Marx Design/Johnny McCormack

ISBN 978-1-90934-286-6

Printed in China